IMAGE VS ARTIFACT
IN
CONTEMPORARY
ART

MICHAEL DYER

Publisher:
MichaelDyerMusic.com
POB 927, Topanga CA 90290
MDyer@MichaelDyerMusic.com

2nd Printing, 2017, with identified errata corrected
Printed by CreateSpace, an Amazon.com company

ISBN-10: 1502904276
ISBN-13: 978-1502904270

DEDICATION

I dedicate this book to *Yvonne Flowers*, my mother-in-law, whose enthusiasm for all forms of contemporary art I have found quite contagious.

I also dedicate this book to *Raul and Emilie de Brigard*. It was a conversation on art (that I had with this very thoughtful couple a few years ago) that inspired me to write this book.

Acknowledgements: Thanks to my wife, Margot Flowers, for listening to me as I developed the ideas in this book, and for her many useful suggestions on earlier drafts.

Thanks also to my daughter Andrea for allowing me to take some very informal photographs of her oil painting ("Butterfly Eyes" © 2013) for use in the making of the front cover image for this book.

TABLE OF CONTENTS

PREFACE

Motivation For Writing This Book

For most of my life I have felt confused about contemporary art. I could not make sense of the sometimes bizarre behavior of contemporary artists, nor of many of the pieces they produced. I was shocked by the enormous sums of money paid for works of art that I felt any "man-on-the-street" could have produced. Then, one day I had an epiphany and suddenly it all made sense. Over the years I have had some additional insights about the nature of contemporary art and I began to think that some of these realizations/observations might be of interest to others (who may also be trying to understand contemporary art).

What I Mean By the Term "Art"

When I use the term "Art" in this book I am referring, for the most part, to static images painted on canvas (or on other types of backing materials hung on walls). I am also restricting myself to *contemporary* art. By *contemporary* I am referring to art produced after photographic cameras became common. I do not feel that Art before the 20th century needs explanation (at least not in that same way that contemporary art requires).

The Shock of the Photographic Camera

The photographic camera was invented in the early 1800s. By the early 20th century cameras had become more and more portable and common. Before its invention, artists labored mightily to produce realistic-looking images. The arrival of photographs forced artists to rethink the entire nature of Art.

Imagine the frustration (and fear) that some artists must have felt when the newly-invented camera could produce a realistic image of a person or scene that is vastly superior to that achieved by any painting that has been created manually. On the other hand, the invention of the camera ended up freeing the artist -- in the sense that artists need no longer pursue realism. Over the last century, surrealistic, abstract, minimalist and impressionistic images have become acceptable forms of art.

What This Book Is *Not* About

This book is *not* about the following:
- How to recognize different schools, genres or styles of art.
- How to acquire various art techniques, such as shading and perspective.
- The history of art.
- An analysis or critique of any specific work of art.
- A philosophical discussion of processes of perception in Art.
- The many roles Art plays (e.g., erotic, religious, political).

Gate Keepers of Art

Occasionally I will refer to "art literati", connoisseurs, "high priests", "upper echelons" or other gatekeepers of art. By such terms I am referring to those multi-millionaires who collect art and act as patrons to Art; to the museum curators who acquire and display art; to those gallery owners who are frequented by the very wealthy and who support specific artists and sell their works; to the professors of art and art history in major colleges and universities, and to those who write about and review works of Art.

I am not a member of any of these groups. For some readers this alone may be reason enough to stop reading any further in this book. For others, my lack of credentials in contemporary art may be a plus. Hopefully you will read on and decide for yourself.

My Approach to References and Footnotes

In this day of the internet, I assume that anyone can find images produced by artists simply by typing those artists' names to a search engine (such as Google or Bing). Instead of references to artists and their works, I supply keywords that the reader can type to a search engine, in the form: [srch: *key-words*; *alternate-key-words*] where "srch:" indicates that the user should use some internet search engine. I have not supplied URLs because, in my experience, over time web pages tend to disappear (or a URL gets replaced by another). The keywords I supply in this book I have tried myself and I believe that this approach will supply the reader with a set of URLs (for more examples or information about the topic under discussion).

There are references at the back of this book; however, I did not intend to have many references to articles about art; nor will there be many references to specific artists or works of art. Instead, I will refer to economists, psychologists or neuroscientists who have made observations about Art.

I indicate each footnote (actually, an endnote) with {ch.n} where ch indicates the chapter in which endnote n appears. All footnotes appear at the back of this book.

I am assuming that the reader already knows something about contemporary art and has encountered examples of it (through media or by having visited various modern art museums). If the reader wants to find images produced by any artist that I mention, the reader need merely type that artist's name (along with the term "art" or "artist") to a search engine.

Hopefully the reader will find the observations in this book to be thought provoking. I hope that, after having read this book, the reader will feel that he/she has attained a greater insight into the nature of contemporary art and can explain the existence of some of contemporary art's decidedly non-masterful-looking so-called "masterpieces".

How to Judge Art

The work of the great masters in past epochs is relatively easy for anyone to recognize and appreciate. Centuries ago, those with tremendous talent in the arts would find wealthy benefactors to support them. Most people today realize, at a glance, that they could never produce one of these masterpieces from the past (such as those hanging in the Louvre), even with years of study.

In contrast, many people today mock common and famous examples of contemporary art, especially those that look like anyone could have produced them with a minimum of effort. For example, there are websites in which the viewer is asked to determine whether an art piece was produced by a famous artist, or by a child or a toddler [srch: quiz toddler modern art].

Other sites ask the viewer to distinguish between works of art sold for millions versus works sold at garage or yard sales [srch: distinguish multi-million dollar art yard sale]

Among other things, in this book I will attempt to supply the reader with a general set of formula schemas for judging the quality of contemporary art; that is, a way of ranking contemporary works of art. For reasons that will be explained later, this attempt can only be partially successful.

Art vs. Music -- A Contrastive Approach

I have found it very insightful, when pondering the nature of contemporary Art, to compare it with contemporary popular music. I will make comparisons of Art to Music throughout this book and I believe that the resulting contrasts will help to shed some light on the nature of contemporary art.

Chapter 1
IMAGE vs. ARTIFACT

An Epiphany

Years ago I was at a gallery. I saw a work of art on sale for about $4000. I was shocked because this particular piece seemed so slap-dashed and messy in its construction. Its backing was a large piece of crude plywood (about 8' x 4' in size). The plywood contained splashes of paint, along with yellow lined-sheets of school paper (with the writing of some child on them). These yellow pages (glued on to the plywood) seemed to be the homework assignments of some elementary school student.

I was horrified. How could something so crudely done, producing such a chaotic, messy image, be expected to sell at such a price?

About 5 years later I found myself back in the same gallery. To my surprise, there was again another piece of crude plywood, again with the same mess of paint speckles and schoolwork on it, but this time, the art piece had a price tag of around $16,000! I couldn't believe it!

Then I noticed a book placed on a table immediately beneath the piece. The book was open to a specific page. I picked up the book. It was a recent book about contemporary art and artists. On that open page was the artist who had produced the work in front of me. Along with a description of the artist was an example of the artist's work -- one that looked similar to the work currently in front of me (and currently affronting my aesthetic sensibilities).

Then an epiphany came to me! The placement of the book (beneath that work and opened to that page) was a way of saying:

"See! This artist has now entered into the *history of art*. This artist has now been vetted by some high priest of the arts (namely, the author of that book). This artist is no longer just any artist, but is now one of *the* artists of our time. Thus, his (or her) works now need to command a price 3 to 4 times higher than before."

A Major Epiphany

With that minor epiphany (above) came a more fundamental epiphany:

Artifact trumps Image in Art

Those who establish the value of works of art are interested mainly in the *artifacts* of art -- *not* in the *images* that appear on those artifacts!

Consider any image painted on a canvas by some artist: There is the artifact -- namely, the physical canvas with the physical paint (or other materials) placed on it and, separately, there is the image -- namely, what could be conveyed via a poster or by some other image replication process, such as a photograph taken of the canvas.

What is it that *impresses* the art connoisseur who collects the works of art produced by some artist? Is it the acquisition of the image of a work of art, or the acquisition of the historical, physical artifact?

Consider scenario SC1: You buy a poster, say, of a work by Matisse (i.e., the *image*). Alternatively, consider scenario SC2: You buy an original Matisse work -- that is, the actual, historical *artifact*. I suspect that any art gatekeeper (i.e., museum curator, gallery owner, wealthy benefactor, etc.) would *not* be impressed in the least by your ownership of the image (i.e., poster or photo), but *would* be impressed by your ownership of the physical, historically authentic canvas (that contains the image on it) -- namely, the artifact.

Is the art connoisseur interested in collecting the *images* created by famous artists? Is the art connoisseur's home (or gallery) filled with posters or photographs (or other reproductions) of paintings? Of course not! What is of value to the art literati -- to the museum curators and other gatekeepers of Art -- is not the image, but the *historical artifact*. Art connoisseurs are in the business of collecting (and displaying) *artifacts*, not images.

Artifact in Music vs. Artifact in Art

Consider music. What is an artifact in music? Music does **not** really have a corresponding historical artifact -- one that is attached to the sound. The closest thing to a corresponding artifact in music would be the physical audio master, such as the master album that would be cut onto a glass or metal disc. In the past, multiple copies of vinyl records would then be created from this master (much like a key is produced by using another key as the pattern to control a key-copying machine).

For those who are too young to have owned vinyl records, those little bumps and troughs in each vinyl groove produce sounds by means of a needle that is traced along them within the groove. This up-down tracing process (over the pits and bumps) causes an electrical signal that drives a set of speakers and thus reproduces the sounds that are encoded in the vinyl.

The major problem with vinyl records is that, each time the needle bounces along in a groove, it wears away some of the vinyl and so the sound degrades over time with each playing of the record. In contrast, CDs (compact discs) contain discrete pits (representing 0s and 1s -- thus a *digital* as opposed to *analog* encoding, such as in vinyl) which are read by a laser, and so there is no degradation with each re-play. In the digital case there is no real difference between a master (the original CD) and any subsequent CD copies. The 0s and 1s are copied without loss of information and then interpreted by a computer to produce the sound.

With the advent of cloud computing and streaming on the internet, CDs themselves are beginning to go the way of vinyl records (they're disappearing). Instead of handing someone a physical CD, music can be transferred now between individuals by downloading (from some website) a digital file that encodes the audio signal as a sequence of 0s and 1s. Alternatively, one could hand someone a thumb-drive in order to transfer a file from one computer to another (or from an iPod or other hand-held device to another).

There do exist historical artifacts that are *related* to music; for example, the sheet music that musicians had to refer to in order to help them perform the music, or a specific instrument that was played by a musician, or the album cover (with its art work and credits), but, in general, there is **nothing** in music like the distinction between the historical *artifact* (that unique canvas-with-paint-on-it) versus the *image* (what the eye sees when it looks at the canvas).

In music, the closest thing to an artifact is the original, historical performance -- which is something that is *unrecoverable*. What is recoverable is a recording of that performance. That original recording is equivalent to all of its copies -- one copy of a recording (in the case of digital files) is just as good as another. (I am assuming here that a copy of a recording is made without any form of compression, since compression can degrade a copy in order to reduce the size of the original, digital file.)

A Hypothetical, Sci-fi Scenario for Art (*SF-Aw/oAF*)

To have a similar situation in Art (as exists in Music) we would have to imagine a science-fiction type of alternate universe in which, the moment an artist finishes painting a canvas, the canvas magically disappears, leaving in its stead some *recorded copy* of the image that was on that (now gone) canvas -- an image that somehow came into existence just before the canvas disappeared.

We will refer to this strange sci-fi world as scenario *SF-Aw/oAF* (that is, *Art without Artifact*). Of course, this is *not* the case for Art in our world. The canvas remains and all *copies* (reproductions) of the <u>image</u> on that canvas are viewed by the *art literati* as something one looks down one's nose at, as compared to the unique, historical <u>artifact</u>.

In this sci-fi scenario an artifact fails to come into existence when paint is applied to a canvas. In this hypothetical universe only copies of images would exist (just as in the case of only copies of sounds existing after a musical performance).

Would Art museums exist? Would thousands of visitors go to the Louvre to see merely an *image* of the Mona Lisa? This image would no longer be unique, since it would no longer be attached to a unique, historical, physical artifact.

The Forgery Effect in Art

Proof that the "high priests" of Art care mainly for the *artifact* (over the *image*) can be seen when a work of Art, that was thought to be an original artifact, turns out to be a more modern forgery. The value can suddenly drop from hundreds of thousands (or millions) of dollars to just a few hundred. [srch: art forgeries]

The image on the canvas has not changed at all. What has changed is what is called the art work's *provenance* (the chronology of ownership, which is used to help establish its historical authenticity). If the art connoisseur truly loved the <u>image</u>, then the value would remain the same even after it is uncovered as a forgery (since it remains the same image). Clearly, it is the historical <u>artifact</u> that has value to the connoisseur, not the image per se.

Distorted Art vs. Transparent Music

This artifact-vs-image distinction in the visual arts has created a psychological *distortion* that simply does not exist in the realm of Music. When someone admires, is impressed by, or emotionally moved by a work of Art -- do they admire the <u>image</u> being conveyed to their eyes, or are they being mainly affected by the knowledge that they are in the presence of a unique, historical <u>artifact</u>? With Art, the answer is not immediately clear and this lack of clarity I refer to as a psychological *distortion*.

This kind of distortion simply does not occur in Music. It does not occur because it <u>cannot</u> occur. When someone admires (is impressed by, or emotionally moved by) a piece of music, they love the *sounds* that they are hearing (not some artifact from which sounds emanate). Music listeners do <u>not</u> love some unique, physical, historical artifact. For example, when a music collector says "I love this song by The Mamas and The Papas that appears on the album *If You Can Believe Your Eyes and Ears*", what they mean is that they love the *music* that they hear. But when an art collector says "I love Salvador Dali's *The Persistence of Memory*", it is not clear whether it is the *image* that Dali produced or the *historical artifact* that is the object of that collector's admiration and desires.

This psychological distortion goes a long way toward explaining many strange social phenomena in contemporary art -- phenomena that do not occur in the realm of music. {1.1} For example, one strange phenomenon is that of a great many people-on-the-street expressing a distain for many iconic and highly expensive works of contemporary art -- works that are considered masterpieces by the art literati. [srch: proof anyone make modern art; modern art anyone could have done; modern art sucks].

Consider how this image-vs-artifact distinction might distort someone's appreciation of art: A viewer is shown an image that looks like it was made by squirting a bunch of thin streams of paint at a canvas. Is the viewer impressed by (or aesthetically moved by) the image?

But first, the viewer is told that he/she is looking at a famous, one-of-a-kind historical *artifact* -- not just the image but also the actual, physical, one-of-a-kind object that was produced by a famous painter [srch: artist Jackson Pollack] and which has recently been sold for $25,000,000. In this case the viewer may not be impressed by the *image*, but the viewer is guaranteed to be impressed by the *artifact*!

One-of-a-kind Art vs. Many-of-a-kind Music

There is nothing like this kind of distortion in music. We may encounter a Stradivarius violin selling for millions of dollars (i.e., the artifact) but we will never find any music (performed on that Stradivarius violin) selling for millions of dollars. When the art literati consider a work of (visual) art to be a great masterpiece, someone within the upper echelons of art (a multi-millionaire or a museum with private or public funds) will most likely have spent a great sum for that *artifact* (but never that amount for any image or reproduction of that artifact).

In contrast, when a piece of *music* is considered a masterpiece, then millions of people (across all echelons of music) will each obtain a reproduction (a copy) of that work of music (whether it happens to be a song or an instrumental piece) -- with each person paying a small sum of money for that music. {1.2}

In Music, the collector is acquiring those sounds that are pleasing to that collector's ears. In Art, however, the collector is *not* acquiring those images pleasing to the eye; rather, the collector is acquiring *artifacts*. (If collectors were acquiring only images, then they could have a fine collection of posters; which, of course, they do not.)

Exclusivity in Art vs. Inclusivity in Music

When a well-known (visual) artist dies, in general, the value of his/her works of Art rise. The accepted explanation is that, upon death, the artist can no longer produce new pieces. Under the theory of supply and demand, if there is a demand for a product and the supply drops then the price for those products will rise, due to the increased demand for them.

In the visual arts it is common, for example, when a lithograph or serigraph (silk screen) process is used to produce a print, for the artist to promise potential buyers that only a limited number of such prints will be created (i.e., that the plates or screens used to produce them will be destroyed). This behavior only makes sense if the buyers are more interested in having an *exclusive* ownership of a *limited* artifact (as compared to owning a non-exclusive image).

The desire for *exclusivity* (that is so prevalent in Art) simply does not exist in Music. The music aficionado is <u>not</u> looking to own a song that no one else can own! The value of the music is unaffected by some limited (or exclusive) ownership.

Desire to Impress vs. Share

Sad to say, but, based on my experience, most art connoisseurs, when they show off their collections, are more interested in impressing the viewer with the *value* of their collection (rather than with the aesthetic *beauty* of the images). This is a common phenomenon and completely acceptable for other types of collections, in which beauty is not an issue. For example, consider coin collectors. They do not show off their collections to impress the viewer with the beauty of their old coins. What they are showing off is the **uniqueness** and **exclusivity** of their finds. (What is more valuable, a common ancient coin with a nice-looking image on it or a **rare** ancient coin with no image?)

In contrast, when music lovers ask others to listen to their collection of songs (or instrumental pieces), these connoisseurs, in this case, are doing so because they want to *share* their love of this music with the other listeners. In this sense, Music is psychologically *transparent* while Art is psychologically *distorted* (due to the phenomena of artifact existence and exclusivity). The music lover is in no way bothered by the fact that anyone else can go and acquire an identical copy of that music. However, would a billionaire hedge-fund manager pay millions for his/her Art collection if others could own identical pieces?

Copying Art vs. Covering Music

There is another distortion -- one most likely due to differences in copyright laws concerning Art versus Music. In the USA, a musical artist (ma1) cannot deny another musical artist (ma2) the right of ma2 to make a derivative copy of ma1's original song.

Making your own arrangement of someone else's song is called "covering" that song and the resulting song is called a "cover song" (or just "a cover" for short). Copyright law allows for the issuing of *compulsory* mechanical licenses. This license enables the derivative artist to perform a cover of the original song without having to obtain permission from the copyright owner.

The license is called "compulsory" because the original artist is *compelled* to allow the cover to be produced. The derivative musical artist ma2 need not get permission from ma1, as long as the derivative artist pays ma1 a royalty (with the royalty rate set by law). {1.3} In the case of the making of CDs, the mechanical license specifies fees that the derivative artist ma2 must pay the copyright owner for each CD that is (mechanically) produced. To my knowledge, there is nothing like this for works of (visual) art.

In music, there are PROs (Performing Rights Organizations), such as ASCAP and BMI, which require musical venues (such as restaurants, dance clubs, coffee houses, etc.) to pay licensing fees when they want to have derivative artists able to cover songs written by other musical artists.

There is a strong cultural tradition, in the area of music, of many people covering songs. (Consider karaoke bars and all those young people posting videos of themselves covering songs on Youtube.com.)

In contrast, in the visual arts, the word "cover" is never used with this meaning; instead, the phrase "cover art" (in the visual arts) refers, rather, to art that appears on the front covers of books, albums, and magazines. Visual artists who are trying to learn new techniques will attempt to copy (in this sense "cover") the works of great artists, but there is no great desire, on the part of those artists, to sell such works.

In Music, the more famous a song becomes, the more it will be the case that different cover versions will be made, bought and sold (and listened to and loved) by music aficionados. For example, one of the most covered songs in the USA is the 1935 Gershwin song *Summertime*. According to Wikipedia, there are over 25,000 different covers of this song. For example, a fan of this song can obtain covers of *Summertime* performed by Billie Holiday, by Ella Fitzgerald, Janis Joplin, Frank Sinatra, Nina Simone, and many more musical artists.

This joy and enjoyment (of covering the work of others) occurs in jazz to a very high degree. Certain songs (referred to as "jazz standards") are covered by a majority of jazz groups, with a great deal of improvisation thrown in.

This kind of sharing (of the love of a song, as performed in different ways by different artists) simply does not occur -- at least in any way to the same degree -- in the visual arts. Art aficionados appear, for the most part, to not be interested in buying thousands of different "covers" of, say, Leonardo daVinci's *The Mona Lisa*.

Artists <u>will</u> create caricatures of famous works of art (when the original works are in the public domain and thus not under copyright) in order to make a political statement, or to show off their skill within a certain style or genre, but such cases are exceptional enough to "prove the rule" that, in general, there is not a culture of creating "covers" in the visual arts (as there is in music). {1.4}

So Art is psychologically *distorted* by its collectors' desires for superiority (in terms of *exclusivity* and monetary value); by its one-of-a-kind uniqueness (affecting supply and demand) and, most fundamentally, by the distinction between a work of art as an historical *artifact* (for collecting) versus as an *image* (for the enjoyment of the eye).

In summary, Music lacks artifacts and thus is judged solely by how pleasing the actual music is to the ear. Unfortunately, Art is not always judged by how pleasing its images are to the eye. In contrast, the act of creation in Art immediately produces a physical *artifact* whose monetary value is often <u>independent</u> of any qualities of the associated image.

Chapter 2
VALUE MULTIPLIERS

Most artists are interested in having their works of art attain greater commercial value. No matter what artists might say, they are happier creating their art if what they create is perceived by others as more valuable.

There are products that are *fungible* (easily interchangeable with their value unaffected) -- examples include different 20-dollar bills or different stock certificates (indicating ownership shares in the same corporation). In contrast, there are products that are not fungible (e.g., a piece of real estate). Posters (showing the same image) are fungible while the original painting, in general, is not fungible.

When an object is fungible and easily reproducible (such as a music CD or a poster), a natural way to increase its value is to produce and sell *multiple copies* of it. In contrast, most works of Art are of limited fungibility.

The *Giclée*

One way to produce copies of a canvas painting is by means of a *Giclée*. I believe that some consumers misperceive a *Giclée* as a unique, one-of-a-kind artifact. *Giclée* is a French word that refers to a spray of liquid. Thus, a *Giclée* is actually a *reproduction* of a painting -- one that is produced by a large, high-quality inkjet printer. By making *Giclées*, the artist can retain the original artifact while still selling each inkjet printing for thousands of dollars.

Mid-level consumers of art (who are not very sophisticated with respect to technology) are often **not** told that a *giclée* is simply an inkjet reproduction (unless they ask the seller outright). "Giclée" does sound so much better than "inkjet reproduction".

In general, however, collectors of Art are interested in one-of-a-kind *artifacts*, not reproductions. The seller of any product naturally wants to increase profitability for a product. Thus, the seller needs some form of **value multiplier**. In general, there are 2 ways of multiplying the value of a product:

1. Create and sell *many reproductions* of that product - that is, a *physical* multiplier.

2. Increase the prestige and desirability of that single product - a *psychological* multiplier.

Musical artists attain financial success via the first method while visual artists mainly do so via the second method.

Inherent vs. Perceived Utility

Objects tend to have both an inherent utility and a perceived utility. The *perceived utility* is set due to its demand or market value. The *inherent utility* of an object is related to how it can be used to fulfill some need. A hammer can drive nails into a board (its inherent utility), but what if our neighbor tells us that he needs a hammer right away. He does not have time to go to the store and he is willing to pay us $200 right now for our hammer. In that case, the hammer has a market value (momentarily) of $200.

There is a common saying: "Something is only worth what someone else is willing to pay for it." (A person can claim that their home is worth $1 million but if no one is willing to pay more than $100,000 for it, then $100,000 is what it is currently worth.) This saying is actually quite insightful, since it is the basis of many a market bubble. [srch: books market bubbles].

A famous example is the tulip market bubble that occurred in Holland in the early 1600s. Investors would buy tulip bulbs and then sell them at a higher price. This profitability attracted more investors. As more investors sought to buy tulip bulbs, that demand raised the price of tulip bulbs, which then attracted yet more investors, which then led to increased prices, and so on. At the height of this bubble, investors were buying and selling tulip bulbs for values that were more than 5 times the value of an average person's *annual* income! (Today, with an average US income of around $40,000, such bulbs would be selling each for $200,000!)

Each investor was willing to pay an outrageous price for a tulip because he felt that he could sell it to someone else for yet a higher price. Once the market became saturated (no new investors to drive up prices), it then crashed and speculators found themselves in possession of tulip bulbs that no one was willing to purchase.

The tulip bulb has only a modest inherent utility (looking pretty as a flower) but, during the market bubble, each bulb had obtained an enormous *perceived* (i.e., market) value. This value, however, was based only on the psychology of the market (which can be very fickle). {2.1}

Like a tulip bulb, a work of art has a very mild inherent utility (that of hanging it on a wall and admiring it each day). The main value of art is in terms of its market value -- what someone else is willing to pay for it.

How can the artist (or subsequent owner of a work of art) multiply its market value? This can be achieved as follows: Convince the potential buyer that he/she will be able to sell it later for much more than it is currently worth (namely, the bubble principle).

There are different ways to accomplish this goal:

1. Convince potential buyers that the artist (who produced the work) will become more and more famous over time and that the artist is a committed professional who will continue to produce unique, interesting works of art.

2. If the artist is already famous and his/her works are selling at a high price, then convince potential buyers that the artist will pass away soon, and thus the work that is currently available will be from a limited stockpile.

In Music, one could argue that perceived value is created the other way around: When millions have bought the music of a musical artist, that might cause others to be attracted to that music. One might refer to this as the "busy restaurant effect" or (more unkindly) as the "sycophantic or lemming effect". (When a restaurant is very busy, more people want to go there with the explanation being that, upon seeing so many customers, others assume that the food must be very good.) In the case of the sycophant, this person wants to curry favor with those who like a type of art/music and, in the case of the lemming, those types of people are unsure of their own taste in art/music and therefore simply follow the crowd.

Psycho-Social Reasons for Liking Art (or Music)

Many people like a work of art (or a piece of music) because:

- Their friends like it and they want to continue to be accepted by those friends.

- They want to become friends with an individual or group and that group likes that type of art.

- They have very little knowledge of art (music) and so they stick to what is tried and true for them (e.g., the art/music they liked as a teenager).

- They notice that the so-called "experts" in that area of art greatly appreciate that type of art (music) and so they defer to them (as a safe path to take).

- They want to feel exclusive so they try to find a form of art (music) that few others seem to like.

- They want to feel superior to others, and so they find works of art that others either cannot afford, or, due to their uniqueness, others cannot obtain.

The last psycho-social reason mentioned above seems to occur only in Art -- not in Music.

I believe that, when it comes to taste in Art *and* Music, the majority of people take their cues from the environment. If those environmental cues indicate that the work should be appreciated, then they will appreciate it, but if those cues indicate that the work is to be ignored, then they will ignore it. There are scenarios, in both areas of Music and Art, to support this claim. For example, when people are shown works of Art by unknown artists, but they are placed in an upscale gallery with so-called experts raving about them, then they will perceive the Art to be of very high quality.

The same is true in Music and in other areas of aesthetic judgment (for example, taste in wines). {2.2}

For example, when the world-famous violinist Joshua Bell performed at a major concert hall, people would pay over $100 to hear him, but when he went into a subway in Washington D.C. and played intricate classical pieces for 45 minutes, practically no one stopped to listen to him. [srch: Joshua Bell violinist subway]

Social Influence in Cultural Markets

Some cultural works become extremely popular while others languish. Experts in areas of popular culture (movies, books, songs, paintings) often fail to predict what will or will not become a cultural "hit". Matthew Salganik (a sociologist at Princeton University) decided to explore this phenomenon. He and his colleagues (Salganik et al. 2006, 2008) wanted to know to what extent the *quality* of a work of art determined its social success and, alternatively, to what extent *random* factors and *positive feedback* determined success. Positive feedback occurs in cases in which initial attention paid to some particular work of art (call it WA1) causes other people to then become aware of WA1, which causes yet more people to then pay attention to WA1, and so on. Thus, attention leads to more attention.

Salganik wanted to address the following potential cultural paradox: if the quality of some work of art determines its success, then it becomes hard to explain why the level of success of many other high-quality works is so unequal and also so unpredictable. However, if the success of any work of art is determined by initial random factors, coupled with positive feedback, then this would provide an alternative explanation.

Salganik found 14,341 participants on the web -- American teenagers who enjoy obtaining free downloads of songs composed by unknown bands. They were asked to rate songs (with 1 to 5 stars) and were given the opportunity to download the songs if they so chose. Salganik set up two broad classes of environments: independent and social influence. In the *independent* environment, the participants were not told what other participants were doing. In the *social influence* environment, the teenagers were told how other participants were rating songs. The popularity of a song was measured in terms of the number of teenagers who chose to download a song.

Salganik and colleagues took 48 songs by different unknown bands and set up multiple, distinct *artificial* cultural environments. Within each, the researchers specified a different set of ratings for the different 48 songs. That is, each teenager was seeing ratings (by other teenagers) that were artificially set by Salganik and his colleagues and the number of "likes" were different for each distinct, artificial cultural environment.

If the quality of a song determines its ultimate popularity, then they expected to observe the same set of songs becoming successful (in terms of downloads) across all the different environments. However, if participants were being heavily influenced by observing how *other* participants were rating songs, then a completely different set of songs would become successful (in terms of number of downloads) within each different environment and that is what they observed.

Salganik pointed out that their study differs from real cultural markets, in the following ways: (1) real markets have product placement and promotion, (2) real markets have an enormous number of products (as compared to just 48 songs).

Salganik's experiments help explain why experts are so poor at predicting what artistic works will become highly successful, because their success is predicated only tenuously in terms of quality, but more strongly in terms of social influence. Salganik and colleagues describe this social-influence effect as a "self-fulfilling prophecy", in which an initially perceived popularity creates yet more popularity.

They also discovered, however, that the very worst songs failed to retain popularity and the very best songs, over time, did manage to recover their popularity, even after having been given initially inverted ratings. However, high quality songs (with inverted artificial ratings) never reached the same level of downloads.

If a song had a reasonable level of quality to begin with, then how well a song did (in terms of downloads) was greatly influenced by what participants perceived other participants to be doing, in terms of their ratings. In their 2009 study, they repeated their experiment with 2930 participants who were older and more international and obtained similar results.

As knowledge of Salganik's ground-breaking work has spread, some commentators in the visual arts have stated that this social influence effect should operate for the visual arts as well. For example, in 2014 Alix Spiegel (on National Public Radio), in a piece titled "Good Art Is Popular Because It's Good. Right?" states that most people think that the Mona Lisa is the most famous painting in the world because "there must be something profoundly special about it ... but is that true?" and then goes on to talk about the effect that random processes, coupled with the positive feedback of social influence, can have on a work's success.

Why Art Installations Often Appear Ridiculous

Over the years I have seen many art installations at galleries and museums. More often than not, they have struck me as idiotic, pointless and/or ridiculous. For years I was confused as to why artists would produce something that, often, had the following properties:

1. It is unsellable.

Why produce something that cannot even be sold? I have seen installations composed of boxes of breakfast cereals with their contents spilled over pieces of furniture and scattered all over the floor. Clearly, such works have a very low probability of ever being purchased.

2. It may have taken a lot of work but the labor (put into making the installation) wasn't worth the overall effect.

I once saw an installation that consisted of hundreds of polaroid photos (of the same naked young lady, from the waist up) all floating in a rubber pool of water. What the point was supposed to be (to this day) escapes me.

3. The effect could have been executed with much greater skill.

Another installation I remember visiting consisted of an unpainted canvas and a few feet away from it was a bunch of string, suspended in space. The string had a series of white, red and blue blobs of paint that had been painted along the string. The viewers where asked to walk between the canvas and the painted strings.

After a brief moment I realized what it was the artist had in mind: The string was supposed to represent the paint (that would normally have been brush strokes on the canvas) and, thus, the viewer was supposed to experience what it would be like to pass *in between* the canvas and its painted image. This is not a bad idea, but the execution of this notion was so poorly done that the installation was less than impressive.

Another installation I recall (which I saw at a museum in Germany) consisted of janitorial materials (a ladder, a broom, etc.). Do you get it? Clearly, the viewer is supposed to consider the role of common, occupational objects -- as Art. I was unsure as to whether it was an actual art installation or whether a janitor had left his tools while in the middle of some clean-up task in that museum room. In fact, there have been cases where highly priced Art has been mistaken for trash. {2.3}

Another Epiphany

I used to wonder why artists would make such wacky, silly, over-the-top installations. Then, one day, I had another epiphany: If artists can increase their *celebrity status*, then those artists can sell their *other* works of art at a much higher price! It does not matter that the installation might be mocked or can never be sold. If the artist receives sufficient publicity from that installation, then that artist's *other*, standard (sellable) works of art will have increased in value.

Role of Celebrity Status in Art and Music

A celebrity is one who is "celebrated" by others. In general, people want to own things that are recognizable by others. If I buy a child's chair I might pay $50 dollars for it, but if I can tell others that, say, the actress Shirley Temple sat in that chair as a child, (and if others know who Shirley Temple is) then those others may be willing to pay thousands of dollars (or more) for such a chair. The value of the chair will rise with its associated celebrity's status. If the celebrity is known world-wide then the associated object will be more valuable than if the celebrity is known only within a small social sphere.

If the celebrity's status is so great that people might even pay to see the object, then it's value becomes even greater. An example (for chairs) would be some poorly designed, ugly, uncomfortable chair that President George Washington happened to have had in his room when he was a child. Such a chair might be worth hundreds of thousands of dollars. This example shows the clear difference between *aesthetic* value (in this case, defined as low -- due to being ugly, poorly designed, uncomfortable) and *artifactual* value.

Art and Publicity

How does someone, who is not already famous, get celebrated? Answer: Publicity. Unfortunately, one of the most expensive things to purchase is publicity. Companies spend millions of dollars every year to make their products known to potential customers, or to keep their products in the public's eye/mind. They will pay millions for endorsements by celebrated personalities. Companies know that certain celebrities attract enormous attention and so, if that celebrity endorses their product, then millions of people will become aware of this fact, and companies are willing to pay very large sums to create the necessary awareness about their products.

Works of Art are as much a product in the marketplace as any other type of product. Consider the wacky things that (very savvy) musical artists will do, in order to attract attention. Recently, the musical artist Lady Gaga received an enormous amount of free publicity by wearing a dress made out of slabs of raw meat. Think of the marketing genius here. As a result of this 'event installation', Lady Gaga was celebrated in numerous news shows and TV talk shows. For her to have bought an equivalent amount of publicity would have cost millions of dollars.

Her increased celebrity status results in more and more people becoming aware of her existence, which translates directly into more people becoming aware of her actual products (namely, her shows and her music CDs), which translates into increased sales.

There is a saying that, when it comes to publicity, bad publicity (notoriety) is just as good as good publicity. Recently, the actress and singer Miley Cyrus was criticized for behaving in a slutty manner (e.g., simulating sexual acts with her tongue sticking out) but the resulting notoriety has increased the public's awareness of her existence way beyond her current fan base, and so can be considered highly successful (in terms of increasing celebrity status). {2.4}

Related Epiphany: Christ-in-Urine Technique in Art

So what is a poor, unknown visual artist to do? The artists who are not already wealthy cannot afford publicity; therefore, they must generate it by "guerilla-marketing" techniques. Some years ago, an artist gained great notoriety by creating a work of art in which a small plastic crucifix of Jesus was placed in the artist's urine. This piece shocked and appalled a great number of devout Christians. From a marketing point of view, however, it was very savvy (like Lady Gaga's dress made of raw meat), because the more people who know who that artist is [srch: Serrano Piss Christ], the more valuable will be any *other* work produced by that artist.

The purchaser of any other work by that artist will now be able to boast (to anyone viewing his/her art collection): "Oh, that piece is by Serrano. You remember, the controversial artist who created *Piss Christ*."

Now, every time I attend an installation that is crude, or offensive, or ridiculous, or idiotic or pointless, or over-the-top in some way, I think to myself: "Another use of the meat-dress and/or the Christ-in-urine technique."

There are millions of works of art (and songs) out there. I am sure that a subset of them are brilliant, beautiful, inspiring and/or emotionally moving, but we will never know because we will never experience them. We won't become aware of their existence because the artists involved (or their agents) did not do a good enough job of publicizing their work.

The artists who succeed in the marketplace are those who are either excellent promoters themselves, or who have the good fortune of attaching themselves to others who are excellent promoters. {2.5} For example, the artist Salvador Dali was known as a shameless self-promoter and, as a result, he became extremely successful. [srch: Salvador Dali self-promoter] Toward the end of his life, his celebrity status was so great that it is said that he could scribble a rough image on a napkin, along with his signature, to avoid having to pay for a meal at a restaurant.

Some artists develop tremendous artistic skill and have great creativity. They hope that a high level of skill will ultimately result in their work being recognized and admired, but this recognition often fails to occur.

There are two, self-promotion techniques that an artist can employ (to avoid the need for having to develop artistic skill and/or visual imagination):

1. Shock and/or offend others with one's art: We have already discussed this technique.

2. Create works of art on a grand scale: If one polaroid nude photo has some effect on the viewer, then perhaps a great number of nude photos may have an even greater effect. (As a result, the viewer is forced to look at a pool with numerous nearly identical nude photos floating in them.)

Many artists have become famous for making hundreds of something. For example, Christo and Jeanne Claude are a married couple who make common, uninspired objects, but they do it on a large scale and, as a result, have obtained art-celebrity status. For example, they have draped an entire large building with cloth; they have placed hundreds of large umbrellas out in the desert; in 2005 they placed large yellow banners throughout New York's Central Park [srch: artist Christo NY gates]. With their increased celebrity status, they can then more easily sell their other, more standard works of art.

The Value of a Good Backstory

Thompson (2014) is an economist and business professor who specializes in the very high-end contemporary art market. He is interested in understanding why certain works sell for $25 million or $2.5 million while others sells for $250,000 or $25,000.

Thompson asks why someone would buy, as a work of art for $2.4 million, a wax mannequin of someone else's wife, which was not even produced directly by the artist (rather, contracted out to technicians) and especially when (given Thompson's analysis of the art market) most high-end art pieces will not increase in value as well as a decent investment portfolio. Also, Thompson claims that such art will probably not be considered as important 25 years later.

His answer is: a good backstory. A "backstory" is a story that the new owner can tell his/her peers that will entertain, shock, amaze or otherwise impress them. A backstory is greatly improved when it involves well-known celebrities. In the case of this particular purchase, the mannequin represents Stephanie Seymour, a supermodel who has graced over 300 magazine covers. Before she married her billionaire industrialist husband she dated Axel Rose, the lead singer of the well-known rock band Guns N' Roses. Her husband is also a celebrity who owns a polo team, an extensive art collection, and publishes the well-known magazine *Art in America*.

Thompson states that, while many art pieces end up on the auction block as the result of death, divorce, bankruptcy, or legal troubles, those types of events rarely appear in an auction house's backstory. He discusses the case of Sotheby's backstory for an Andy Warhol piece titled *Brillo Soap Pads Box*, which sold in 2012 for over $700,000.

Sotheby's backstory emphasized how the work represents a revolution in art, with a profound influence on the notion of art authorship.

Thompson tells a different backstory -- one that he points out was not used by Sotheby's but that could be considered more factual -- namely, that an artist named James Harvey designed the Brillo box for the Brillo Company in 1961, as a container design. Warhol then took Harvey's design and re-titled it as art.

This backstory would probably not be what a new owner would want to use to impress his peers (and if it had been used at auction by Sotheby's, might not have helped with the sale of this particular piece).

Chapter 3
RECORDINGS of ARTIFACTS

In Chapter 1 we discussed a hypothetical, sci-fi-like scenario (referred to as *SF-Aw/oAF*) in which no artifact would be left after an artist painted an image on a canvas. In that scenario Art becomes like Music -- in the sense that any labor performed by the (visual) artist fails to result in an artifact.

A Sci-Fi Scenario for Music (*SF-MresAF*)

Now let us consider the flip side of this scenario, which we will refer to as sci-fi scenario *SF-MresAF* (*Music results in an artifact*). In *SF-MresAF*, we imagine a strange world in which, whenever a musical group (or individual musician or singer) performs, there magically appears a unique, physical artifact for that performance. Later on, whenever anyone interacts with this physical artifact, they experience that original performance -- just as though they had attended the actual, historical performance.

Furthermore, in scenario *SF-MresAF* this physical artifact cannot be reproduced without a great of loss in fidelity; therefore, it is a one-of-a-kind object. This feature is critical for such objects to be sought after and collected (just as physical paintings are collected by wealthy art patrons and museums). In this scenario, we would expect museums of music to come into exist and for wealthy collectors to spend large sums of money -- in order to own these unique, one-of-a-kind, physical, historical artifacts of music.

Relationship of Reproduction to Artifact

Let us examine the relationship of reproduction to artifact in Art more closely. Why is the painting on the canvas usually a unique and non-reproducible physical artifact?

The answer is that, as the result of being painted, the canvas now contains (in most cases) an enormously complex physical surface -- one created by layers of little bits of strokes and blobs of paint, positioned on the canvas due to a set of very idiosyncratic forces (arising from the particular motions of the artist's hands and tools, such as brushes and palette knives).

To perfectly reproduce such brush strokes (for the vast majority of art pieces) becomes nearly impossible.

Consider just one brush stroke made across a portion of the canvas. If someone tries to copy this stroke then, if the amount of paint is just slightly different or if the motion is just slightly variant, the result will not be identical. Multiplied by many strokes, the chance of reconstructing a physically identical artifact (by hand) becomes vanishingly small.

Furthermore, if the paint used (say, by an inkjet copier) is just slightly different from the original paint used, the copy could be recognized as different merely through an analysis of the material that was used to reproduce it.

What are the main differences between a *reproduction* (a recording) of the artifact and the *artifact* itself? There are two main differences:

1. *2D vs. 3D* -- The reproduction is mainly an attempt to capture what is perceived by the sense of *sight* (the eyes). (Most people are not allowed to *feel* works of art that hang in museums and galleries.) The recording reproduces only the image of the artifact, usually with its 3D surface (and its weight, its materials, and the physically of its backing, etc.) being left out.

For example, a poster of a painting is a *degraded* representation of a painting due to the fact that the poster is flat while the surface of the canvas is 3-dimensional. This flatness will cause the poster to reflect light in a manner that is different than that of the 3D paint surface on the canvas.

2. *Level of resolution* -- Consider again a poster. It is usually produced by some inkjet process, which may result in a degradation in precision -- in terms of how closely the pixels on the poster correspond to the colors from the brush strokes of paint.

The precision of a recording can be described in terms of the number of colored pixels per inch. The more pixels per inch, the smaller the pixels must be and the higher the magnification needed to spot each pixel within the reproduction. The precision is also affected by the range of colors of the pixels. A pixel may be one of just 3 colors, or it may be one out of, say, 10 (or 100 or 1000) possible different color shades.

In digital recordings, the number of possible colors (the digital palette, so to speak) is based on the number of bits that make up each pixel. A pixel made up, for example, of 4 bits (0000 up to 1111) can represent 16 different colors while one made of 8 bits can encode up to 256 different shades of color. Thus, greater precision requires more information (in terms of number of bits).

So artifacts are *superior* to their reproductions in the realm of Art, in terms of both *physicality* and *precision* (*resolution*).

Reproductions of Music

Now let us compare reproductions in Art with reproductions in Music. In the case of Music, the closest thing to an "artifact" is the original, historical *event*, which is the musical performance. Outside of our sci-fi scenario *SF-MresAF*, no physical artifact remains, so only some recording will remain (if one was made during the performance). Like a recording in Art, a recording in Music is a *degraded* reproduction of the original performance. Even if the recording includes video (i.e., images of how the performance looked from one or more angles of viewing) it still fails to capture all aspects of the physicality of the performers or of an audience member experiencing that performance.

Let us consider a recording that contains only the audio (music) information from a musical performance. This recording was made by placing microphones at various positions during the performance. These microphones will necessarily alter the original sound (that reached a listener's ears) in some way.

Precision/Resolution in Music Recordings

In digital recordings of Music the number of bits will determine the audio features of a note (which could be the tonal quality of a musical instrument or of a human voice). In Music, for example, it is common to compress an audio file (with loss of fidelity) in order to have the file take up less space in computer memory, or take less time to transmit the file to another site on the web (or to download it onto a laptop). An example of this type of *lossy compression* is an mpeg file. In such a file, fidelity is lost, as compared to the original audio file (used to make a CD). The CD reproduction itself is also usually a compression of the original recording. (The original recording of the performance might have been done using 32 bits, but a standard CD employs only 16 bits.)

Is an Artifact Always Superior to its Reproductions?

An interesting difference between recordings in Art and Music is that, in Art, the artifact is <u>always</u> considered <u>superior</u> to the various reproductions of its associated image. In contrast, many audiophiles prefer the reproductions of a performance (as compared to the original performance) because, in a music studio (that is, on a computer that is programmed to behave as an Audio Manipulation Device or AMD), the original recording can be *enhanced* in various ways. For example, via computer software, a variety of music effects can be applied, such as increasing a sense of sound volume (through adding a slight artificial "echo" or "reverb"). Similarly, if a singer was a bit "pitchy" (i.e. sang a slightly flatted or sharped note) then *auto-tune* software can correct this error. Since there is <u>no</u> original artifact of a music performance (in the sense that there is in Art), the musical artist is always working with a (degraded, imprecise) reproduction of the original (ephemeral) performance, and so is free to modify the reproduction in a wide variety of ways. {3.1}

In contrast, modifications of reproductions of Art are almost always restricted to attempts to represent the original artifact with as much fidelity and verisimilitude as possible.

Imagine if a recording expert were to attempt to sell a Salvador Dali poster in which all of the colors had been changed, in order to make some part of the image "stand out better". How shocked art connoisseurs would be!

A major goal of reproduction in Music is to *enhance* the sound (by some subjective criteria). The main goal of reproduction in Art is to stick to the original image (associated with that artifact) as much as possible.

So, in Music, the artist is much freer in the manipulation of the recordings of performances, since there is no original, "gold standard" artifact against which to compare those recordings. In Music it is always the case that a recording is being compared only against some earlier recording. What the musical artist (and the musical artist's producers) feel "sounds best" will end up being what is sold to the listening public, and that product will further become degraded as listeners compress those audio files to produce mpeg files (for easier storage and transmission).

In contrast, in Art the image (associated with the artifact) is always considered the "gold standard" by which to judge any image reproduction. In a sense, Art functions within a straightjacket (as compared to Music) when it comes to the creation, and manipulation of reproductions. Subjective "enhancements" of the artist's artifact are rarely tolerated. {3.2}

These differences, in how reproductions are valued and treated in the areas of Music vs. Art, are quite deep. While it is acceptable to make a singer (or instrument) sound fuller in a music recording, I have never heard of an artist's painting receiving enhancements (of color, shading, perspective, balance).

Consider the image on the front cover of this book. It contains an inserted, smaller image of the actual artifact (a painting by Andrea Dyer, titled "Butterfly Eyes" © 2013). The main image, taken of the artifact is, in this case, somewhat different from the image on the artifact itself.

First, to produce the image, the artifact was photographed outdoors, with spots of sunlight falling on it (e.g. light areas on lips and cheeks do not occur on the original artifact). Second, the aspect ratios, of both the main image and the inserted image, were altered in order to fit the image to the 6"x9" dimensions of the book cover.

Is the main image, on this book's cover, superior or inferior to the image associated with the actual artifact?

For the art connoisseur, the answer to this question must be, almost by definition: "It is inferior."

Personally, I think that, once an artifact has been produced, other art lovers should be allowed to make "covers" (see Chapter 1) of the artifact, by creating photographic and digital variants (as long as the original work is properly acknowledged and the original artist is properly compensated – as is done in Music).

By the way, the artifact was *not* thrown away in the trash! This trash placement was done only temporarily, for the purpose of contrasting the notion of *image* as compared to that of *artifact*.

Chapter 4
THE IMAGE SPACE

Three decades ago I was having lunch in a cafeteria at a major East Coast university and I happened to strike up a conversation with an Art professor. As a joke, I stated that, within a few decades, technology would advance to the point where flat-screen displays would exist. Once that happened, I declared, there would no longer be a need for artists to create new works of (canvas) art because the owner of a flat-screen display device could just start out with an all-white screen and then have the screen cycle through all combinations of colored images, until it had finished the cycle and reached the final image of an all black screen.

In between an all-white and an all-black image, there would exist all other possible colored images, including the Mona Lisa, all of Impressionism, all cartoon images, etc. Not only would the flat screen display all known images, it would also display all images that had not yet been invented, thus eliminating (at least in the area of static, canvas Art) the need for any artists!

I stated that the flat screen could be programmed to display each image for a second and then for it to systematically cycle through all possible images. Whenever the viewer liked a particular image, that image could then be downloaded to some storage device for subsequent, more leisurely viewing.

The art professor became very upset and agitated. I tried to then explain that the image space was too large and that I had just been joking but I could tell that I had put this art professor in deeply disturbed state of mind.

Size of The Image Space For a *Tiny* Canvas

Well, the years have passed and people now *do* own flat screens; however, they do not use them to cycle through all possible images. Why not? Just how many different possible images are there "out there"? What is the size of this image space and what is its overall structure?

Let us consider an extremely *tiny* canvas -- one containing just 9 pixels (each indicated here by an asterisk):

```
        *   *   *
        *   *   *
        *   *   *
```

In general, the precision (or resolution) of a standard image contains 72 pixels per inch and so our 9-pixel image above would be very tiny indeed -- much smaller than a tiny fraction of a postage stamp!

Let us assume that each pixel (of these 9) can consist of one of just 10 different colors (white, yellow, red, blue, ... up to black). Let us assume that a computing device will display the number 0 as white, the number 1 as yellow, 2 as red, and so on, up to the number 9 displayed as black. How many different possible images exist in this tiny-canvas image space (of just 3x3 = 9 pixels per image)?

Well, if we place all 9 pixel positions (from this tiny canvas) in one horizontal row, then we have something analogous to a car odometer with 9 positions. An all white canvas would be the number 000000000 and an all black canvas would be the number 999999999. The number 000999111 would be a canvas where the top row is white; the middle pixel row is black and the bottom row is all yellow. There are 1,000,000,000 or 1 billion of these tiny images (i.e., the 999,999,999 images, plus the image consisting of all zeros, add up to 1 billion).

As we can see, in an odometer, for each number (color) in a given position, there are 10 different colors that can be chosen for the positions next to it. Thus, to calculate all possible images (numbers) we must multiply the number of possible colors times itself for every position. In the case of the odometer, there are 10 different numbers (possible colors) per position (0 through 9) and since there are 9 positions in total, there will exist $10 \times 10 \ldots \times 10 = 10^9$ (that is, 10 multiplied by itself 9 times) different numbers (or images). 10^9 equals one billion. {4.1}

What happens if we were to have, instead of 10 different colors per pixel, say, 100 different colors (i.e., different shades of yellow, red, blue, white ...)? Then, for a tiny canvas of just 9 pixels, we would have $100 \times \ldots \times 100$, that is, 100 multiplied by itself 9 times, which is $100^9 = (10^2)^9 = 10^{18}$ different images. So there are *1000 quadrillion different images* possible on such a tiny canvas (when we allow for a 100 different colors to be used per pixel).

Image Space for A Standard-Sized Canvas

Let us now scale our canvas up to an average size (one that might be common in peoples' homes). Nowadays a flat screen TV will commonly have around 1920 pixels (in length) times 1080 pixels (in height), which is somewhat more than 2 million pixels. For simplicity, let us assume that a flat screen's size is exactly 2 million pixels and that each pixel can display one out of 100 different possible colors. Thus, the image space (total possible number of different images that can be displayed) is equivalent to a car odometer that has 2 million positions, in which each position can have a value (color) between 0 and 99. The total number of images in this space is: $100^{2,000,000} = (10^2)^{2,000,000} = 10^{4,000,000}$ or 10 multiplied by itself 4 million times!

Just *how big* is such a space? The only way to get a sense for such a number is to compare it to some other very large number. For example, suppose we were to tightly pack the known universe with atoms. That is, we take all the empty space between the stars and galaxies and fill this empty space tightly with atoms. How big a number would we get and how does it compare to $10^{4million}$?

The known universe is an immense object. According to most physicists, the known universe began with a "Big Bang" around 14 billion years ago and the light from that event has been traveling outward in all directions ever since. {4.2}

Light moves at an enormous speed. If it were made to go around the Earth, light would circumnavigate the earth over 7 times in just one second! Light travels over 186,000 miles in just one second. In one year light travels around 6 billion miles!

Since the Big Bang, light has been traveling (in all directions) for around 14 billion years. The distances in the universe are so vast that scientists talk about "light years" -- which are the distances that it takes light a year to travel, even at its tremendous speed. So the universe could be viewed as a gigantic sphere -- one that has a radius of 14 billion light years (or a diameter of around 28 billion light years across). How many atoms could be packed into a sphere of this immense size?

One can fit more than 100 million atoms along an inch. Therefore, in a cubic inch there would be at least $100million^3 = (10^8)^3 = 10^{24}$

atoms. All we now have to do is to calculate the number of cubic inches in a sphere the size of universe and we will have the number of atoms that one could fill the universe with (as though one were filling an enormous spherical jar with very tiny marbles). The number one arrives at is approximately 10^{120}.

Now let us compare this number (although truly enormous) against the image space that we arrived at earlier, which is $10^{4,000,000}$ -- which we will abbreviate as 10^{4M}.

We have already seen that the number 10^{120} is enormous; but how does it compare with $10^{4,000,000}$? Let us refer to 10^{120} as PUA (packing the universe with atoms) and refer to 10^{4M} as FSIS (Flat-screen Image Space). How much bigger is FSIS than PAU?

To determine how much bigger one number is than another, we usually divide the smaller number into the larger number, to see how many copies of the smaller can fit into the larger. So let us divide FSIS by PAU. When we divide numbers with exponents we simply subtract the exponents. For example, $(10^5) / (10^2) = 10^{(5-2)} = 10^3$ (since $100,000 / 100 = 1,000$). Let us do this for FSIS and PAU.

FSIS / PAU = $10^{4M} / 10^{120} = 10^{(4,000,000-120)}$, which equals $10^{3,999,999,980}$. As we can see, we have hardly put a dent in FSIS! So PAU goes into FSIS nearly as many times as the original FSIS number itself! So it would take $10^{3,999,999,980}$ *universes*, with each one tightly packed with images (in which each image takes up only the space of an atom!) in order to store all the possible images in FSIS (our flat-screen image space)!

Imagine, instead, that we packed the known universe with atoms and then *for each atom* we created an entire, new universe (of the size of our known universe). Now, imagine that we associate a different image with each atom in each of these different universes. Would we be able to use up all of the images from our image space?

There are roughly 10^{120} atoms packable in our known universe. If we create that many universes (one entire universe per atom) then we will have $(10^{120})^{120} = 10^{(120 \times 120)} = 10^{14,400}$. This is still *nothing* when compared to FSIS -- the number of possible images that can be displayed by a standard-sized flat screen.

Displaying The Image Space Over Time

Suppose we attempted to display a different image (in the flat-screen image space) every second. (This is what I had told that art professor, decades ago). How many images could be displayed within some time interval?

Suppose a flat-screen TV managed to already exist at the start of the Big Bang -- therefore having 14 billions years of time in which to display different images. If a different image were displayed every second, how many images could be displayed (out of the total number in FSIS)? This is the same question as asking how many seconds there are in the span of 14 billion years. In seconds, the universe is roughly 10^{17} seconds old, so even if we had the entire age of the known universe at our disposal, we would only be able to display 10^{17} images out of the (super-humongous!) $10^{4,000,000}$ images that exist in the flat-screen image space!

Notice that, in our thought experiment (about FSIS) we are doing something quite different from what most artists (and art connoisseurs) do. Instead of thinking of ways of creating new images, we are considering *all possible images* (of a given canvas size). From this point of view, every image already exists (as a possibility) and is "out there" -- available to be discovered -- even if a given image has never been created (or even conceived of).

In any case, now that we have an appreciation for the mind-boggling *immensity* of the image space, no artist ever need worry that all possible images will be generated automatically (and thus eliminate the need for artists).

But what about the content and structure of FSIS? What type of content does the image space contain and how are images related to each other?

Large-Scale Structure of The Image Space

In terms of content, within the image space there will exist all the kinds of images that sighted people have experienced: all forms of photographs (of scenery, plants, portraits of people, buildings, social events), cartoons, sketches, all types of paintings found in museums (abstract, surreal, impressionistic, religious, etc.), even all types of text (e.g. a photograph of a page of a book, or of a sign on the street, or of a work-sheet containing cursive handwriting), and so on.

Let us consider one category of images -- selfies (self-portraits taken with a hand-held device). FSIS will contain, not only all current selfies in existence, but also *all possible* selfies that could even be imagined (including selfies taken by real or imaginary alien species). These self portraits will include, for any one individual (whether or not that individual ever existed) all possible expressions and selfies of that individual at all possible ages.

Let us consider another category -- images of the content of any closet containing just clothing. FSIS will contain all possible images of real and imaginary clothing closets (including all combinations of items in those closets where, for example, some subset of the shirts are hanging upside down, or in which the shoes are floating in the air, or in which every suit is horribly frayed or has holes in it (with images of suits with holes of every possible size and in every possible combination of hole-locations).

The most surprising fact about FSIS is that the vast majority of images in FSIS will look like *noise* (what one's TV set looks like late at night when there is no signal).

Let us set *each* of the 2 million pixels (each with 0-99 different possible shades of color on our flat screen) to a *randomly* chosen color value. The resulting image will most likely look like a grayish, amorphous, noisy "mush".

Let us now change the value of just <u>one</u> pixel. This will give us a completely new image (because, technically, if just <u>one</u> pixel is different in one position, then it is a different image). Let us call our first random image Rand1 and the new image Rand2. These images will look identical to the eye but they are different (that is, they have a different color at <u>one</u> pixel position). How many images are there that look nearly identical to Rand1 but differ by only one pixel value? Well, if we choose one particular pixel position there will be 100 variant, noisy-looking paintings (because we have assumed that each pixel can take on 100 different shades of color). If we do that across all 2-million pixel positions, then we will get 100 x 2-million image variants, all which look nearly identical to Rand1!

But we can go further. What if we were to change <u>two</u> different pixel positions at the same time? Suppose we pick a pixel position somewhere in the upper right corner of the image and a second pixel position somewhere in the middle of the image. Clearly, if the image already looks noisy then it will still look noisy after changing just 2 pixels. How many combinations of 2-pixel-altered images are there? Well, since each pixel can take on 100 different values (colors), *combinations* of 2 pixels will have 100x100=10,000 different values. So there will be 10,000 times the two million image variants, all which will still look nearly identical to Rand1. This process (of selecting 2, then 3 pixels, then 4 pixels, then 5 pixels to alter simultaneously) can be done, each time producing enormous combinatorial subspaces of images, all of which will continue to look like Rand1 (our initial, random, noisy image).

Now suppose we alter *every* pixel (all 2 million) at once, all altered randomly. The chances are very good that we will still have a noisy-looking image! Only if we select our pixel positions in a *non-random* way (say, selecting all pixels that happen to fall in a horizontal line) and select a reasonable portion of these to have a non-random set of color values (say, all the same shade of red) will we start to see an image that starts to look less random.

For example if we were to select a 200 (horizontally) wide by 6 (vertically) deep set of pixels to all have the value 35 (assume that 35 is a bright red color), then we might see an image that looks like noise everywhere -- except that there would be a horizontal red line somewhere on the image.

So, in general, the image space is dominated by *random* (mushy, gray, noisy) images! Images that are interesting to human eyes are actually only a very, very tiny fraction of all of the images in the image space. Consider a non-random image, such as a painting of a dog lying down. This image is like an oasis in a vast desert of sand (where each grain of sand is an image that looks like noise). Remember, however, that we can alter many combinations of selected pixels at random and our painting will still look like a dog lying down, so this oasis is a *region* (not a point) in the image space.

Imagining Image-Space Structure as a Physical Space

Here is a way to imagine the image space: Think of our universe. Our universe is known to consist mostly of vast regions of empty space (which will represent for us all those noisy, uninteresting "mushy" random images), with galaxies (as oases of interesting images) interspersed between the "mush" (empty space). Each star in a galaxy can represent a clean, clear image of some sort, where related images are closer to one another (by physical distance) than to unrelated images. For example, a dog looks more like other dogs (than like cats) and will look more like other 4-legged animals (than like fish). Flowers will look more like other plants than they look like insects and so on.

Astronomers now know something about the large-scale structure of our universe. Its structure is one of clusters of galaxies that are connected to other galactic clusters by thin tendrils or filaments of visible matter. In our image space, these filaments can represent a *morphing* function.

Morphing is the process of altering an image (of some object) over time so that it gradually turns into an image of a different kind of object. For example, one can give the image of both a cat and a dog to a morphing function and it will produce a series of intermediate images that, when played in sequence (as a video), will turn the cat image into the dog image. So, in our vast sea of uninteresting images, there "float" oases of interesting images with tendrils/filaments of intermediate images that transform one oasis (cluster of similar-looking images) into a different image-cluster. If we consider the center of a "star" as analogous to a clear image of some specific object, then, as we move way from that image, the image will become noisier/messier in some manner, until finally, as we reach the dark space around it, the images in this dark area will now consist of those "mushy" images that look like noise.

There are many ways in which an image (one with a clearly defined structure) can be made to look less structured, or noisier. Consider some painting of a dog. We could shoot a spray of dirt at that painting; we could pass a brush (with some color of paint on it) over different areas of the painting; we could make the colored blobs/strokes in different areas of the painting take on random colors. These kinds of operations would serve to make the dog image look "dirtier", blurrier or less distinct (and less clear and less recognizable).

Some Implications of the Image Space

By examining both the size and structure of the FSIS image space, we have arrived at some conclusions:

1. The image space is mind-boggling enormous, probably beyond any enormity every considered (except for the concept of infinity itself).

2. The image space is dominated by noisy, dirty, mushy-looking images,

followed next by noisy/blurry hard-to-recognize "dirty" variations of recognizable images, with clean recognizable images being the *rarest* of the images.

3. Images that are recognizable (or otherwise interesting to humans, such abstract, geometric patterns; images from Nature; images of dreams, such as surrealistic images, etc.) constitute only a tiny, tiny, tiny fraction of all images.

What are the implications (for artists and for Art) of these properties of the image space?

One implication is that, since the vast majority of images are featureless, noisy images, it requires the imposition of *constraints* to select out *interesting* images from the vast sea of uninteresting images. For example, if we place a simple constraint, such as that of forcing all pixels to be of the same color (say, blue), then we get an all-blue image, which is of some, (albeit minor) interest. As we add more constraints, we can generate images with more interest. For example, if we add the three constraints of: (1) circularity, (2) same color within the circle, and (3) different color outside the circle, then we will produce an image that could be described as a blue background with a yellow circle located (somewhere) on that background.

Another implication is that, noisy ("mushy", "dirty", featureless, vague) images should be considered inherently less interesting (since they are so common) when it comes to judging such images (that is, ranking them in terms of other images).

Image Sub-Spaces

The above constraints in our 3-constraint example are still somewhat underspecified. We have not specified *where* the circle is to be located on the canvas, nor have we specified the *size* (radius) of the circle. For example, if we select a center for the circle to be placed somewhere on the right side of the canvas and select a radius that is larger than the height of the canvas, then only a portion of the circle will appear on the canvas. We will now be the proud owners of a *partial* yellow circle on a blue canvas.

The *under*-specification of constraints leads to creating, not a single image but to a *set* of possible images. In the above case, the set consists of all images of a given color with one circle of a different color, where the size and location of the circle can vary. This set of images (generated from these constraints) constitutes an image *sub-space* (of the original, immense image space).

The more constraints we specify, or the more detailed a given constraint happens to be, then the smaller the image sub-space will become, in terms of the number of possible images that make up that sub-space.

A very detailed constraint, such as that all pixels on the canvas (or flat screen) must be blue, except for one (which, let us say, must be white), will create an image subspace with 2 million different images. How did we calculate this? Well, if there are 2 million pixel positions making up our original image space, then there will be 2 million different positions in which the color white (as a single pixel) can appear (with the rest of the pixels set to blue). If we allow for, say, 10 different shades of white, then the image sub-space would grow to be 2-million x 10 (or 20-million different images in that particular sub-space).

Consider again the image sub-space of yellow circles placed on a blue background. This is a larger image sub-space. To produce any specific image from this sub-space we must decide on the *location* of the center of the yellow circle and the *size* of the radius of that circle. Consider an added constraint in which the circle's radius cannot be greater than 200 pixels in length. Since we can place the circle's center at any pixel, we will have 2 million possible centers to start with. Since there are 200 different sizes that the radius can be (from 1 up to 200), we therefore have 200 x 2million = 400 million different yellow-circle-on-blue images in this particular sub-space.

Constraints and Their Origins

What types of constraints exist in Art and where do they come from? Some constraints are *geometrical* in origin: straight vs. curved lines; different types of geometric objects, such as circles, rectangles, triangles; the projection of 3D geometric objects onto 2D surfaces, etc.

Other constraints are *process*-based: the stroke of a brush; the movement of a finger or palette knife against a blob of paint already on a canvas, etc. Some constraints relate to the positions or sizes of different objects within an image (or canvas). Other constraints relate to the types of objects to be drawn (e.g. a cat vs. a tree) or the number of objects allowed (e.g. a constraint that no more than 18 cats can appear in the image sub-space).

The potential number of constraints may appear limitless but, in fact, the number of constraints that artists think up and use is many, many times smaller than the number of images in the image space. Remember that the main purpose of a constraint is to *restrict* the image space in some way (since the vast majority of images in the image space are uninteresting, amorphous, noisy images).

One may describe the process of creation that the artist goes through as that of creating more and more constraints until the constraints have reached a point of restricting the image sub-space to a single image (or to a very small set of images).

For example, an artist (call her Jenn) might first decide to draw a cat. Jenn then decides that the cat will be sitting (which further restricts the sub-space -- in this case, to a sub-space of seated cat-like images). Jenn then decides to paint the seated cat floating in a cloud which is above a tree on a wheat field.

Each decision here consists of placing more and more constraints on the nature of the image. Let us say that Jenn starts by painting first the cloud. As she paints she is deciding how much of the canvas will consist of cloud (along with the type of cloud). This decision will mostly likely influence what other constraints she decides to place on the location and size of the tree, and so on.

From this example we can see where constraints come from. They come from both the artist's conscious and subconscious mind. They also come from experience with Nature. In the above examples all of the constraints were based on natural objects. The constraints, however, could have been abstract (e.g. patterns of splotches), geometric (e.g. lines for 3D perspective) or process-based (e.g. Jenn decides to dump a gob of paint on a canvas on the floor and then press her foot down on that gob).

Interesting vs. Uninteresting Images in the Image Space

Throughout this discussion I have assumed that, for most humans, images that look like noise will **not** be considered very interesting. What are *interesting* images? One just has to look at past images (produced by artists, designers, photographers, cinematographers, cartoonists, journalists) to see the kinds of images that interest humans. We live in environments created by both Nature (weather, plants, animals, rivers) and by civilization (buildings, freeways, rock concerts, churches, roads, etc.) and we all have to learn to survive in this combination of both natural and man-made environments. Therefore, it is predictable that we will find images, both relating to Nature and relating to human affairs, to be of interest to us. In fact, we are so accustomed to restricting ourselves to just the sub-spaces of interesting images that we might never realize just how much more immense (and, in general, uninteresting) is the space of *all* images.{4.3}

The same applies in the area of Music. Musicians (and other lovers of music) do not sit around listening to the crackling of staticky, buzzy noises on an empty radio station late at night. They greatly prefer songs and instrumental pieces that, when compared to such noise, are highly constrained and structured.

The constraints in Music include patterns of repeated rhythms; sequences of certain types of chords; sequences of certain notes (e.g. scales and scale segments); note pairs and triads with different types of harmony, and so on.

Why are so many constraints applied by the mind so effortlessly? I think that the answer here is that the human brain itself has a structure (constrained through processes of survival and evolution) that subconsciously impose numerous mental constraints. (See Chapter 13.) Other constraints arise over time, through learning. (See Chapter 15.)

Another part of the answer is that Nature appears to follow laws (e.g. gravity, refraction of light, friction, laws of heat, etc.) and so Nature itself is far from random. Whenever we store (in memory) images from the Natural world, we are obtaining images that are already constrained. Any image that is based on Nature will be following whatever constraints those natural laws happen to impose and those natural laws will constrain the kinds of images we experience.

It is for the above reasons that we find it relatively easy to avoid the uninteresting images (that dominate the image space FSIS of all possible canvas images of a given size) and to concentrate on that tiny subset of the more *interesting* images.

An obvious, final consequence (for Art) is that, the more an image looks like noise, in general, the more we will tend to be unimpressed and find it inferior to other images. (See Chapter 8 on judging images of art).

Size of 3-D Image Space

All canvas art actually is 3-dimensional (at least to some extent) because the little bits of paint (left by a brush or other tool) create a 3D surface of bumps, ridges and troughs. These 3D surface features are not captured by a 2D reproduction. In this chapter we have concentrated on the size of a 2-*Dimensional* image space (for images up to 2million pixels in size; obviously the image space grows rapidly as the size of the canvas is increased). If we were to want to capture *3D* images, what would that take and what would be the size of this space?

To create a 3D visual experience requires sending two slightly different images at once -- one to each eye. The brain then constructs a 3D experience from these slightly different images. The more variant the images are (within a given range), the more depth of field the viewer will experience.

However, one cannot send two arbitrarily different images to each eye and experience a 3D effect. For example, one cannot send an image of a dog to one eye and an image of a cat to the other eye and expect to see something in 3D. What is needed are two *similar* images (but shifted by the effect of parallax, which is due to the fact that each eye is seeing the same image at a slightly different angle). If image pair similarity were not needed, then it would be easy to calculate the 3D image space for canvases of the size we selected. We saw that, for 2 million pixel-sized images (with 100 color possibilities per pixel), the image space is $10^{4million}$. With the need for 2 images (one for each eye), there would be 10^{4M} for each eye, which is $10^{(4M+4M)} = 10^{8M}$.

However, since the image sent to the second eye is constrained to be very similar looking to the image to the first eye, the 3D image space is nowhere as large as this number. As a very rough calculation, we will assume that the second image is selected from within the top 10% of images closest to the first image. Given this very crude assumption we can calculate the 3D image space (for images up to 2 million pixels in size) to be: $10^{(4million+(10\%x4million))} = 10^{(4,000,000+400,000)} = 10^{4,400,000}$.

So the 3D image space is *much* larger than the 2D space -- that is, $10^{400,000}$ times larger (which is a 10 with 4 hundred thousand extra zeros after it!). However, it still a space that can be calculated and whose content can be reasoned about and imagined.

For any *pair* of 2D images, we can imagine a "3D region" surrounding it. 3D images in this region would look similar to the 2D image, but each would display a different level of depth.

Imagine two photographs taken of some rocks on a beach, each from a slightly different angle. As we vary this angle, the entire image will jut out at us (in terms of depth). Now imagine that we vary regions within each photograph. This variation will cause different rocks within the image to appear to be coming "at us" (or to be receding from us).

One conclusion here is that canvas art in 3D (vs. 2D) does not constitute any insurmountable hurdle. One could have a flat-screen device display 3D images and then one would wear 3D glasses in order to appreciate these images. {4.4}

Chapter 5
DESCRIBING ART
OBJECTIVELY

It is a common saying: "A picture is worth a thousand words." This saying can be interpreted to mean (a) that a picture conveys a great deal of information or (b) that, no matter how many words one uses, the image cannot be adequately captured by words. In spite of the difficulty of describing Art, art literati continue to attempt this feat.

Objective vs. Subjective Descriptions of Art

Almost all descriptions of works of art by art connoisseurs are *subjective*; that is, they convey how the work affects the person writing the description, or how the work compares/contrasts with other works of art by that same artist (or as compared to the works of other artists). In contrast, an *objective* description of a work of art would be one that could be used to faithfully *recreate* that work!

In some *subjective* descriptions there may appear some elements that are partially objective. For example, someone writing a review of a work might state that there appears in it "a large orange half-circle near the left-hand corner". This is a partially objective description, but it would have to be filled out in much greater detail, before someone else could use this description to recreate that orange half-circle. For example, the exact color of orange would have to be specified, along with its exact size and location on the canvas, along with other features, such as its orientation, and so on.

It may be of surprise to some, but for *every* image (at some level of precision/resolution -- i.e. in terms of number of pixels associated with each small area of the image), there exists an *objective* description -- one capable of recreating that image!

At a basic level, each digital image can be represented as a sequence of numbers, where each number represents a pixel value. An image composed of, say, 2 million pixels can be encoded using 2 million numbers. This sequence of numbers is an *objective description* of a particular image, in the sense that, if these numbers are given to some entity capable of interpreting these numbers as an image (i.e., decoding them -- as colors to be placed in their correct positions on some flat screen or canvas), then the original image will be reconstructed.

Description Languages: Natural & Artificial

Any description, whether subjective or objective, must be made using some *language*. To decode an *objective* description (and thus reconstruct the image) requires an ability to understand the language within which that description is being made.

In the case of most *subjective* descriptions, the language used is a *natural language* -- i.e., a language that has arisen during human evolutionary history, such as English, French, Mandarin Chinese, Japanese, Swahili, etc.

Natural languages are extremely complex because humans are so complex. Human languages have very large vocabularies and complex grammatical constructions. Human languages contain many ambiguous words and phrases. Such "natural languages" can get away with ambiguity because the entities who understand such languages (namely, humans) are highly intelligent -- they are capable of rapidly applying context and reasoning to infer which meaning in being intended in a given context.

For example, suppose someone says to you: "John picked up a bat and hit Bill. There was blood everywhere." You immediately understand these sentences to mean:

   a. John grasped a bat with his hand (that is, "pick up" does not mean the case of "pick up" someone socially in a bar).
   b. John grasped the handle end of the bat with his hand.
   c. John hit Bill *with* this bat that he is holding.
   d. "Bat" refers to a baseball bat (as opposed to a vampire bat).
   e. "Bill" is the name of a person (as opposed to a form that refers to a debt).
   f. It is Bill's blood that has spilled (not John's).
   g. "Everywhere" refers just to the area on and surrounding Bill's body. (It does not refer to all points throughout the universe.)
   h. Some of Bill's blood is now outside his body due to the damage caused by the force of the blow.

None of the above is stated explicitly in the original two sentences. Thus, natural languages rely on the intelligence of their users (who able to rapidly infer all of the unstated or ambiguous information not being explicitly stated).

The words/phrases of natural languages refer to complex concepts -- involving both concrete and abstract entities, such as: time, space, authority, relationships, visual images, goals, plans, actions, physical objects, processes, etc. Within the term "natural language" we include technical vocabularies (from law, medicine, engineering, etc.) that enable a more efficient transmission of technical knowledge in specialized areas (e.g. the term "hydrochlorothiazide" refers to a medication to treat high blood pressure in the area of medicine; "hysteresis" refers to an effect in certain materials in the area of engineering; "escrow" refers to a type of account used during the sale of real estate in business, and so on.)

In contrast, all *artificial languages* (those created by mathematicians, computer scientists and engineers) -- at least those created thus far -- are much simpler than natural languages. Artificial languages are usually designed to be interpretable by some program running on a computer.

There are two major approaches in designing artificial languages that can *objectively* describe (and thus recreate) images:

1. Describe the resulting images themselves.
2. Describe *processes* that, when carried out, produce the resulting images.

Below is an example of the first type of approach. It is an extremely simple artificial language -- one for specifying a very restricted set of images.

A Simple Language for Stark Black/White Images

For example, suppose we have a (tiny) canvas that is 8x7 = 56 pixels in size, in which each pixel can be either white (represented by 0) or black (1). There are no colors (or gradations of gray) allowed in these images. Thus, I call these black & white images "*stark*" images.

Here is a simple artificial language we could use to *recreate* any *stark B&W* rectangular images of any size:

[Specify, in binary, using commas to separate the following: the number of pixels across, the number of pixels down, the sequence of 0s and 1s that make up the content of the image -- in the following order: row-1 row-2

… row-n].

For a tiny canvas that is, say, 8x7 pixels in size, there would be 8 rows, with each row containing 7 bits (a *bit* is a binary digit, which is 0 or 1). Let us call this artificial language **L-starkB&W**.

This is an extremely simple (artificial) language, as compared to a human natural language. But it is a *language* nonetheless, in the sense that, once we understand it -- that is, once we know how to interpret it (decode it), we can recreate any stark B&W image (of any size) that was specified (encoded) as a description using this particular language.

Let's try it out. Below is an encoding **E1** of some image **Im-1** . The encoding **E1** (using language **L-starkB&W**) is:

E1 = [1000, 111, 0000101000100100100010101011011001101000
110100011010000000]

The resulting image **Im-1** (see Figure 5.1) consists of a stark B&W image that is composed of 8 rows x 7 columns = 56 black/white pixels. The image contains a black vertical line along the right-hand side of the canvas and a diagonal black line near the upper left-hand corner. It also contains a black rectangle near the lower center of the canvas.

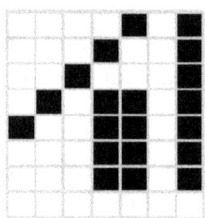

Figure 5.1: Image **Im-1**

How do we know that the image is 8 rows by 7 columns in shape? Well, in the encoding **E1** above, 1000 is 8 in binary, followed by 111, which is 7 in binary. In this particular language, we interpret these first two numbers to specify the size of the canvas (in terms of number of binary pixels -- as rows and columns across and down). Given the first two (binary) numbers, the remaining numbers are interpreted (in this **L-starkB&W** language) as the content of each row, in which each row contains 7 binary pixels. Within each row, each 1 is interpreted as a black pixel; while each 0 is interpreted as a white pixel.]

So, given an artificial language (along with a method for interpreting descriptions within that language) and a description (of some image) in that language, we can interpret (decode) that description to generate (or recreate) the corresponding image.

Thus, our a description E1 above is completely *objective* -- in the sense that, any person (or machine) who understands the language (in this case **L-starkB&W**) will be able to read descriptions in that language and produce (recreate) the corresponding images.

Different Description Languages for Stark B&W Images

Let us refer to artificial languages of the above sort -- languages that provide *objective* descriptions of images -- as *description languages*. If one thinks about it for a moment, it should become evident that there are a great many, potentially different types of description languages that could be invented for encoding stark B&W images.

For example, a slightly different description language might specify the size information at the end (instead of at the front) of each description. An alternative description language might separate each row with a comma, or list the bits in column order (vs. row order).

The use of commas in a description language could be eliminated if the language is limited to describing images on canvases that are less than some fixed, maximum size. For example, if any canvas is restricted to not being bigger than 1024 pixels in length (or width), then the first 10 bits could specify the width; the second 10 bits could specify the pixel length and thus no commas would be needed to separate these two binary numbers.

Using this type of language, if the bit sequence at the front were, say, 00001000001000000000, then this would indicate that each row of the canvas is 32 pixels wide (because 0000100000 in binary equals 32) and that there are 512 rows (because 1000000000 in binary equals 512).

Universality of Binary

A different description language might use decimal numbers (or other types of symbols) but it is important to point out that *binary is universal*, in the sense that *any* type of digital encoding can be replaced by an equivalent binary encoding. {5.1}

An "existence proof" for this claim is that all forms of media (Art, Music, Literature) are stored today in computers as binary files and then later displayed by programs that know how to interpret the description languages that were used to encode those forms of media.

Even a 3D object (say, a sculpture of a frog) can be encoded as a sequence of "bits" (binary digits). To achieve this, one would first decide on the kind of description language to use to encode the frog; then abstractly 'slice' the frog's body into many thin slices and encode each slice as a binary image. The resulting description could then be used to reconstruct the entire frog sculpture.

Capturing Image *Structure* with Description Languages

The most basic form of description, as we have seen (with our **L-starkB&W** language), is that of "paint-by-number" -- at the pixel level. However, there are two problems with this approach:

1. The descriptions tend to be very long (large). A canvas that contains 2 million pixels, in which each pixel can take on, say, a color (from a palette of, say, 256 different colors), will require a description that is 16 million bits in length! {5.2}

2. The descriptions fail to convey any information about the *structure* of the image.

For example, suppose an image consists of a blue sky, a green field of grass and a solitary tree, then it would be nice if an *objective* description could, not only recreate the image, but also indicate that structure in its description.

When I used the word "structure" I am referring to objects and patterns (that can represent concrete or abstract image components) that exist above the pixel level. For example, if an image contains a large black square, then that image has some structure. Images that consist of a noisy, random scattering of different-colored pixels will be said to have little (or no) structure.

There are two general approaches that have been used to capture structure in images:

1. *Use of Compression:* The general technique of compression is to notice that, whenever a pattern of bits repeats multiple times, it can be replaced with a sub-description -- one consisting of that pattern, along with how many times that pattern is repeated. For example, if a million-bit image happens to have a section within it, consisting of a subsequence where the pattern: 010 is repeated 1024 times, then this 3x1024 = 3072 bit-long sequence can be replaced by a much shorter sequence, such as: [1111, 010, 1000000000], which is only 17 bits long.

In this case we are imagining some description language that employs the format: [1111, b, c] where 1111 represents the command to repeat a pattern, b represents the pattern itself, and c represents the number of repetitions of that pattern. (Note that 1000000000 in binary notation equals 1024.)

The result is that the 3072-bit-long sequence has been *compressed* into a 17-bit-long sequence, without any loss of fidelity.

2. *Use of functions:* A function is a type of mapping (from inputs to output). A function takes a set of inputs and returns some type of object as its output. The types of inputs used are call the parameters of the function and the values passed to those parameters are referred to as the arguments.

The functional approach to describing images falls into the second major approach of describing images objectively; namely, the approach of describing a set of *processes* that, when carried out, produce the final image. These processes are carried out by functions.

There exist a great variety of functions -- that both create and modify images (or image segments). For example, a Circle function might have 4 *parameters* (radius, color, fill, loc).

An *argument* passed to radius would be a number specifying the size of the circle. An argument passed to color might be the name (or numeric code) of a specific color shade. The argument passed to fill might be 0 (to indicate only coloring the circumference of the circle with the specified color) or 1 (indicating to fill the entire interior of the circle with the specified color). An argument passed to loc would be a pair of numbers, indicating the (x, y) coordinates where the center of the circle should be located on the canvas.

Description by Means of Functional Composition

Multiple functions can be used by executing them in sequence or by *composing* them with each other. Functional composition is the process of taking the output from one function and feeding it, as input, to another function. Here, we will use a function composition format called "Polish prefix". In this format, the function to be used appears inside a pair of parentheses, with the arguments following it (in some pre-specified, agreed-upon order). For example, in Polish prefix, an execution of our circle function, with color yellow4 filling its interior, of radius 3, at location (43, 54) would be encoded as: (circle 3 yellow4 1 (43 54)).

Suppose that we had another function -- one that twists images in some way. Let us call this function twist. Let us assume that it has 2 parameters: (a) the image to be twisted and (b) the angle of an axis along which the twisting will occur. Then we could compose twist with circle in order to produce an image of a twisted yellow circle, in which the twist occurs along a 45-degree angle, as follows:

(twist (circle 3 yellow4 1 (43 54)) 45)

Here the execution of the circle function supplies an image to the function twist (as the first argument to twist).

Let us now imagine some particular *functional image-manipulation language (FIML)*, consisting of, say, 100 different types of functions (that create and/or modify images). These functions might stretch an existing image, or cause one image to partially overlap another image; or densify an image (i.e., make an image more transparent/opaque) or bend an image in some way, or blur an image, and so on. Other functions might delete a portion of an image, or create part of an image by, say, producing a kind-of simulated brush stroke, e.g., by smearing pixels (all of one color) in a mild arc, and so on.

Different functional expressions would construct (or reconstruct) different images. Some functions could be specialized to produce specific types of complex patterns or objects. A face function might contain parameters that draw a wide variety of human faces [srch: police sketch software; facial composite software].

If such a function were composed with other functions -- that move, stretch, grow/shrink images (passed to them as arguments) then all sorts of surrealistic human faces could be created anywhere on a canvas. A place function might take another function (as one of its arguments) and place the image (specified by that other function) at some designated location on the virtual canvas.

In fact, popular image construction/manipulation software (such as Adobe Illustrator, Corel DRAW, Photoshop) operates by means of image-manipulation functions, mediated by a user interface. For example, when an artist selects a brush size and then moves a finger over a touch-pad (or over a touch-sensitive screen) the software composes and executes the corresponding image-creation and manipulation functions. The user interface makes it easier for the artist to create an image, via the use of virtual brush strokes (as opposed to having to directly type in a brush-stroke function and pass to its parameters the argument-values that the artist wants).

The interface software takes the artist's motion on a tablet input device and turns that motion into the corresponding calls to the appropriate sequence of composed functions. The artist using such software is (perhaps without being aware of it) actually generating a sequence of function calls to an image-manipulation, functional, description-language interpreter.

An *interpreter* is a computer program that is able to decode these descriptions and carry out the computations necessary to produce the resulting image that is being described.

There are two ways that the resulting image can later be reconstructed and displayed: (1) as a "raw" file of the resulting pixels (*binary-pixel description*) or (2) as a description of those *functions*, that were sequenced and/or composed onto each other (which, when interpreted by the interpreter that understands that particular description language, reconstructs the image).

In each case there is a different language (one of pixels vs. one of functions). The advantages of the *functional description* approach are: (a) that it will re-create the image in exactly the same way as the artist created it and (b) the functional description will most likely be much *more concise* (fewer number of bits) and easier to understand than the raw pixels.

In contrast, the pixel description approach -- while also able to reconstruct the image -- lacks a description of both how the image was originally formed and lacks any description of its structure (i.e., any patterns above the pixel level).

One goal of this book is to propose generalized formulas (called *schemas*) for judging art images (see Chapter 8). One aspect of an image is its *complexity*. In the next chapter, we will see how image complexity is related to the objective descriptions that we have just discussed.

Chapter 6
IMAGE COMPLEXITY

For the purpose of this discussion, let us restrict ourselves to images of the same size, say, 2 million pixels. If we were to judge image complexity in terms of the number of pixels, then all images (of the same size) would have equal complexity. But we want to capture our *intuitive* notion of image complexity. For example, an image that is an all-white canvas, or that has a single black square in the middle of white canvas, will not be considered very complex. In contrast, an image of a rider astride a unicorn with wings will be considered more complex. But all of these images will contain the same number of pixels -- so pixel size is not a good measure of complexity.

What is a good measure of complexity?

We want an *objective* measure that will capture our intuitive notion of image complexity (and we will later use this measure when judging images).

Complexity in Terms of Image Compression

Perhaps we can use our already-mentioned notion of compression to help us refine our intuitive notion of complexity: namely, an image that can be highly compressed would be one that would be *less* complex than an image that cannot be as compressed. Using this notion of complexity, the more one can compress an image (without loss of information) the simpler the image. Let's try out this notion of complexity. Assume we have three images:

1. *Black-Square-On-White-Canvas:* This type of image can be compressed into a very short description -- one in which we describe the location and number of black-pixel repetitions (for the black square), along with the locations and repetitions of white-pixels (for the background). This compressed description will be much smaller than the original, 2 million pixels making up the image.

Since we have been able to compress the image into a much smaller description (one that can still completely reconstruct the original image), the image must be quite simple.

2. *All-White-Canvas:* This is probably the least complex image and it will compress down to a very short description; namely, a description consisting of a code for the shape of the canvas, the color white and a number indicating the size of a contiguous sequence of pixels of that color.

3. *Rider-Astride-Flying-Unicorn:* Let us assume that this is an image of a rider on a flying unicorn. The unicorn has outstretched wings. Both rider and unicorn are flying in a clear blue sky, high above a meadow of grass. This image will be much less compressible: We *will* be able to compress the blue sky into a shorter description (for all the repeated blue pixels) and we will be able to compress the grass (assuming that the pattern of grass blades is highly self-similar and so can be replaced with a number and a pattern indicating the number of repetitions of some green-grass-blade pattern), but the rider and unicorn will be much less compressible.

As a result, the compressed description of *Rider-Astride-Flying-Unicorn* (although much less than 2 million pixels in length) will still remain much larger than the compressed description of *Black-Square-On-White-Canvas*, which will itself be a longer description than that for *All-White Canvas*. So this notion of image complexity *does* seem to have a close relationship with the notion of compressibility -- in general, the more compressible an image, the less complex.

Problem -- Complexity of Random Images

Unfortunately, a random (noisy) image -- one in which all of the 2 million pixels have their color values set at random -- is completely incompressible! Why is this the case? Well, since every pixel is set at random, there is going to be little (or nothing) in the way of repeated patterns or structures within the image. From a compressibility stand-point, a noisy image would have minimum compressibility and therefore *maximum* complexity, but this is not the result that we intuitively want! We want complex images to look, well, complex, but we don't want random, chaotic (noisy, "mushy", featureless) images to count as more complex. They shouldn't count as complex because, in some way, they are actually easy to generate (just throw dice and fill in each pixel).

Complexity in Terms of Functions

Let us approach this "random-image problem" from the *functional* perspective (as described in the prior chapter). From this perspective, each image consists of a sequence of functions that are possibly embedded inside other functions (i.e., functions whose arguments are obtained through the execution of yet other functions). An image M-1, whose functional description is larger than another image M-2, could be said to be more complex.

Let us consider an example to see if this approach works. To keep things simple we will restrict ourselves to a language with just four functional expressions:

1. **(PLACE x y fcn)** -- the function **PLACE** can place an image (created by function **fcn**) at location (**x,y**) on the canvas.

2. **(SQUARE color side)** -- the function **SQUARE** can draw a square of size **side**, filled in with color **color**.

3. **(CIRCLE color radius)** -- the function **CIRCLE** creates a circle with a radius size of **radius** and with **color** as its interior color.

4. **(BACKGROUND color)** -- the function **BACKGROUND** creates a background with the background color being set to **color**.

Now consider two image descriptions: M-1 and M-2. Which resulting image is more complex?

M-1:   (BACKGROUND white3)
         (PLACE 30 40 (SQUARE red5 10))

M-2:   (BACKGROUND black)
         (PLACE 100 200 (SQUARE blue9 15))
         (PLACE 500 500 (CIRCLE grey3 44))
         (PLACE 240 60 (SQUARE green2 100)

Functional description M-1 creates a canvas with a single square (painted some shade of red), appearing on a whitish background. M-2 creates a black canvas with 3 objects on it. Clearly M-2 is a more complex image and its description is also *longer*.

Can we now define image complexity in terms of the size (length) of the functional descriptions needed to reconstruct a given image?

Complexity in Terms of Description Length

We still have some problems. One problem is that the *name* of a function could be extremely long. To be perverse, suppose we were to name a function with a name that is 100 letters long. Then a description using that function would look like it is longer than some other description (that does not use that particular function) merely because the first description uses a function with a very long name.

We can solve this problem by encoding our functional language into binary. For example, suppose that our functional language contains 1024 different functions. Then we could encode each function as a binary string that is 10 bits long (since there are 1024 different binary patterns consisting of 10 bits in length). In that way, no function would have a longer name than any other function.

There is another problem. It might be possible to create the same image in a more verbose way. For example, consider image description M-3.

```
M-3:    (BACKGROUND black)
        (BACKGROUND black)
        (PLACE 100 200 (SQUARE blue9 15))
        (PLACE 100 200 (SQUARE blue9 15))
        (PLACE  500 500 (CIRCLE grey3 44))
        (PLACE  500 500 (CIRCLE grey3 44))
        (PLACE  240 60  (SQUARE green2 100))
        (PLACE  240 60  (SQUARE green2 100))
```

This image is much longer than M-2, but if you look at it closely you will see that it is *redundant*. It executes the same functions twice. Thus, description M-3 produces the *same* image as M-2, but by employing a much *longer* description.

We do not want to consider the image to be more complex just because it uses a highly redundant description to create it.

Complexity in Terms of *Minimal* Description Length

We can solve the above problem by specifying image complexity in terms of *minimal* description length, which we will abbreviate as MDL. {6.1} But we still have two remaining problems: (a) that of random images and (b) fractal images. Let us consider fractal images first.

Fractal images (e.g., [srch: Mandelbrot set images]) have wonderful complexity and, yet, they are specified and created by extremely concise formulas! How can this be? The answer is that, although the formulas are very concise in their description length, they are executed (repeatedly) an enormous number of times to produce the image. Each time, the output of the prior execution is fed back, as input, to the next iteration.

So we need to expand our notion of complexity to include, not only the functional description length, but also the *computational complexity* (CC) of an image. The computational complexity is defined as the number of computing steps that are required to recreate the image. Those steps are usually specified in terms of some standard type of computer. {6.2}

Complexity as MDL + CC

Let us compare the complexity of images, not only in terms of the *minimal* description length of the functional specification -- used to create (or recreate) the image -- but also in terms of the number of computations that must executed to construct the image.

For example, let us add a new function, called ITERATE:

(ITERATE from to counter fcn) -- the function **ITERATE** repeatedly executes function **fcn** while increasing a **counter** from start value **from** up to end value **to**.

For example, assume that, to produce some image M-4, we execute the functional expression:

(ITERATE 1 1000 c (PLACE c c (SQUARE c green4)))

In the above case, ITERATE will repeatedly execute (PLACE c c (SQUARE c green4)) with c=1; then increasing c to 2; then to 3, etc. until c=1000. For each different value of c, ITERATE will execute (PLACE c c (SQUARE c green4).

For example, the first execution will be of (PLACE 1 1 (SQUARE 1 green4)). The second execution will be of (PLACE 2 2 (SQUARE 2 green4)) and so on, until finally executing (PLACE (1000 1000 (SQUARE 1000 green4)). The result will be an image with a *thousand* different green squares, each placed at different (x,y) locations. Those (x, y) locations will be at: $(1,1), (2,2), (3,3,)$ up to $(1000, 1000)$.

As we can see here, this rather *concise* functional description represents a 1000 executions of different versions of the PLACE and CIRCLE functions. Clearly, image M-4 is a much more *complex* image than image M-2, even though its description length is probably a lot shorter. It is a more complex because it specifies more computations to be performed.

By including the number of *computations* required, we are factoring in the amount of labor (by a person or a computer) required to create the image.

Minimal Interpreter of a Description Language

There is another problem. An image could be created using a different description language. Let us imagine that two such languages exist: DLan1 and DLan2. DLan2 might have some command CMD that executes the same function F1 twice in a row. Since DLan1 does not have this CMD command, when some program needs to compute the equivalent of CMD it will have to explicitly repeat the function F1 twice, which will make the description length of that program be longer.

We can handle this problem by looking also at the description length of the *language interpreter* used to decode and execute those commands of that language (that will create the final image).

By including the length of the minimal description of the *interpreter* of a description language (**DLan**), we can account for the fact that one description language may have *more efficient descriptions* of how functions are applied than another description language (e.g., an ITERATE command requires a less lengthy description when executing the same function over and over again, but this command must be interpreted by a more sophisticated description language interpreter).

Returning to the Complexity of Random Images

Our remaining problem is still that of how to treat *random* images. The reason that we tend to not be impressed (at least from a complexity standpoint) by random images is that, in such images, we don't really care whether or not a given pixel has a given value.

Let us define a function FILL-RANDOM. This function will receive a location (or region) and throw (simulated) dice to fill in each pixel at this location (or within this region). Thus, although two regions may have different pixel values, from the point of view or our *interest* in that region, each set of values is of equal interest (or disinterest). Now, two executions of FILL-RANDOM may result in distinct pixel values, but they will have *similar* functional descriptions.

Putting It All Together

Finally, we can incorporate our ideas of compression into our functional description language by creating a *function* called COMPRESS. What COMPRESS will do is to receive, as input, a region of an image and look for any repeated pixel patterns in the region. COMPRESS will then replace those pixel values with a description of the locations (where the patterns occur), along with the number of their repetitions within those regions.

Now we finally have a workable definition for the complexity of any image Im:

$$Complexity(Im) = MDL(Im) + CC(Im) + INT(DLan)$$

where:

MDL(Im) stands for the *minimal description length* (in binary) of the functions that, when executed, produce an image *Im*.

CC(Im) stands for the *computational complexity* of an image *Im*, which will be the number of steps required when repeatedly executing those functions (that will produce/recreate *Im*).

INT(DLan) stands for the minimal description length (in binary) of the interpreter that is able to interpret the description language (DLan) in which the descriptions of images are specified.

So, to compare the complexity of two images, we now <u>add up</u> the following for each image:

1. The number of bits that were used to encode the functional description of each image (assuming that each image is encoded in binary using a *minimal* description).

For example, instead of having 1000 repetitions of the functional expression (PLACE ...) above, it will be much more concise to use some description language that contains ITERATE, so we assume that this has been done.

2. Count the number of execution steps used by the description-language interpreter INT when *executing* those functional descriptions (that are described in some language DLan).

3. Add the length (in binary) of the interpreter program INT that was used to execute commands in the language DLan that contains those functions.

The image with the *larger* number of bits should look (and be) more complex. For example, the minimal description length for a fractal image may be very short, but if we count the number of execution steps required to produce that image (i.e., the computational labor required) then the source of the complexity of that fractal is now revealed.

Notice how MDL, CC and INT capture three major features of our intuitive notion of image complexity:

1. MDL -- The smaller the description (i.e., the more compressible), the simpler the structure of the image.

2. CC -- The more labor required (in terms of execution of functions), the more complex the image.

3. INT -- The more sophisticated the description language, the larger the interpreter (for that language) will be.

Some functions will require more computation than other functions and the amount of computation required may depend on the arguments given to a function. An obvious example is the function **ITERATE**. If it is passed 10,000 (as opposed to 10) as the argument to the parameter **to**, then it will perform 1000 times the amount of computation (because iterating something 10,000 times is 1000 times more work than iterating just 10 times).

An Intuitive View of Image Complexity

Let us now try to describe the above in non-computational terms: "The complexity of an image depends on: (a) the amount of *structure* in the image, (b) the amount of *labor* that is required to produce the image and (c) the amount of *skill* needed in carrying out that labor."

Let us examine what we mean by "the amount of skill needed in carrying out that labor".

Consider a Zen-style ink painting (such paintings were greatly influenced by calligraphy). A master of this style may be able to, in one stroke, produce a masterpiece within this style, but it may have taken years of labor to reach this point. So, even though the image is being produced quickly, we must factor in the years of labor required to reach this level of skill.

Thus, we need to include the (minimal) description length of the *interpreter* used in executing the functions that produce the image. This interpreter is, itself, another computer program.

In our final, image complexity formula we are including the *interpreter* that is capable of interpreting (executing) the functional descriptions (of some description language). We have called this program INT. In the case of the Zen-calligraphic master, that interpreter is the experienced human calligraphy artist (who has acquired more skill than some novice).

An *objective* description of the calligraphic master's skill would consist of a computer program that can perform image-creating actions with the same skill as the master. The computational complexity of such an INT program (i.e., that can simulate the master) will be more complex than that for a novice. Such an INT will have a longer description length than that of some other novice-level interpreter. Thus, we are including the capabilities of the master (i.e., his skill level) in our notion of complexity. {6.3}

In summary, image complexity involves adding up all the bits that it takes to encode: (a) the minimal functional description (that when executed, produces the image) plus (b) the actual execution steps required to generate the image plus (c) a minimal description of the interpreter that is used in executing those functional descriptions.

Now let us imagine that we are looking at paintings in a museum or gallery. How complex is a given image? We examine an image and see that there are a great many different shapes, objects, patterns, etc. in it and we find out that the artist studied many years to obtain the skills required to paint these various components. We decide that the image is of a high level of complexity.

We examine another image: It consists of what appears to be of a single, large, calligraphic stroke. We attempt it ourselves but can't seem to reproduce the effect. Again, we find out that many years of study were required. We conclude that the painting is also complex (although, at first glance, it appeared simple), but not quite as complex as the first image. We conclude that it is more complex (than it at first appeared) because we are factoring in the skill level required in producing it.

Finally, we examine a painting that consists of a red square on a white canvas. We learn that the painter produced it within a short time period and with little prior skill acquisition. We conclude that this painting's image complexity is very simple.

The claim in this chapter is that the notion of image complexity developed here (in terms of minimal description length, computational complexity and interpreter sophistication) matches up very well with our intuitive notions of what image complexity should measure. Note that the measure of complexity we have produced here is a totally *non-subjective* measure. It is completely objective -- in the sense that one could program a function (call it IM-COMPLEX) that would take, as input, the following:

1. a minimal functional description (in binary) of an image Im, specified in a description language DL,

2. the length of an interpreter INT that is capable of carrying out descriptions made in language DL.

IM-COMPLEX would cause INT to carry out the computations (to produce the image Im) and keep track of the number of computational steps employed. It would then add this number to the number of bits that make up the descriptions of INT and Im. IM-COMPLEX would then return a number representing the image complexity of image Im.

In the next chapter we will develop two distinct schemas for judging (ranking) works of Art and so when we refer to image complexity in that chapter, we will be referring to the (objective) notion of complexity developed here.

Note that I am not the inventor of such notions (of computational complexity and minimum description length). These are standard notions in Computer Science, and in its various subfields (such as the subfield of Artificial Intelligence and Machine Learning). [srch: minimum description length; computational complexity]

Art Without Artifacts

The image complexity formula (above) works best on *digital* art; that is, art that has been created on a computer -- art produced by manipulating *virtual* brushes and *virtual* paint (or by employing other, digital effects via computer) to create a digital image on a digital canvas (which exists inside the computer's memory).

Notice that this digital art-creation process *fails* to leave an artifact! Thus, this process is very similar to the process of creating music -- in the sense that neither leaves behind any physical artifact and in the sense that one digital copy of the image (or music) is just as good as any other (assuming also that any compression that has been applied to the digital file makes use of non-lossy compression techniques). {6.4}

Even though we cannot apply our IM-COMPLEX function to standard artifacts of Art, conceptually, the same process applies. There are two ways in which we can judge the complexity of an image that is associated with a *physical* artifact:

1. If we take the *results*-oriented approach, then it is easy -- We simply take a digital photograph of the artifact and then run a compression function on the digital image. To the extent that the image is compressible we will obtain a reasonably good sense of how complex it is.

2. If we take the *process*-oriented approach, then it is more difficult -- we have to either have access to information about how the artist produced the artifact, or we have to imagine or reconstruct this process. We could then examine our (pseudo-) functional description of this process to conclude how complex the resulting image is.

We would also have to factor in an assessment of how much skill was required in creating the artifact under consideration.

In the case of digital images, our image complexity calculations could, in principle, be completely objective (and thus be accomplished by computer programs). In the case of images that result from the construction of physical artifacts, our analysis of an image's complexity will have to remain somewhat subjective.

Digital Art vs. Analog Art

Analog Art is what a traditional artist does -- that is, employing actual physical bushes and paints (whether acrylics, oils, water colors or other, physical materials). *Digital Art* comes about whenever an artist uses a *virtual* canvas (i.e., inside a computer's memory) and creates images by employing *virtual* brushes using a *virtual* palette, etc.

More and more artists are using computers to generate digital images. In these cases the artists cannot make money by selling one unique artifact (since none exists) and so they must survive by selling (or licensing) multiple copies (just as in the sale of multiple song downloads in the audio domain).

Some visual artists attempt to have both worlds. What they will do is, first, take a digital image and make a Giclée of it (see Chapter 2) and then, second, attempt to turn that Giclée into an artifact; namely, by adding some gobs of paint to it, here and there.

Clearly, it is much less labor to add a few brushstrokes to a Giclée than to have to produce the original image by the standard, "old-fashioned" process of painting on an actual canvas with an actual brush and using actual paint.

The digital process offers the artist tremendous convenience. For example, if the artist has generated a background color (as a virtual layer) for the digital canvas, then, even after the artist has added other images to the digital canvas, the artist can decide to alter that background color with the touch of a virtual button.

Consider the realm of digital vs analog photography. For years, many old-style photographers argued that digital photography would never be able to compete with chemical (emulsion, darkroom) photography, but digital cameras now dominate over analog cameras.

When you snap a photo with an analog camera, you can't tell if the image is any good. You have to wait until you can get into a dark room and start to chemically develop it. You can't immediately share it over the internet with your friends. In the dark room you are greatly limited, in terms of the types of effects you can employ and you have to deal with messy chemicals.

For the most part, dark rooms have disappeared and more and more professional photographers use digital cameras and manipulate their digital photographs in computers, via software functions. {6.5}

I believe that, over time, digital Art will dominate analog Art.

Chapter 7
ISSUES in JUDGING
IMAGES of ART

Some people want just to *enjoy* Art, without ever having to judge any works of Art, but for the most part this approach is impossible because, in general, people want to maximize their enjoyment of life and that requires making judgments. Suppose we have two movies that we might be able to see at the cinema and we think that movie-1 will deliver less enjoyment for us than movie-2 (all other things being equal, such as cost of theatre tickets, convenience of show times, etc.). In that case we will choose to see movie-2.

We make these kinds of judgments (where we rank something to be above or below some alternative) all the time. The same will have to be the case for Art. All other things being equal, we will prefer to experience (or purchase) works of Art that, in some way, we feel are superior to their alternatives; so making judgments about Art cannot be avoided.

What do I mean here by "judging Art"? I take "judging" to mean the forming of a *ranking*, so a judgment is something that is comparative. One cannot judge an image (or work of art) in isolation. One judges an image by declaring it superior (or inferior) to some *other* image (or images).

Relations for Ranking Objects

It turns out that making judgments about Art can be extremely difficult. We will see why below, but first let me clarify what I mean by a *ranking*.

The basic relations in any ranking will be: $>$, $<$, $\sim$, and $<>$. When we say "$w2 > w1$" (or $w1 < w2$) for two works of art, we are declaring that work $w2$ is ranked above (superior to) $w1$. When we say "$w3 <> w4$" we are declaring that $w3$ and $w4$ are equivalent (in terms of ranking) in that neither can be ranked above/below the other. When we conclude $w1 \sim w2$ then we are stating that they are not comparable. Let us, for the moment, restrict ourselves to objects that are comparable.

The use of the relations of $>$, $<$ and $<>$ can form different types of ranking structures. The simplest is a vertical line, such as the line created by stating: w9 > w7 > w10. In this case, w9 would be physically above w7 on a vertical line with 3 nodes (those nodes being w9, w7 and w10).

We can conclude from the above relational structure that w9 > w10 even though it is not explicitly stated. Thus, the relation > is transitive; that is, (a > b) & (b > c) implies (a > c). If we add to the relations above the additional fact that w9 <> w8 then we can conclude also that w8 >w7 and w8>w10.

Trees and Lattices

The standard kind of ranking (that the relation > creates) is that of a *hierarchy* (or inverted tree). Here is an example of a hierarchy where, for example, w44 > w77, but there is, as of yet, no comparison between w44 and w55. {7.1}

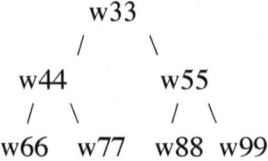

```
            w33
           /    \
       w44        w55
       / \        / \
    w66   w77  w88  w99
```

Figure 7.1

In a hierarchy, each entity has only one entity directly *above* it, but any entity can have many entities directly *below* it. (By "directly", we mean that there must be a line drawn between the two entities under discussion, with no entity in between).

Another common ranking structure is that of a *lattice*. In a lattice, any entity can have multiple entities directly above it. See Figure 7.2.

```
        w55  w44
        /  \  /
    w99   w98 w97 w96 w95
      \   / \  / \ |  /
       w88  w77   w66
```

Figure 7.2

Here, w66 has 3 entities (w97 w96 and w95) that are directly superior to it.

It turns out that the ranking structures formed (when art judgments are made) tend to be lattices (not hierarchies).

Why Judging Art Images is Difficult

There are two fundamentally different forms of ranking: (a) the ranking of *images* and (b) the ranking of *artifacts*. (We will discuss this distinction more at length later on.) For now, we will restrict ourselves to the ranking of *images*. There are 4 reasons why the task of ranking images of Art is difficult:

1. Rankings occur along multiple dimensions.
2. Rankings are weighted by individual preferences.
3. Rankings occur within genres.
4. Rankings are dependent on prior knowledge and context.

Rankings Are Multi-Dimensional

Rankings occur along multiple dimensions. Consider ranking two movie theaters. Theater-1 may have better popcorn than theater-2 but theater-2 may have more comfortable seats than theater-1. Theater-1 may have a better sound system while theater-2 is a bit easier to drive to. Thus, each theater has dimensions of: [popcorn taste, seating comfort, sound system, driving distance]. Comparing theaters requires making comparisons along these multiple dimensions.

If object-1 is superior to object-2 along *all* relevant dimensions then it is easy to rank object-1 > object-2, but this is rarely the case. Usually only some of the dimensions of one entity are superior to the other.

When we examine any two works of Art, they will most likely vary along multiple dimensions. Work1 might have a nicer sky in its image than work2 but work1 may have more crudely executed scene of a meadow than work2. Work1 may have a superior sunset to work2 but work2 may also have an annoyingly poor image of someone sitting by a tree watching that sunset, while work1 may lack this annoyance.

In general, it can be very difficult to decide which work ranks higher when one work is superior to another only across a subset of all of the relevant dimensions.

Individual Preferences

There is the famous Latin saying: "*De gustibus non disputandum est.*" This saying means that there is no disputing taste; namely, each to their own. For example, I may prefer coffee ice cream over chocolate ice cream and hate pistachio ice cream, while some one else will love pistachio and hate coffee ice cream.

One might therefore conclude that ranking anything is impossible. However, that is not the case. It just means that each person's formula for ranking will have components that are weighted (valued) differently. So each individual can clearly judge (rank, rate) different objects. However, *across* individuals rankings may vary. Note that the elements (components, dimensions) used to form those rankings will remain largely the same across individuals -- it is just that they will be weighted differently.

A standard kind of ranking formula has the form:

$$\text{Rank} = w1xC1 + w2xC2 + w3xC3 + \ldots + WnxCn \qquad [1]$$

where each w is a weight (a coefficient indicating how important that component is). Each C is a different component (feature or dimension). The formula [1] is really a formula *schema*, since the specific weights and components are not yet specified.

For example, suppose we rank two foods in terms of the components: Texture and Flavor, then the formula (for some individual named Alan) might be:

$$\text{Taste}_{\text{Alan}} = -2x\text{Texture} + 30x\text{Flavor} \qquad [2]$$

Formula [2] indicates that Alan weighs Texture negatively and Flavor positively and that, for Alan, Flavor is many times more important than texture.

Formula [2] is still more of a schema than a formula because we have not yet specified what we mean by Texture or Flavor, nor have we specified what the details of the formula are for a specific food. Here is an example of an actual formula:

$$\text{Taste(FF)}_{\text{Alan}} = 0.7\text{Texture(FF=crunchy)} + 0.3\text{Flavor(FF)} \qquad [3]$$

Formula [3] states that: (a) it is Alan's formula, (b) that it is concerning french-fries (FF), and that, for Alan, 70% of the Taste comes from its texture (when its crunchy) and 30% from its flavor. Theoretically, we should be able to hand Alan a mushy french-fry FF-1 and a crunchy (but poor flavored) french-fry FF-2 and Alan would apply the above formula to tell us which french-fry he prefers (which would depend on just how mushy one was compared to how poorly flavored the other one was).

The formula schema shown in [1] can be applied to images appearing on works of Art. That is, we will expect individual differences (i.e., different weightings) but the components that are used to make the rankings will be largely the same (at least, within a given art *genre*).

Rankings Occur Within Genres

Try to compare these two movies: *Alien* and *All That Jazz*. It is impossible. Why? Because they exist within completely different genres.

Alien is science fiction horror and outer-space monster movie. It is probably ranked as having 5 stars (out of 5) by most fans of that <u>genre</u>. In contrast, *All That Jazz* is a musical and dance movie. It is probably also ranked 5 stars by fans of this genre, but these two movies really can't be compared to one another.

Within the genre of musicals *Alien* would be ranked extremely low (and within the sci-fi genre *All That Jazz* would also be ranked extremely low).

The same is true for works of Art. One cannot compare a minimalist work with a classical, medieval religious work. One cannot compare an impressionist work with a surrealistic work. These statements imply that the kinds of components that are considered for weighting are going to be different across different genres.

The existence of genres is part of the reason that rankings tend to form lattices, because, even if there exists a strict inverted tree-like structure within a given genre, once multiple genres are included, one will get sets of trees and cross-connections across trees, which will start to look like a lattice. For example, although *All That Jazz* is a musical, it is also about death and dying, and so this movie will also have a place within a ranking lattice of other movies -- ones that are not musicals, but happen to also be concerned with death and dying.

Rankings Are Dependent on Prior Knowledge and Context

This is one of the trickier aspects involved in making ranking judgments. Consider the first James Bond movie, *Dr. No*. When this movie came out, it was 5 stars (within the Bond secret-agent genre). However, as the years have gone by, subsequent James bond movies have incorporated more special effects, more exotic secret agent gizmos, and more thrilling action sequences. As a result, *Dr. No* now looks quaint when compared to later versions; so how should it be ranked?

If we do not take historical context into account, then it will lose its 5-star rating. If, however, we include the dimension of historical innovation (as a component to appear in schema [1]), then it will retain its high ranking. This component takes into account the historical context in which *Dr. No* was produced -- recognizing that it is much easier to produce a good Bond secret agent movie *after* the ground has already been broken by the production of the first one of its genre.

Our prior *knowledge* also affects how we make judgments. This will be true in all areas, including Art. Years ago I saw some very large, minimalist works of kiln-cast glass by Czech glass artists. I was unimpressed. But a few years later I had done some glass blowing and glass casting of my own and I learned about the requirement that glass must be annealed (cooled down on a special, computer-controlled temperature schedule) to avoid later cracking.

It turns out that, the thicker the glass, the longer the required annealing time. Extremely large pieces of glass can take *months* to anneal and, as a result, it can be quite difficult to produce such large, single-piece sculptural forms. Given this additional knowledge, I had to modify my judgment of these monumental glass pieces.

In the area of canvas art, the same will be true: Our judgment of a piece will be dependent on our knowledge of the difficulty (and thus the corresponding skill and effort) required to produce the piece. Thus, knowledge of both a piece's historical role -- in terms of innovation -- and its difficulty in production, will have an affect on how it is rated against other, comparable pieces.

Image Quality vs. Artifact Value

The final reason it is difficult to judge Art is that there exist two completely different domains in which these judgments can be made. I will refer to these domains as the *Art Image Domain* and the *Artifact Investment Domain*. It turns out that the formulas for judging Art are completely *different* in these different domains. That is, the components used when judging *images* are almost completely *different* from the components used when judging *artifacts*. The goal of judging images is to rank some images as superior to others. The goal of judging artifacts is to predict which artifacts will grow the most in monetary value over time.

Structure of the Image-Judgment Landscape

Let us imagine that judgment rankings form *physical* landscapes (with superior images being located physically above inferior images). For the moment, let us restrict our landscape to just 2 physical dimensions. These 2D landscapes can have different structures. One simple structure is that of a single, smooth mountain with one peak (Figure 7.3a). In this case, making judgments would be easy, since there would exist one image (at the peak) that is superior to all images below it and there would exist 2 genres (one on either side of the mountain) in which, within a given genre, the images placed farther up on a given side would be superior to the lower ones. The peak image would be considered superior to images from both genres (i.e., sides of the mountain).

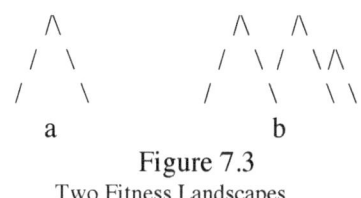

Figure 7.3
Two Fitness Landscapes

However, a (slightly) more realistic landscape (for image placement and thus rankings) is Figure 7.3b, which consists of a range of mountains. Here, there are multiple peaks (with some higher than others). Rankings across different mountains would not be comparable.

When scientists imagine objects being ranked (according to some criteria) and placed in an imaginary landscape, they refer to such landscapes as *fitness landscapes* (because objects placed higher on a landscape are considered superior, and therefore more "fit" than others, according to the selectional criteria).

The *image* judgment landscape happens to have the structure of being very rugged. A *rugged landscape* is one in which the landscape has a fractal property -- that is, on each mountainside there exist rugged regions, each with its own rugged mountainous subregions. That is, as we attempt to climb up the slope of such a mountain, we would encounter paths the also drop down (as we go up and over sub-peaks, that are themselves placed along the side of the larger mountain). Thus, each slope is never smooth, but has its own rugged terrain, with its own sub-peaks, plateaus, ridges, etc. Each sub-peak has multiple sub-peaks, and so on, as illustrated in Figure 7.4.

In fact, the image judgment landscape is much, much more complex than this. First, the image fitness landscape is not 2-dimensional (as in Figures 7.3 and 7.4). Consider a physical mountain range, which is 3-dimensional. Instead of just being able to move up (or down, as in the 2D case) on an actual, 3D mountain range, one can move laterally across a given mountain side. Such 3D landscapes can have plateaus, ridges, crevices, crags, cliffs, etc.

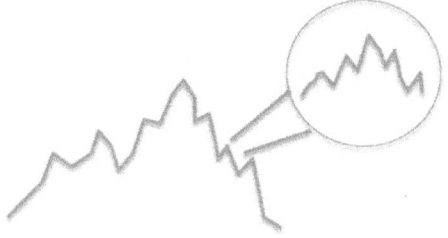

Figure 7.4
Rugged Landscape:
Each side is itself rugged, as shown in the expansion of a segment.

Furthermore, since images can have many dimensions (along which rankings/judgments are made), the landscape we are attempting to imagine will have to be an n-dimensional rugged landscape (in which n is greater than 3). Imagining a physical landscape of this sort is very difficult to do, so let us restrict ourselves to 3D rugged, mountainous landscapes, with images scattered across them.

Given millions of images, figuring out the ranking structure of those images would be like trying to figure out the detailed, rugged structure of the landscape on which these images "reside". If we knew that landscape (and the position of each image on it) then we could answer any question about which image is superior (or incomparable) to any other image. Even if we knew the dimensions (being used for making judgments within each genre), this would be an extremely difficult task.

Are There Objective Dimensions for Judging Art?

The fact that each person will prefer (weigh) different features of art differently implies that the structure of the image judgment landscape will differ for each individual. However, this does not imply that all hope is lost in having objective measures for judging art across individuals. I claim here that, although the weighting on each feature (measure) of art may vary for each individual, most people should be able to agree on the features (measures, components, dimensions) themselves. {7.2}

What might these dimensions (features) be? Well, it will depend on whether the judgments are within the Art Image Domain or the Artifact Investment Domain. Within each domain, it will further depend on what type of genre is being judged.

We will first consider (in the next chapter) those dimensions relevant for judging *images*, and then we will later consider (in Chapter 11) dimensions for judging *artifacts*.

Chapter 8
DIMENSIONS for JUDGING
IMAGES of ART

Here is my (partial) list of dimensions for image judgment: (1) complexity, (2) engagement, (3) framing, (4) scale, (5) historical innovation, and (6) conceptual content.

Image Complexity

We spent all of Chapter 6 on this dimension, mainly because it is a very important one. According to our definition of image complexity, this dimension has factored into it already the skill and labor required to produce the image. In general, simpler images will be judged to be inferior to more complex images. Simpler images take less time, labor and skill to produce and, in general, will engage the viewer less. {8.1}

Image Engagement and Processing Fluency

I have spent some of my time, in various major museums in the U.S. and Europe, looking *not* at the works of art, but at how *other* people interact with those works. In general, those images that I personally believe to be inferior, appear to have a very short engagement time with other viewers. For example, I have watched many visitors to the Tate Modern in London approach some Rothko painting and then, within seconds, turn away. In contrast, I have observed many viewers examining Salvador Dali paintings for many minutes at a time.

Given the existence nowadays of facial targeting and recognition software, it should now be possible for a museum to attach a face-tracking system to one or more paintings and have the system track how long visitors spend observing or examining various paintings. I believe that this approach would provide a fairly good approximation of an image's power to engage a wide number of viewers.

Of course, individuals will vary, in terms of how much a given image engages them. The level of engagement will be due to a number of preference factors, including genre preferences, and also how much a person has viewed an image (or set of images) in the past. Just because a particular viewer quickly turns away from an image does not necessarily mean that this viewer has a low opinion of the work -- it might simply be the case that the viewer, while being a great admirer of the work, has spent a lot of time *in the past* examining it, and so now has no need for allocating more time. But, averaged across many individuals over long periods of time, the overall engagement ability of an image should be able to be accurately assessed.

Image engagement is determined both by the goals of the viewer and the amount of subconscious and conscious "cognitive processing labor" that the viewer must allocate when viewing an image. This kind of mental labor has been called *processing fluency* by those researchers who want to understand the cognitive processing that underlies aesthetics in general, and the appreciation of Art in particular (including emotional responses).

The term "fluency" refers to how skilled a viewer has become at interacting with an image (or genre of images). The more a viewer examines a genre of images, the more cognitively fluent the viewer becomes and thus, less cognitive labor is required. That is, over time, the viewer's brain learns to process this class of images more efficiently. One theory of aesthetics states that, as processing fluency increases, the viewer receives more pleasure. This is the same type of pleasure that is experienced by anyone as they become more skilled at any task (for example, playing a musical instrument).

Some images will have features that the viewer's brain is already accustomed to, such as symmetry and balance. Such images will tend to be pleasurable. Other images, however, may cause a viewer to experience cognitive processing *disfluency*. For example, an artist may, on purpose, create images that lack symmetry; that are unbalanced, perhaps with chaotic elements added, in order to create this disfluency *on purpose*, e.g. [srch: Dadaism]

The viewer, when experiencing this disfluency, will either turn away from the image (experiencing displeasure) or will become intrigued and will make a conscious decision to examine the image more analytically; that is, relying less on the automatic processing of the subconscious and more on conscious, self-aware cognitive processing. Whether or not the viewer does this will depend on the viewer's goals or desires.

So image engagement alone is not a sure-fire method for determining image quality. For example, many viewers have built-in sexual goals/desires and therefore erotic images may cause the most amount of image engagement (and yet not be considered images of the highest aesthetic quality).

After going through a stage of processing disfluency (with respect to an image) the viewer may gain increased fluency and thus, over time, change his/her judgment of an image. That is, an image that, at one time, required more cognitive labor to appreciate, may now elicit pleasure more readily. As a result, the viewer will now find a new class of images more appealing, more engaging, with a corresponding increase in emotional and aesthetic pleasure.

Image Framing and "What is Art?"

This is a interesting dimension of judgment and I was unsure what to call it. I decided to call it "framing" because it has to do with whether or not the viewer can even tell if the work *is* Art or not, and that has to do with how something is framed. For example, we do not tend to think of a toilet bowl or urinal as a work of art. However, if an artist places a frame on a wall and attaches that toilet bowl to the frame, then it suddenly becomes viewed *as* work of Art. [srch: Marcel Duchamp fountain]. The artist has made it into Art simply by *framing* it as Art. In this case the artist is asking the viewer to consider a common, manufactured object *as* Art. For example, the genre of *Found Readymade Art* relies heavily on processes of framing.

Framing does not require that an actual, physical frame be placed around the object. For example, just placing an item (or arrangement of items) in a museum will cause viewers to treat it as Art (since Art is what is expected inside a museum).

We must remember that the vast majority of images that we encounter throughout our lives are *not* images *of* Art. You get up in the morning and get out of bed. You look back and see your unmade bed. That image (projected onto both your retinas) -- you do *not* consider to be an *Art* image. You drive to work. All those images (of roads, traffic, buildings, pedestrians) that enter your eyes, you do *not* consider to be Art. You come home and watch the news (more images, again, not considered Art). So the process of framing is actually *essential* when it comes to judging images of Art.

However, if I encounter an image, framed *as Art*, that I would not normally consider to be Art, then I tend to judge that image more critically. For example, I tend not to be impressed by works of art made of found items -- unless those items have been altered in some way and there is great skill displayed in the way they have been altered, or in the way those items have been placed in relation to each other.

Image Scale

Many an artist has gained recognition for producing works that are unusual with respect to their size. For example, many *Pop Art* pieces consist of common objects that have been blown up to a very large size, e.g. [srch: pop art giant toothbrush] or shrunk to a very small size, e.g. [srch: tiny art].

van den Berg and Pasero (2012) discuss the increase in the number of large-scale works of art. They supply a variety of reasons for why works seem to have grown in size, including: (a) the globalization of the Art market, with the internet enabling a global focusing of media attention, (b) the application of techniques from heavy industry, (c) the emergence of curators who control large spaces (within which large pieces end up being constructed), and a weakening of the distinction between *high* Art (in museums & galleries) and *low* Art (i.e., commercial Art).

This weakening is largely a result of Andy Warhol's successes in the areas of Pop art and readymade art (i.e., manufactured products that are re-contextualized/re-framed as Art).

Personally, it annoys me when some inherently uninteresting item is blown up to an enormous scale. An example is the work of Richard Serra. He creates works made of enormous (rusting) bent steel plates. At the Los Angeles Country Museum of Art (LACMA), in the Broad Contemporary Art Museum a large portion of the bottom floor is taken up with one of these sizable bent walls. If this rusted wall were sitting at a steel yard or a construction site it would garner little interest, but when framed *as Art*, I guess it is supposed to engender some sort of awe. However, as members of the 20th and 21st centuries, we are surround by truly enormous structures (e.g., expansion bridges, skyscrapers, cruise ships, jumbo jets) which are inherently more interesting and have an even larger scale, but they are not normally framed *as Art*. {8.2}

In the area of (canvas) art, it is a well-known psychological fact that very large canvases tend to be treated, psychologically, with more respect than small canvases. In this case the artist is saying "Look at the greater effort (and risk) I have taken, in producing my image on a very large canvas. Since I have put in the increased effort to augment its scale, you, the viewer, need to take it more seriously."

At the other end of the scale, extremely tiny works can also cause viewers to pay more attention, and can lead to commercial success for the artist. For example, Willard Wigan creates extremely tiny sculptures of iconic personages (e.g., Superman, Snow White) and celebrities (Elvis Presley). These sculptures are so tiny that they easily fit inside the eye of a needle! Wigan has created only around 200 such pieces and they are so tiny that he uses the hair of a housefly when painting them. His pieces have sold for over $100,000. [srch: Willard Wigan micro-sculptor gallery]

Historical Context and Innovation

As we mentioned in Chapter 7, images cannot be judged outside of their historical context. Some images were the first of their kind. This fact must be acknowledged and taken into account when ranking images. In general, it is much easier for an artist to improve on a pre-existing image than to have broken entirely new ground by coming up with totally novel images, e.g. [srch: Picasso innovations].

Let us imagine that an artist (Alice) has created a very new image (or category of images), but her renderings of these images are crude and simplistic. Another artist (Amy) comes along and discovers Alice's work. Amy then creates images that, although derivative with respect to Alice's work, are more sophisticated and engaging than Alice's original images. Which images are superior?

This is a difficult question, due to the fact that Alice's images rank higher on one dimension (historical innovation) while they rank lower on other dimensions (complexity and engagement). In this case, a person who weighs historical innovation most highly will judge Alice's images as superior, while someone who discounts historical innovation will rank Amy's images as superior to those produced by Alice.

As result of this thought experiment, we can conclude that it can never hurt to become more educated in the area of Art (in any area, for that matter). We can conclude also that, as we become more knowledgeable in the history of Art, our rankings of images will change.

I am always fascinated when I encounter someone who is more knowledgeable about an area of Art than I am and who has a much higher opinion of the work of some artist than I do. In those cases I try to find out from that person why their opinion is higher. Sadly, in most cases, they are unable to offer me any convincing support for their position.

I am afraid that many Art connoisseurs may be obtaining their opinions, not from a careful and thoughtful examination (and self-examination) of any underlying criteria for how their judgments were made, but simply because, at some time in the past, they were told (probably by some other Art connoisseur) that this particular work is important and is to be ranked highly.

The above criteria we have just mentioned are relevant for judging Art in general. However, within a given genre there will be more specific criteria. Judging impressionistic images will require additional, distinct criteria than for judging realistic images (vs cartoon images, surrealistic images, etc.)

Conceptual Content of an Image

Artists (and those who collect their art) in general do not like to think of the images they produce (or collect) as being *ad hoc* (and therefore lacking any connection to some larger conceptual statement or theory). I believe that, many times, an artist will produce a work and then, *after* the fact, search for a good "just so" story, statement or theory to make that work seem more important and appealing. {8.3}

In many cases, also, once an artist has arrived at a novel theory for some work (or genre) of art, the artist will then use that newly invented theory to guide himself/herself in the making of new works of art.

I have observed students in art classes producing statements, *after* the fact, to characterize and elevate the conceptual status of their pieces. For example, a glass artist might be attempting to produce a vase, but due to a mishap (or lack of skill) the vase comes out all distorted. The artist then comes up with a statement (title, story, description) to make it appear that the vase was *intended* from the start to be distorted in exactly this way, in order to produce a broader comment on some aspect of the world.

Consider the conceptual statements made by two contemporary artists, concerning their own work: (a) Michael Salerno and (b) Liz Hickok.

Salerno has been producing large, abstract canvases filled with many layers of blobs and squiggles. His underlying conceptual theory is that he is allowing his subconscious to produce the images by trying not to plan out what his arm is doing while generating an image. He claims that the resulting images themselves then become objects that enable others to access their own subconscious imagination. Personally, I feel that this is a tenuous argument -- there is no reason to believe that something created by the artist's subconscious will serve to enhance subconscious processing in others.

Hickok has been producing art pieces by filling rectilinear molds with different colors of jello. She then places the resulting jello solids together to form city-like conglomerations. She then casts light through these structures and photographs them. Her conceptual statement has to do with how the ephemeral and weak nature of jello corresponds to underlying weaknesses in human cities. She speaks of how her jello creations "become a metaphor for the transitory nature of human artifacts". [srch: artist Liz Hickok statement]

Personally (that is, in my own formula for judging images) I weigh the dimension of Conceptual Content very lightly. To many others, however, this component is extremely important. Many collectors seem to have been seduced by conceptual theories espoused by artists (as "just so" stories to enhance the importance of their art).

Dimensions Not Included Here

The reader will notice that there are many dimensions -- ones that might seem obvious to any artist -- that I have not included in my list for judging (ranking) images. These include, among others: color, perspective (e.g. vanishing lines, occlusion), shading/shadows, types of brush strokes, and so on.

Clearly, use of color can enhance many images. Perspective-based techniques (along with shading and shadows) will give an image more depth; so why have I left these dimensions out?

They probably should be included but, at this time, I do not have useful objective measures for how to use these dimensions when performing judgments. I cannot at this time specify, for example, how adding more red to some class of images would make them superior. Similarly, I cannot state how adding perspective will improve an image (or class of images). There exist many flat images that happen to be more appealing and interesting than images containing perspective. There exist many black and white images that are superior to color images.

There probably do exist sophisticated measures (involving color and perspective) that would specify under what circumstances the above features would enhance an image, but such measures most likely require a complex analysis of the structure and inferred conceptual content of an image. It is for this reason that I leave off these dimensions.

Process of Image Creation

When artists create images, they have internal, imagined visual constructs in their minds, along with non-visual, conceptual ideas (about both future image content and methods for achieving that content). As the artist begins to create the image, there is a feedback process: As the artist examines what he/she has created so far, that examination triggers changes in the artist's imagined visual constructs, along with changes in whatever non-visual concepts are currently associated with those mental image constructs. This feedback process -- the act of creation altering the direction of future creation -- continues until the artist decides that the image has reached completion.

As the artist examines his/her own incomplete creation, the artist makes judgments about the current quality of the image. If the artist judges a technique to have made the image inferior, then the artist will erase (or in some way cover over) what has just been done. Thus, the artist is constantly judging a sequence of newly created image versions (each considered incomplete by the artist). When the artist starts out, there is some overall goal of what the artist wishes to accomplish. This overall goal is usually a complex mental structure -- one that is most likely underspecified and consists of many subgoals that are loosely interrelated to one another.

Therefore, the overall creative "loop" is:

1. Focus on a mental, visually related goal (from that mental structure will arise multiple, interrelated subgoals).
2. Select a technique for realizing a subgoal.
3. Apply that technique to the canvas.
4. Judge the result (which will modify the overall goal structure).

5. Repeatedly apply steps 1 - 4 (each time with modified goals) until the judging process (in step 4) determines that the image is now complete.

In Chapter 15 we discuss how the above processes of creation might be specified in a much more detailed manner, along with what the consequences, for the future of Art, might be as a result of any success in this specification enterprise.

Chapter 9
CONCEPTUAL ART
VS IMAGE CONTENT

Most artists believe that some conceptual content is conveyed to the viewers of their works. Certain artists, years ago, decided to play around with the idea that the concept (associated with their art) might be as (or *more)* important than the art itself. One of the first proponents of this theory was Sol LeWitt. [srch: conceptualism LeWitt] The resulting genre of art is now referred to as "concept art" or "conceptual art" and this genre has dominated the last half of the 20th century and into the 21st century. Taken to its logical conclusion, in Conceptual Art the image can be completely done away with, leaving only the concept!

I recall attending an art conference at Aix en Provence in France and seeing numerous examples of Conceptual Art. In one case an artist had set up a fax machine, in which a message was faxed to various people in different cities around the world. The art work itself was mainly an explanation as to how these faxes created lines-of-communication through the center of the world; thus creating a kind of abstract, 3D geometrical form inside the Earth. {9.1}

It's wonderful for the artists (and their agents) if they can convince collectors to purchase inferior images by convincing those collectors that the images themselves don't count!

Some artists do not want to just generate works of aesthetic beauty or interest. They want their works to critique (or subvert) existing institutions, attitudes or accepted customs of everyday life. Some artists want their works to be self-reflective; that is, to comment on the processes and relationships (including economic and social) that the artist had to go through in order to produce the art in the first place. Some artists dislike the success of other artists in the current market, and therefore dislike (or disapprove of) how the Art market currently operates (with its interwoven web of galleries, art fairs, museums, curators, dealers, auctions, patrons, connoisseurs, and so on). These artists object to the commoditization and commercialization of Art (with its use of branding, advertising hype and other art-promotion events).

87

Over time, the reactions of such artists have resulted in works of Art that are, in some way, attempting to be non-Art. Genres that tend to have this goal include: conceptual (dematerialized) art, Pop art, readymade art, found art and performance art.

In 1917 the artist Marcel Duchamp submitted a urinal (titled "Fountain") as a work of art and helped to start the genre of readymade art. In 1962 Andy Warhol exhibited works titled "100 Soup Cans" and "100 dollar bills" and helped to start Pop art. He had succeeded in turning *low* (i.e., commercial) art into *high* (i.e., museum/gallery) Art by having his works of art comment on the commercial aspect of Art itself. In 1965 Joseph Kosuth exhibited a work titled "One and Three Chairs" -- consisting of a physical chair, a photograph of a chair and a dictionary definition of a chair. He had helped to continue the development of conceptual art. The term "concept art" was not coined until 1961. [srch: Henry Flynt coin concept art]

As stated in the Preface, artists were profoundly affected by the invention of the photographic camera, which could render vastly superior realistic images. On the positive side, the camera freed artists and enabled them to explore non-realistic styles, such as Cubism, Impressionism and Surrealism. However, these genres did not degrade the role of the *image* in Art.

In contrast, all forms of *conceptual* art seem to result in a degradation of the image. This occurs because, in conceptual art, the concept (i.e., the message, joke, self-reference, commentary on society, subversion, textual content, etc.) is often considered *more important* than the rendering of the image. Some forms of readymade art, Pop art and minimalist art can be viewed as sub-genres of conceptual art. Most forms of performance art are also often conceptual in nature (in the sense that the concept dominates the quality of the execution of the performance).

Image degradation *need not be* an essential feature of conceptual art. For example, it should be possible for a painter to create a work of *great visual interest* that, at the same time, contains a self-referential (or subversive or critical) message. Unfortunately, in such a case I don't think that Art connoisseurs would actually recognize it *as* "conceptual art"!

Interesting Images Await Discovery/Invention

Conceptual art has had an enormous impact on Art in the last half of the

20th century (and also at the start of the 21st century) and, in my opinion, it is an unfortunate effect because, over all, the quality of images (in spite of their enormous sale prices) has gone downhill.

Recall Chapter 4 and reconsider how immense the image space is! We imagined that each interesting, clearly specified image to be a star and a galaxy of stars to consist of related images. We imagined tendrils between galactic clusters acting as morphing functions, which transform one set of images (a galactic cluster) into another set of images (a nearby galactic cluster). Finally, we imagined the immense stretches of black space (between starts and galaxies) to be filled with amorphous, undifferentiated, noisy, (and thus largely uninteresting) images.

Even after focusing only on the stars (interesting images), there are over 100 billion stars in each galaxy and over a 100 billion galaxies in the known universe, and we saw (in Chapter 4) that even if we replaced each speck of empty space with another entire universe, we would not begin to touch upon all of the potentially *interesting* images in the image space! So there is no need to produce degraded, poor images (in which an idea is paramount and, for most conceptual art pieces, that idea usually lasts for only seconds in the mind of the viewer) when there are *so many* unexplored, yet highly interesting images still waiting in image space!

There must exist images that are glorious, amazing, inspiring *and*, at the same time, convey very complex and interesting concepts. They are out there, in the image space, waiting to be discovered/invented. Instead, Art collectors pay millions of dollars to own a Warhol image of a dollar bill. As an image, it is not very exciting and, as a concept (i.e., critiquing our money-oriented, consumerist society), it is a concept that only stays interesting for a few seconds. Perhaps Art collectors prefer images whose concepts can be quickly understood. Personally, I would prefer to view an image of sufficient interest and complexity that it might take days (or years) to understand its corresponding conceptual content. (Salvador Dali paintings are both conceptual and have high quality, complex images, but since the images are of high quality, Dali's work is rarely considered to fall into the category of "conceptual art".)

Competition with Other Conceptual Media

A fundamental problem with Conceptual Art is that, as its associated images become dominated by conceptual content, those works of art enter into realms traditionally controlled by media not normally considered a visual art (such a novels, scientific and technical articles, essays, philosophical works, poems, etc.). In general, these literary/linguistic media are vastly *superior* to (visual) Art as a way of conveying complex ideas (e.g., the story plots of *Harry Potter* novels, Darwin's theory of evolution, legal argumentation by supreme court justices, etc.).

It is the height of hubris for an artist to think that the concept(s) conveyed in a single image will be able penetrate as deeply into the realm of ideas such as those that are conveyed by hundreds of sentences (which can communicate religious ideas, humorous situations, advice on child-rearing, investment strategies, political manifestos, and on and on.)

For readers not familiar with conceptual art, here is an example -- "investment art". In this sub-genre of conceptual art, the artist makes an investment (say, in the stock market) and then, *as Art*, displays documents related to the investment (such as stock shares, or purchase transactions, or documents indicating how the investment has risen or dropped in value). The viewer of these documents is then (I guess) supposed to think about how the process of producing Art for later sale (hopefully for profit) is similar to that of buying a stock that will later be sold (hopefully also for profit), e.g. [srch: artist Les Levine Profit Systems I One]

Don't get me wrong -- I am happy that a work of art makes some comment on (or criticism of, or subversion of) some aspect of society or life. I just don't want that comment to become an excuse for a crude (or shoddy, or dashed off or amorphous) image. If I were an artist who had produced something less than a masterpiece, I would (of course) try to "dress it up" with conceptual clothing.

Rather than embrace and revel in that conceptual clothing, as many art critics and reviewers seem to do; instead, critics should take an inherently skeptical stance toward conceptualism; namely, the more conceptual the art, the more likely one might be to "smell a rat" -- especially if there is an inferior image (or no image at all!). Unfortunately, the opposite seems to occur more often, resulting in mediocre images that are placed high onto conceptual pedestals.

There exist words that seem to have a great impact on certain art connoisseurs. Two examples that come to mind are the words "exploitation" and "subversion". Consider the former. I can cast *any* economic interchange between people in a negative way by using the word "exploitation". For example, I can cast the role of the employer (who is employing others and thus providing them a livelihood) in a profoundly negative way by referring to it as an employer "exploiting" those workers. (No wonder those, who dislike any kind of imbalance in the accumulation of wealth, tend to love that word.)

Art as Subversive

Now consider the use of the word "subversive" in Art. I think this must be a favorite word for conceptual artists. A conceptual artist can elevate *any* garbage-y image that he/she has produced -- simply by claiming that the image (or the process of producing that image) is intended to "subvert" some aspect of current human cultural (or institutional) affairs.

A straightforward example of "subversion" is the *money* paintings of Reena Spaulings, which consist of crudely created banknotes that are defaced in some manner. {9.2}

In contemporary art it is common for artists to seek attention by defaming respected cultural or religious icons (a flag, a crucifix). Unfortunately, the concept conveyed usually lasts (in the mind of the viewer) less time than a one-note samba.

A Comment on Performance Art

In my opinion, the greatest performance art pieces of the 20th century are full-length, motion-picture films. They take millions of dollars to produce and involve the collaborations of hundreds of highly skilled individuals (in acting, directing, costumes, software special effects, music orchestration, staging, etc.). In contrast, the videos produced by most performance artists are really not worth the time it takes to view them (even if they only last a few minutes).

The problem with most current performance art is that, for a performance to really move people it usually requires those elements found in motion pictures and stage productions: likable and richly portrayed characters (that the viewer will care about), goals of different characters that are in conflict, character growth and emotion, plot structure with unknown elements that generate curiosity on the part of the viewer, suspense, and so on. Such elements are usually lacking in conceptual artists' performance pieces.

Performance art's weaknesses become ever more apparent as this sub-genre of concept art attempts to penetrate into areas dominated by traditional film and stage. The best we can state, at this time, is that performance art (and their associated videos) are still at a very early stage of development.

Minimalist Art (and Music)

The theory of Minimalism argues that it is important to strip Art down to its essential design elements. Unfortunately, when taken to its logical conclusion, the most valuable images would then become ones with, say, a single black square on a white canvas, (or just a white canvas!).

From the point of view of minimalism, the most prized work would be, not even a white canvas, but perhaps a frame with nothing in it! Actually, that is still not minimalist enough (since there is still the frame and the wall it is hanging on). Perhaps it is just a dark room with nothing in it!

I recall reading, some years ago, a review in *The New Yorker* by art critic Peter Schjeldahl (2002) of a minimalist installation (by artist David Hammons) in which there are several unlit, black rooms. Each viewer was given a small, cheap little flashlight with an incandescent bulb (this was before the existence of LED-based flashlights). The viewers were sent in to see the works of art and, lo-and-behold, there was no art, only the other viewers, who were wandering about, each hoping to see the art (perhaps they *are* the art -- get it?). Apparently Hammons was unhappy that many of the viewers were absconding with those cheap, little flashlights.

I believe that many have been seduced by the *theory* of minimalism to the extent that the resulting works that they admire have very little image quality to them.

Three other areas, in which conceptual theories sometimes dominate over image quality, are those of (a) *Abstract Art*, (b) *Word Art* and *Pop Art*. In Abstract art, images are produced that have little relation to "visual references in the world" [srch: Wikipedia abstract art; Wikipedia nonrepresentational art]. In Word art, the images tend to be dominated by words, phrases or sentences. Both of these theories, when taken to the extreme, will result in inferior images. In Pop art, degraded versions of commercial images (e.g., brand icons, images of commercial products) are treated as museum-quality art.

It is due to the above types of dangers that I personally assign little weight to the theoretical statements that are created by artists, agents, or art theorists to explain, justify or in some way enhance the intellectual scope or appeal of images (or genres of images) that are of questionable quality.

Did the theory of minimalism affect Music? In classical music, the theory of minimalism reached its logical conclusion rather quickly, in a composition titled *4'33"* (pronounced "4 minutes, 33 seconds") that was composed by the John Cage in 1952. The score of this piece directs the musicians to *not* play their instruments for 4 minutes and 33 seconds. Ostensibly, this musical silence causes the audience to become aware of background sounds in their environment.

Another minimalist American composer is Terry Riley. Listen to his composition, titled *In C*. You can find on Youtube.com. Judge for yourself (my own ears find it monotonous).

Abstract Art

Art historian Alfred Barr (1936) states that there are two types of abstract art: (1) pure-abstractions, which consists of geometric shapes or amorphous forms and (2) near-abstraction, which consist of real objects that have been transformed into nearly abstract forms.

The goal of abstract art is to focus the viewer onto forms, colors, light and shading. In terms of this goal, the use of natural objects could be considered as a distraction. Barr states that the abstract painter will often make an analogy to music since music (when a human voice singing lyrics is removed) evokes moods and associated thoughts without any overtly conceptual content.

While one could view abstract art as impoverished when compared to the full range of possible images, one can also view abstract art as a concentration on structure and on forms of organization (as in pure music). Barr argues that, in this sense, abstract art can be viewed as an *emancipation* from realism.

From the point of view of Chapter 4, abstraction consists of a restriction; that is, restricting the artist to a subset of the image space. It is only an emancipation from an *historical* perspective (since, historically, western Art had also restricted itself, until the end of the 19th century, to mainly realistic images).

Art historian Meyer Schapiro (1937) states that arrival of abstract art has often been explained in terms of dialectics -- that is, realistic art became boring and exhausted and thus abstraction came about as a reaction to realism. He claims, however, that the exhaustion-and-reaction theory provides an inadequate explanation because there are many cases in which some novel approach to art pre-existed, in an undeveloped form (sometimes for centuries) but without ever developing into a coherent movement.

He argues that how one reacts to something depends on how that something is defined. For example, the work of early Impressionists was attacked with the claim that the canvases looked the same whether or not they were right-side up or up-side down. They were also attacked because critics felt that abstract images exhibited a lack of clarity -- and also for their unconcerned, relaxed approach toward the process of applying brushstrokes.

Schapiro states that, while abstract painting may look like the work of a madman or a child, it is the result of a purposeful design process in which the artist is trying to release inner processes of fantasy and spontaneity (in a state that is free from worrying about adult responsibilities). By deliberately applying techniques of impoverishment (such as obscuring and distorting forms) the artists opens himself to "his repressed interior life".

Schapiro states that the spread of abstraction in Art was influenced by societal changes at large. For example, during colonialism, primitive art became available to Westerners but inspired little aesthetic interest during a time, in the 19th century, when rationalism was dominant. As a respect for technologically primitive peoples grew, so did the influence of primitivism in abstract art. Thus, Schapiro argues that an artist's philosophy of Life greatly influences an artist's philosophy of Art.

Abstraction vs. Realism in Art and Music

How do Music and Art compare along the dimension of abstraction vs. realism? In Art, realism is the depiction of actual (e.g. natural and man-made) objects, events and actions. Realistic examples include a man patting a dog's head and a rusted car from a traffic collision. In Music, realism includes music with lyrics (and dialog segments that are sung in operas).

On the abstract end of the spectrum, examples from Music include all forms of music that are lacking lyrics. Examples from Art include arrangements of colors, lines and forms that do not depict any recognizable natural (or man-made) objects, actions or events.

An artist can be inspired by the natural world in order to create an abstraction. For example, an artist might think of a train coming toward her from the upper right. She would then use the recall of this natural event to inspire the drawing of a series of partially overlapping, empty squares -- ones which start out small in the upper-right part of the canvas and then grow as they are placed toward the center.

The resulting image is not recognizable as an approaching train but, nevertheless, that is what inspired this particular abstraction. Given the abstract nature of the image, a viewer will probably not be able to extract this concrete information from the abstract drawing (i.e., that it started out as a train) without knowing what originally inspired this abstract image.

Art historian and critic Varnedoe (2006) points out that many pleasures in life (food, music, sex) are enhanced by the user becoming more knowledgeable in those corresponding areas. In the case of abstract art, the more we know about this area, the more we will project conceptual content into abstract works of art. Varnedoe worries that, perhaps, art connoisseurs are being played for fools (i.e., being educated into seeing what is not there). He says that this anxiety is heightened in him by the fact that abstract artists are known to enjoy playing around with absurdity and emptiness.

Decoding Art's Conceptual Content

Let us grant that works of art often convey meaning to its viewers and that this is a feature of Art that should not, in itself, be denigrated, but rather, should be celebrated. All things being equal, a work of art that has conceptual content (or stimulates ideas in the minds of its viewers) should be considered superior to works that do not.

Let us, for a moment, examine standard messages -- namely, those of language. Words and sentences are the standard conveyors of meaning. How is this transmission of meanings accomplished?

When we say that each word "has a meaning", we are really speaking quite loosely. In fact, meanings exist only in the minds of people and words to not possess meanings themselves; rather, they excite or trigger meanings in the minds of those who hear (or read) those words. After all, a word is just a bit of ink, or an image of the word, or a sound pattern. Words *evoke* meanings and those meanings exist only within minds.

It is difficult to constantly speak this way, so we tend to just say that words "have" meanings. In fact, each word will evoke slightly different meanings in the minds of different listeners (or readers), but there is usually enough overlap in these meanings so that people can still communicate.

To understand a message in language requires the mind of a receiver of the message to apply background knowledge in order to decipher the content of the message. Recall our example of "John picked up a bat and hit Bill." in Chapter 5. To figure out what meaning this sentence is conveying requires that the listener already know about the consequences of hitting someone, about cave-dwelling (vs. baseball) bats, about what standard first-names people tend to have, and so on.

Contextual knowledge is also needed. For example, if we happen, at that moment, to know that John is collecting live bats in a cave with Bill, then what John hits Bill with is most likely *not* a baseball bat but, rather, a flying mammal.

Background knowledge and inferential mental processes are also required to extract conceptual content from images. Consider the image in Figure 9.1. To one viewer this image might convey the concept of a road receding into the distance (with a cross-walk).

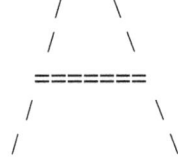

Figure 9.1
An ambiguous image

To another viewer (say, given a visual context of a large letter "C" to its left and a large letter "T" to its right), this image could convey the concept of the letter "A" (as part of the word "CAT"). However, if a large "T" happened to be placed on the left of this image, with a large "E" on the right, then this image might be interpreted as the capital letter "H".

Images are, in some sense, like poetry -- they will convey different meanings to different people, all based on the different background knowledge that different people bring to them. As a person accumulates more knowledge of various genres of Art, then art images (within those genres) will convey more (and different) meanings to those more knowledgeable individuals.

Explaining Art Requires Knowledge and Theory

Let us refer to the knowledge needed -- to extract a given meaning from a work of art -- as an *explanation*. The reason I am selecting this word is because I am imagining a person (Paul), who is incapable of seeing a given meaning (M1) in a given work of art (WA1), while another person (Saul) does extract this meaning M1 from work WA1. How might Saul enable Paul to *also* extract meaning M1 from work WA1?

Saul would give Paul an *explanation* as to how and why Saul sees meaning M1 in that work. This explanation would convey to Paul whatever background knowledge Paul is missing, and also whatever reasoning Paul needs to apply, to now be able to "see" work WA1 in the same way that Saul is seeing it.

The reasoning portion of this knowledge is usually referred to as some type of *theory* of Art. Background *knowledge* is usually acquired by taking an Art history appreciation course (or reading an associated book) and the reasoning required is usually obtained by learning about various theories of Art.

Should Explanations Accompany Works of Art?

To what extent should Art need (or require) accompanying explanations? At one extreme, no explanation is supplied -- the work is untitled and with no accompanying explanation of how (or why) it was produced. It is then completely incumbent on the viewer to bring whatever background knowledge and/or Art theory he/she possesses in order to appreciate and/or assess the work.

On the other extreme, an art piece would always be accompanied by a detailed explanation (which is considered an integral part of that work) of the artist's motivations; of the theoretical underpinnings and goals of the work, and so on. In the extreme case (of conceptual art), the work itself may consist *only* of that explanation! The question here is: To what extent should the viewer be supplied with this kind of explanatory background knowledge and/or theoretical constructs?

One could argue either way: One could argue that there should *never* be an accompanying explanation; that the viewer should always be made *to work* at viewing a piece of Art. On the other hand, a counter argument is that an knowledgeable viewer has already done a lot of prior work (in terms of seeking out this background knowledge from other sources) and so why should this information not also be made available to other viewers, at the time of viewing?

I suspect that, the more impressively rendered an image, the less likely that an explanation is needed, and when it is needed, the less likely it will be that people will disparage the receiving of this information. Examples of this situation abound -- in the realm of famous masterpieces from past centuries (such as those hanging in the Louvre). Many of those masterpieces can be appreciated without any explanation about the artist's underlying conceptual theory (because the skill of the artist is so immediately evident).

The explanations that *are* usually needed in such cases (and appreciated by the viewers) tend to be explanations of the *story or conceptual message* that the art is depicting. In many cases, masterpieces from the past depict a famous event, either from actual history or from ancient Greek or Roman (or religious) myths. The famous events depicted include: battles, coronations, births, the founding of cities, the journey of explorers, etc. The explanations that accompany these works (as supplied by museum curators) tell the viewer about the myths, famous heroic deeds or other events that the images are depicting.

In contrast, with contemporary art, since much of it is dashed off, it requires explanations that, not only explain its message, but also attempt to elevate its conceptual contribution.

These explanations are sometimes supplied along with the work; often they are left for the viewer to obtain from other sources (e.g., books on contemporary art history and theory).

Conceptual Content in Art vs. Music

Conceptual content *in Art* is conveyed through the recognizable objects, actions and events that are depicted. It can also include language elements (e.g., the painter can insert words/phrases in an image). As a result, images can transmit a great deal of conceptual information -- both visual and linguistic. In the case of *abstract* art, since there are no recognizable elements, what is being conveyed is more likely to evoke emotional responses (or concepts by means of subconscious association).

In the case of pure Music, its conceptual content is similar to that of abstract art, in that it conveys mainly emotional content (see Chapter 14). For example, diminished chords often convey suspense; minor chords played slowly often evoke sadness; fast rhythmic patterns with major chords evoke happiness, and so on. The way that Music conveys conceptual (as opposed to emotional) content is through the instrument of the human voice, which can transmit linguistic information along with musical content. Thus, the lyrics of a song can tell a story (of unrequited love, of revenge, hard times, political aspirations, and so on).

The conceptual content of an image tends to be revealed all at once, from a single viewing (although, in a high quality image, more content will be revealed with subsequent viewings).

In contrast, the conceptual content of a song cannot be extracted in a single moment, but must unfold over time. While one part of the brain is perceiving the music (and responding emotionally), another part of the brain will be decoding the message (that has been encoded as lyrics in a given language). In general, the more complex the conceptual content, the longer the song. To convey more concepts requires combining multiple songs into a longer work (such as an opera or musical).

A similar technique can be used in Art -- the artist displays a series of canvases (that are meant to always be displayed together) or the artist breaks up a single, large canvas into regions, in which each region has a temporal relation to the other regions. Using such techniques, a single canvas can also, literally "tell a story".

Amount of Information in Art vs. Music

In general, for any fixed amount of time (that a viewer is perceiving one or more images, or that a listener is hearing a song), the medium of Art has the potential to convey much more information than the medium of Music.

There are two meanings of the word "information": (1) in terms of meaning(s) conveyed and (2) in terms of the number of "bits" (binary digits) used to encode the medium. Here we will restrict ourselves to the second use.

Let us assume that it takes 5 seconds to view a canvas and let us consider a canvas that is 12 times larger than our standard canvas of Chapter 4. Our larger canvas will contain 12 regions that the viewer will examine in sequence. Thus, the viewer will take 1 minute to examine all 12 regions (that is, 5 seconds per region x 12 regions = 60 seconds). In Chapter 4 we assumed that there were 100 different colors. Here we will assume that there exist 256 colors, which can be encoded using 8 bits (since $2^8 = 256$). An 8-bit sequence is called a "byte" and the size of digital files are commonly expressed in terms of millions of bytes or "megabytes" (MBs).

In examining the 12 regions, the *viewer* of the large canvas will have processed, visually, the following number of bytes in one minute: 2 million bytes per region x 12 regions = 24 million bytes = 24MB.

How does this compare to a *listener* who listens to a 1-minute long song that is encoded as an mp3 digital file? On average, an mp3 song file that is one minute in length will contain around one million bytes (1MB). Thus, the *viewer* is taking in 24 times *more* information (in terms of bytes during the same minute) than the *listener*. Thus, the visual medium has the potential to convey much more information (during any given time period) than the auditory medium.

Chapter 10
THEORIES of ARTISTIC
APPRECIATION

There are researchers who are trying to establish a *science* of the aesthetic experience and to understand the nature of the cognitive processes involved in the appreciation of Art. These researchers consist of psychologists and neuroscientists who want to model those mental processes (conscious and subconscious) that underlie Art appreciation. They present Art materials to subjects and perform experiments in order to develop models of what the brain/mind might be doing. This field is sometimes called "empirical (neuro-)aesthetics". In contrast, traditional scholars of Art tend to understand people's appreciation of Art in terms of an historical perspective.

Recently, Bullot and Reber (2013) have offered a general theory in which aesthetics and Art appreciation are understood in terms of both theories of mental processing and use of historical context. {10.1}

They argue that there are three different modes of Art appreciation: (1) the *exposure mode* -- aesthetic appreciation resulting from viewing Art images without any other context, (2) the *artistic design mode* -- examining a work of art from the point of view of the artist; this is, gaining an appreciation of a art piece by understanding both how and why it was constructed (i.e., artist methods and goals), and (3) the *historical-context mode* -- appreciating a work of Art in terms of its historic role and context. {10.2}

They claim that any theory of aesthetics and/or appreciation of Art is incomplete if it lacks any of these three modes.

Within the field of *empirical aesthetics*, psychologists present art stimuli to subjects, make measurements concerning their responses and attempt to create theories of how/why Art leads to emotional experiences and other, more conceptual forms of appreciation.

The subfield of *neuro-aesthetics* also involves giving subjects Art stimuli, but the theories developed tend to be more oriented toward processing theories of Brain (e.g. neural activity in an MRI), as opposed to Mind (e.g., reaction times or conceptual or emotional responses).

Aesthetic Experience vs. Art Appreciation

In general, art *appreciation* is a set of complex, cognitive processes (both conscious and unconscious), involving input mainly from the visual sense. It includes memory processes (such as when a work, that has been seen before, is recognized or recalled) and reasoning (as when judgments are made). The *aesthetic experience* is an emotional response (usually of heightened pleasure, but it can be displeasurable) as the result of the process of appreciation.

Art Universals

Some cognitive scientists believe that there are "Art cognitive universals" (that is, cognitive abilities shared by all humans). These universals include imagination, creativity, and style, where *imagination* is the ability to create hypotheticals (alternative pasts and futures); where *creativity* is the ability to invent something new (at least new for its creator) and assess its degree of novelty, and where *style* is the ability to recognize sets of attributes that are associated with sets of created objects. What they term "style" we have been discussing under the term "genre". {10.3}

Importance of Historical Context

Bullot and Reber (2013) argue that psychologists and neuroscientists tend to ignore the historic-context mode, which tends to be emphasized by philosophers and historians of Art and of Art appreciation. This approach is referred to as *aesthetic contextualism*, which focuses on the uniqueness of artifacts -- that they are created by individuals within a given historical social/cultural context and are intended to achieve specific goals or purposes of the artist within that context. Contextualists argue that current neural and/or psychological theories of Art appreciation are fundamentally incomplete because they lack a model of the historical/contextual processes that appreciators of Art employ.

Bullot and Reber give the example of Andy Warhol's *Brillo Soap Pads Box* (created 1964). They argue that an examination of the image alone cannot explain how/why certain Art connoisseurs became so passionate about it. They state that, from a neuro-processing point of view, the Brillo pad image would look similar to a standard image of a Brillo box in a supermarket and yet the brain of the connoisseur is responding in a very different manner. This difference can only be explained by taking its historical context into consideration. {10.4}

The historical context consists of past and present situations, including: the artist's actions and mental states; what Art institutions (and other social institutions) are in existence at the time that the artist creates the work; what kind of market for Art exists at that time, and the geographic region in which the artist is functioning. For example, the goals of an artist (residing in the former Soviet Union), in terms of having his/her art comment on communist institutions, will be quite different before (versus after) the fall of the Soviet Union.

Bullot and Reber talk about the importance of the fact that the artist is creating a unique *artifact*. This artifact comes about only because the artist is able to take certain actions, and make use of certain resources that are available to the artist -- in terms of support (or competition) from other individuals or institutions.

Once an artifact exists, it can be co-opted for purposes unintended (or even antithetical) to those of the artist who created it. The artifact can easily outlive the artist and be re-examined and re-evaluated in novel, future social contexts. An understanding of changing historical contexts is therefore needed to understand and appreciate how the artifact functions in society and how those functions might change over time.

Bullot and Reber (2013) argue that psychologists and neuroscientists must incorporate this contextualism into their theories of cognitive processing. They state that, when a connoisseur appreciates a work of Art, the connoisseur is extracting conceptual information from the work that does *not* itself reside in the image, but rather, in the historical context associated with the creation of the artifact on which that image resides.

This context includes the past life of the artist (leading up to the creation of that particular artifact). Why an artist does what he/she does will depend on how the artist has been formed (by the era and region in which he/she grew up) and how he/she responds to his/her subculture and surrounding institutions. For example, a black artist who is a member of a motorcycle gang within a capitalist society will tend to produce art different from that produced by an artist from a Jewish subculture residing within, say, a Muslim society.

Extracting Conceptual Content from Artifacts

Extracting conceptual content from an artifact requires reasoning. Bullot and Reber give the example of inferring the age of trees by counting the number of tree rings. Concluding the age of a tree requires knowing how tree rings are causally related to tree age and then applying this reasoning to a particular tree. In the same way, reasoning about cause/effect with respect to an artist's actions involves inferring the mental states (goals and plans) of the artist at a given point in time.

Assessing Effort

Bullot and Reber argue that reverse engineering an artifact (i.e., figuring out how it was made) is not possible without understanding, to some extent, both the artist's intentions and the labor employed to produce the work. They give, as an example, the time and effort that Jackson Pollock put into making artifacts that are intended to look chaotic and slap dashed. Knowledge of this increased effort by Pollock made some art connoisseurs raise their assessment of Pollock's work.

In general, knowledge of increased effort leads assessors to value a work more highly. For example, psychologists Kruger et al. (2004) discovered that when they told subjects that a poem had taken 18 hours to write, then the subjects rated the poem much more highly than when they were told it only took a few minutes to write.

In Chapter 6 we discussed, as a feature of complexity, an image's *computational complexity*, which is the amount of effort that a computer program would have to go through (in terms of number of computational steps, such as iterations of image functions) to produce the image. Furthermore, we refined this notion to be restricted to the *minimal* description and minimal number of steps required to produce a given image.

These notions correspond to the mental and physical effort that a human artist employs to produce an image. This effort (as discussed in Chapter 6) includes any training that the artist had to go through to acquire the skills needed to perform the labor that results in the artistic work.

Without a notion of minimality, the measurement of time and effort could easily become distorted and misleading. For example, let us imagine that four artists, James, Jeff, Joel and Jacques each set out to produce an *identical* digital image -- one that consists of the digital canvas being all the same shade of blue (containing nothing else). To produce this very simple image James selects a single color function. He specifies the color, the area for that color and, presto, the image is created as the computer repeatedly executes a color function and fills in all the pixels of the canvas with that shade of blue.

In contrast, Jeff spends a lot more time (and effort) creating the same overall effect, because in his case, he uses a different instance of the same function for each small, different region of the canvas. Therefore, he must specify the same color function repeatedly -- one for each small area. As a result, Jeff puts much more time and effort into producing the *same* final image.

Joel does exactly as Jeff, but, in between specifying each function, Joel (with much determination and effort), forces himself to stare into space while counting downward, from 100 to 1. As a result, Joel takes *much* longer than Jeff (in terms of time) to produce an *identical* image.

Finally, Jacques produces the same final image, but he does so by creating multiple, different images. For each different image, he either erases it and starts over, or he covers it over with a new image. Although he produces many new images, none of them are retained or appear in the final image.

With respect to the quality of the image, should we reward Joel, Jeff or Jacques for having expended much more time and effort than James? Certainly not! {10.5}

Thus, while effort in producing an image is, *all other things being equal*, a reasonably good indicator of image quality, it is not a sure-fire dimension of quality because (a) much effort can be generated to produce an uninteresting image and (b) any image can always be created by very inefficient or time-consuming behaviors.

Therefore, any description of an artist's effort must be analyzed critically, by asking ourselves if we can think of any alternative, more efficient ways in which the work could have been created (along with asking ourselves whether or not all that effort was worth it in the first place).

That is why our notion of complexity seeks *minimality* -- in terms of: description length, prior skill, and number of execution steps.

Appreciation Mode of Basic Exposure

As a person is repeatedly exposed to a set of images, that person's brain will extract regularities across related images and extract features that are associated with them. These regularities and associations will lead that person to form generalizations and expectations about future works of Art. (Regularity extraction, generalization and expectation formation are capabilities also of artificial neural networks. See Chapter 15.)

These capabilities exist for both auditory and visual senses and exist across species. For example, pigeons are able to learn to discriminate underwater images of different types of fish. Pigeons can do this even though they did not encounter such images during their evolutionary history. {10.6}

Pigeons have also been trained to discriminate impressionist paintings by Monet versus cubist paintings by Picasso, see Watanabe et al. (1995). Once they were trained to perform this discrimination, they were able to *generalize* -- that is, they were able to discriminate novel Picasso and Monet paintings (ones the pigeons had not been shown during their training).

The more people are exposed to the work of an artist, the more they are able to recognize other works by the same artist. The same is true for exposure to paintings across different artists within a given genre.

Appreciation Mode of Design Stance

In this mode of appreciation, the viewer appreciates the work by acquiring knowledge about how and why it was produced.   For example, psychologist Deborah Kelemen (1999) has shown that children commonly interpret artifacts from a teleological point of view (i.e., inferring that the artifact was created for a purpose).

The inferring of mental states in others (in order to explain the past behavior of others or to predict future behavior) is often called "mind-reading" in the psychological and philosophical literature. This fundamental human capability is applied constantly in daily life and therefore would be applied also to works of Art, e.g. Carruthers (2006, 2009). When engaged in mind-reading, the viewer produces causal mental structures.   These structures supply explanations for why/how the work came about.

Appreciation Mode of Historical Context

In this mode, the appreciator attempts to evaluate the work by comparing it to others within the same historical context. This mode of appreciation is fundamentally normative (as opposed to descriptive). In normative theories, a set of standards (for evaluation) are developed and justified.

In order to evaluate something, one must have a set of dimensions along which one forms judgments of value.

The philosopher Robert Stecker (2005) states that there are many types of value. One can value an object for sentimental reasons, for aesthetic reasons, for financial reasons, etc. Stecker discriminates between *aesthetic* value and *artistic* value. When defining *aesthetic value*, Stecker restricts himself to the ability of the work to create an aesthetic/emotional experience on the part of the viewer. *Artistic* value includes aesthetic value, along with: (a) the cognitive or conceptual value of the work, (b) the ethical value (e.g., when one agrees with the moral stance of the work), and (c) the historical value (i.e., how the work contributed to the development of Art in general, or to some genre within Art).

Stecker specifically *excludes* what he calls "external" values of Art. External values include: (a) the monetary value of a work, (b) the fame of certain artists, (c) non-art related functions of a work, such as using a work of art as a door stop, and (d) sentimental value (e.g., the work being viewed at the time that the viewer was on a first date with the person who would later become his/her spouse).

Stecker argues that Art is not *intrinsically* or *essentially* valuable. Something of intrinsic value would be something that sustains life. Something that is essential would be something that cannot be replaced by other things. According to Stecker, works of art are *instrumentally* valuable (as opposed to intrinsically valuable) because Art is created and employed by people in order to satisfy a variety of goals (e.g. obtain erotic pleasure, impress others, make a political statement). Art is also non-essential because any goal (that works of Art are intended to achieve) can be achieved by other types of objects. For example, works of literature can make political statements or provide erotic pleasure.

As a viewer considers a work of art along these different modes (exposure, design stance, historical context), the viewer's appreciation is then enhanced.

Forgeries and Historical-Contextual Appreciation

If viewers only appreciated the image (i.e., basic exposure mode), without consideration for design stance or historical context, then appreciators would appreciate a forgery (or look-alike image) just as much as the original. However, this is not the case and can only be explained by postulating both design-stance and historic-context modes of appreciation.

When the look-alike image is produced, the forger's design stance is going to be completely different than that of the original artist. For example, the original artist might have produced an image that attacks some aspect of capitalism. In contrast, the forger is producing the image for completely different reasons (perhaps to make money by selling the forgery to a gullible purchaser).

From an historic-context point of view, the original work may have been the first to apply a given visual technique (e.g. cubism) in Art. In contrast, the look-alike is completely derivative. This analysis can only be made if the appreciator is taking into account the work's historical context. For example, the discovery that works (ostensibly painted by Vermeer) turned out to be forgeries by van Meegeren caused appreciators to reassess these works, e.g. see Coremans (1949).

Processing Fluency in Artistic Evaluation

As the brain repeatedly performs any task, it attempts (a) to perform the task more efficiently and (b) to generalize its performance to related tasks. Thus, over repeated exposures, the brain's processing fluency increases. The experience of increased processing fluency is usually perceived as pleasurable (e.g., whether it happens to be a more effortless game of ping pong, or solving crossword puzzles more quickly, or recognizing a novel piece as being produced by a certain artist).

In the area of Art, increases in aesthetic fluency has been examined by psychologists Lisa and Jeffrey Smith (2006). They are educators and psychologists who conduct research on how visitors to art museums view art and how those experiences affect their relationships with others and with society in general. They liken increased aesthetic fluency to increasing one's vocabulary when learning a new language. Notice that, since effort and fluency are related (increased effort gives rise to greater fluency), it makes sense that appreciators will assign a higher value to works that require greater effort to produce.

Artists may use standard features of beauty (balance, order, harmony) or violate these in order to manipulate aesthetic fluency. That is, artists may employ, on purpose, features such as: chaos, imbalance, absurdity, disorganization, violence, etc. In such cases, the appreciator must know (or infer) the artist's goals, in order to accurately assess how well these goals were achieved.

Many artists hope to contribute to Art by coming up with novel genres. One way to achieve this is to violate whatever artistic norms are currently in fashion. Thus, works that create disfluency on the part of viewers may signal novelty to Art connoisseurs (Cho and Schwarz 2006). Disfluency in an image may also signal anger, alienation or an attempt at subversion of some aspect of society on the part of the artist.

How do these modes of appreciation (basic, design, and context) relate to the dimensions that I proposed in Chapter 8?

I believe that the *context* mode of appreciation is related to the dimensions of historical innovation and conceptual content. The *design* mode of appreciation is related to the dimension of complexity and the *basic* mode relates to the dimensions of framing and engagement.

Chapter 11
DIMENSIONS for JUDGING
ARTIFACTS of ART

Within the *Artifact Investment Domain* (as mentioned in Chapter 7), the dimensions for judging *artifacts* are very different than those for judging *images*. Instead of judging the *quality* of an *image*, we are, in this chapter, going to judge the *monetary value* of an *artifact*.

Here are the major dimensions (components, factors) used in judging *artifact* financial value: (a) authenticity, (b) attention, (c) current price, (d) demand by wealthy collectors, (e) demand by investors (f) representation by top dealers/agents, (g) display in influential galleries, (h) display at international art fairs, (i) personality of the artist, (j) geography, and lastly (k) image quality.

Years ago, I ran into a gallery owner (who asked to remain anonymous). She told me that she never considers the image quality of a work of art when deciding on whether or not to consider it for her gallery! She told me that image quality has nothing to do with how much demand there will be for a piece or its price.

She stated that other factors are much more important and these factors include: (a) What types of galleries are carrying works by that artist -- certain galleries have connections to very wealthy collectors and so they have great influence on the price/demand for certain works. (b) What she called the artist's pedigree, which consisted of the types of venues and publications in which the artist's works have already appeared.

Authenticity - Authorship - Uniqueness

Grampp (1989) {11.1} refers to the extent to which a work is deemed as authored by the artist as its "autographic" dimension. The highest-valued art tends to be produced solely by the artist. Reduced levels of autography are: (a) partly done by the artist and also partly by his assistants or students, (b) done in his/her workshop (i.e., not by the artist, but under the artist's influence), and (c) not done by the artist at all but done in the artist's style. In the last case, the work is not authentically the artist's. Grampp points out that, the less autographic the work, in general the lower the monetary value.

Uniqueness refers to how many other works (by that artist) exist that are highly similar (as in the case of prints). In general, the greater the number of nearly identical pieces, the lower their value.

Attention - Prestige - Celebrity

Attention, prestige and celebrity of an artist (i.e., the artist's "pedigree") are determined by who displays an artist's work, and by who writes about it.

In general, there are three broad classes of Art critics: (a) the Art professors and professional writers who publish books on art history/theory and articles in Art journals, (b) the critics and reviewers who maintain Art blogs and write for newspapers and magazines and (c) TV/movie documentary makers, who may choose to review an artist's life and/or body of work.

Consider reviews: some reviews are merely descriptive; others make evaluative judgments. In general, the more that is written about an artist's work, the more valuable that artist's pieces will become. It probably does not matter that some critics don't like the work. As the saying goes: "There is no such thing as bad publicity."

The Wagners (2013) have written a recent book on how to collect Art. They state that they are surprised that many Art critics do not think that they have much influence on the market.

I think that this is not surprising. Each critic has probably had the experience of panning works that later are sold for dizzying sums. What the critic may not realize is that, it is not what the critic has said, but simply the fact that the critic is focusing on *that* artist. That is what counts the most.

The greater the attention that an artist (or some work by the artist) garners, the more that other people will recognize that artist's name (or that piece) when a connoisseur shows off his/her collection to friends and associates. If the artist has produced outlandish work (or behaved infamously) then that just adds a good story that the collector can tell to entertain his/her social peers. Thompson (2008, 2014) refers to this story as the "backstory".

For contemporary and living artists, the value of works of art are related to the number of prestigious venues in which the artist's works have appeared, such as major museums, secondary museums, and in what prestigious Art journals the artist's work has been discussed. Grampp (1989) states that, in the 1970s, the late economist and Art journalist Willi Bognard assigned numeric points to these prestige components and then ranked painters in terms of them. He compared artists' numeric prestige rankings with the prices of their paintings. A regression analysis of these two lists indicated that the price of a painter's work was consistent with the painter's prestige.

The prices set (and sought) by different collectors and museums will vary; mainly because their goals will be different at different times. For example, one museum may already have representative samples of a given artist and so not be willing to pay as much for a work as another museum (that is trying to obtain it first representation of that artist).

The prestige of an artist will change over time. Two major ways of boosting an artist's celebrity status are: (1) a best-selling book written about the artist and (2) a TV or movie documentary produced about the artist's life and work. For example, after the book by Herrera (1983) on Frieda Kahlo became a best seller, Kahlo's pieces began to sell for much more.

In the case of documentary films about artists, their impact will depend on what distribution (in theaters or on television) the documentary receives, which will depend on the prestige of the film's producer/director and any awards that the film itself garnishes.

Bull (2011) states that the German economist Georg Franck argued that there are actually two different markets for Art: (1) the standard market -- of supply/demand for sale/acquisition of paintings and set by price, and (2) a market of attention -- indicated by exhibition venues and appearances in Art publications. {11.2} Bull analyzed how these markets are currently related to each other, by examining two web sites: *Artfacts.net* and *Artprice.com*.

Artfacts.net ranks thousands of artists (living and dead) in terms of their exhibition data since 1998 and so this measures an artist's success in obtaining attention. In contrast, *Artprice.com* maintains information about price of sales (of artists' works) at various art auctions. Bull then produced a snapshot of the current structure of both the price and attention markets.

Currently, the U.S. and Europe dominate the attention market, with 65 of the top artists coming from the U.S., Germany, France and the U.K. However, on Artprice.com, the top 100 artists include 16 Asian and 5 Russian artists.

Bull attempted to find correlations between the top 250 (living) artists on *Artfacts.net* and the top 500 (living) artists on *Artprice.com*. Bull discovered that only 16% appear at the top of both rankings. Thus the two markets are not highly correlated.

Part of the explanation (for this lack of correlation) is that many Asian artists are selling well in the *price market* but are not receiving as much attention (in the *attention market* of exhibitions and Art journals).

According to Bull, in the price market, painters do better than sculptors, who do better than photographers, followed by video and then performance pieces. In the attention market, no specific medium dominates. Bull discovered clusters of artists (in terms of similar regions and techniques) in L.A., Germany, and the U.K. He argues that both indices are useful because artists who have won the *Praemium Imperiale* (a global arts prize awarded each year, since 1989, by the Japan Art Association) tend to appear at the top of both rankings.

Current Price of an Artist's Work

In the area of Music, the price range is very narrow (e.g., in the range of one dollar for downloading most songs). In contrast, works of Art can range from a few dollars to hundreds of millions of dollars.

Current prices of an artist's work tend to set a baseline for how that artist's future work will sell. I recall an art conference in which I attended a panel for gallery owners concerning how to price a work of art (by unknown artists). One panelist, who was also a gallery owner, stated that, when some piece is not selling, consider *raising* its price fourfold! For example, if some piece is priced at around $4000, raise it to $16,000! His argument was that, psychologically, it would attract a different class of customer. There are individuals, he stated, for whom purchasing a work at $4000 is like the rest of us spending $4 on something and thus, to purchase a work for a mere $4000 requires no real psychological commitment to that work. On the other hand, spending $16,000 might make them feel like they have really *done* something that day -- made a real purchase decision that took some nerve and commitment.

This panelist stated that raising the price fourfold again (to $64,000) will cause (yet again) an even higher-class of collector to now consider that piece more seriously (while closing it out for consideration by the lower classes). He reminded the audience that, the higher the price, the more it indicates how highly the gallery owner values that item.

Ullrich (2009) {11.3} states that one might expect that, as the price of a work of art soars, Art experts would examine it more closely, like detectives, and argue for how much greater the image quality of that work must be, but apparently this never happens. He states that, as higher and higher prices take over an Art submarket, price becomes a replacement for words and image analysis.

Art reviewers and connoisseurs no longer attempt to describe, in words, the qualities of a work; instead, they wax eloquently about its astronomical price, as though price is now equivalent (a replacement) for quality. He states that record prices make it more and more incomprehensible why anyone would pay so much and why that work would be so special as to justify such a price.

Demand by Wealthy Private Collectors

If you can discover that a very wealthy, obsessive collector is looking for a certain sub-genre of Art, or work by a certain artist, then you can "ride coattails" by purchasing work within that sub-genre of that artist. In the same way that a very important wealthy person (VIWP) will have many people who earn their incomes by supplying services to that VIWP; in the same way, hobnobbing with the very wealthy (or getting information from some who can do so) can lead to information on what type (or pieces or sub-genre) of art to purchase.

Wolf (1968), in an essay on some of the social aspects of Art, argues that the exclusive Art market (as opposed to Art images purchased by the masses) is created mainly by two classes of people: (a) those from the established families of old wealth and (b) those who have obtained new wealth and are trying to become accepted by the old wealth through the vehicle of Art.

If a new-wealth outsider can become an expert in an area of new Art, and amass a secondary fortune (secondary with respect to whatever original fortune made him/her become *new wealth*) by collecting this new type of

Art, then, maybe he/she can become accepted into that exclusive club of *old wealth*.

The new wealthy can not only show their insight through art purchases, but also through commissioning art. If one of the new wealthy can supply patronage to various new (and as yet, unknown) artists, then not only can the patron create new wealth for himself/herself, but also help direct the future of Art itself.

How might the wealthy impress their friends (and those with whom they want to become friends)? Well, they can impress them with both the daring and the *price* of their purchases. In terms of daring -- that might involve the purchase of an avant-garde form of art -- one before it might have much value. As it becomes much more valuable, then the purchaser gains "boasting rights". In terms of price; that's easy, the higher the price, the more one will impress one's peers. Such psychological phenomena help to drive the high-end Art market.

Baudrillard (1981) describes the art auction as a space within which aristocratic peers engage in economic rivalries -- ones in which one is the conqueror and the other is the vanquished. He argues that the Art auction interchange is one in which signs (auction signals) represent status, pedigree and forms of fetishism over the value of artifacts. {11.4}

Fred Wilson (2001) is a black artist based in New York. He comments that, once his work has joined a private collection, it says more about the *collector* than the artist and he feels as though his work (and its meaning) often becomes lost once it enters into a private collector's hands. He relates a story in which a piece of his -- one that had an Anubis head and Hermes body (and so was intended as a statement about how ancient Greece and Egypt are related to each other) -- was described, (once it was in the collector's home) as being of value because it looked like the collector's dog.

Wilson states that, in the collector's home, his work "... seems to function there as a trophy acquired in a foreign land, as if it has been bagged during an art safari." (pp. 54-5). He also states that, since the collectors of his work are usually white, the viewers will tend to assume that he, the artist, must also be white. When he is struggling with his identity (as a black man) in many of his works, those works can be misinterpreted as being racist -- or negate the black perspective which was intended when producing those works.

Over a century ago, Veblen (1899) wrote that a *gentleman* (a man of leisure) must cultivate his tastes in the finest forms of consumption and be able to discriminate between the noble and ignoble, in terms of goods -- to become a connoisseur of "beverages and trinkets, in ... apparel and architecture, in weapons, games, dancers and narcotics." He should cultivate things of beauty and that most works of art are beautiful and, therefore, he should display good taste in Art. {11.5}

Saatchi (2011) is an art collector and founder of the Saatchi Advertising Agency. He says, of the stupendously rich: "Do any of these people actually enjoy looking at art? Or do they simply enjoy having easily recognized, big-brand name pictures, brought ostentatiously in auction rooms at eye-catching prices, to decorate their several homes ... in an instant demonstration of drop-dead coolth and wealth. Their pleasure is to be found in having their lovely friends measuring the weight of their baubles, and being awestruck ... The new collectors, some of whom have become billionaires many times over ... are reduced to jibbering gratitude by their art dealer or art adviser, who can help them appear refined, tasteful and hip, surrounded by their achingly cool masterpieces."

Imagine, today, that you are a self-made billionaire. You have built, say, a global software firm from the ground up and with your newly acquired great wealth, you start to enjoy the finer things in life. As a result, your children are born into a life of multiple mansions, quick trips to the Alps for skiing, exclusive private schools, their own sporty cars at age 16, shopping at the most expensive stores and boutiques, etc. At this point, there are two paths along which this story can develop. In path-1, the billionaire takes great pains to inculcate in his children a joy of the common things with common people (hotdogs, biking along a beach or park, camping, etc.) or alternatively, in path-2 his children are infused with a sense of superiority. After all, they own $1,000 dollar purses; they go to $500 events; they only associate with others of the same class, in their neighbors' mansions.

The attitudes developed in path-2 will become more pronounced with each generation of leisure and privilege. Image if, at some point, that wealth is lost and the last generation has to give up this life style. They might claw and kill to maintain what they have come to believe is an essential way of life -- along with their attitudes about what is most important in life.

While some multi-millionaires have pledged a large portion of their wealth to philanthropic causes, many others from this group have not and they possess more money to spend than they know what to do with.

What does one do after obtaining (and maintaining) several mansions in different cities around the world and partying on one's own private mega-yacht (run by one's own private crew)? The answer: Become a collector of something. Art is probably the largest market -- much larger than coins, stamps, or old automobiles. Thus, the wealthy can show off, to others of their own class, their remarkable taste and acumen in their purchases. The wealthy can purchase Art both to show off their superior taste (along with its natural exclusivity of class) -- and as an investment strategy.

Many banks have branches that cater to the wealthy. Their experts educate and advise their clients on how to collect Art as a financial investment. [srch: banks experts art investment]

It is not very controversial to state that wealthy collectors (along with institutions, such as museums and foundations) create the Art market in which 100 million dollar sales shock and amaze the rest of us. If an artist can penetrate that market, then his/her success is assured (assuming, of course, that the artist is not self-destructive in the management of his/her professional career). For an eye-opening description and analysis of this world of Art (by the top 1%), see Thompson (2008, 20014).

Demand by Art Investors

Wagner and Wagner (2013) distinguish between collectors (who acquire art because they love the art they collect) and investors (who purchase art to later sell it for a profit). Collectors believe in their own taste (i.e., have confidence and conviction in their art purchases) while investors believe in the authority of the market. If one believes that the art market is highly efficient, then one will believe that high-priced works are actually higher quality Art than lower-priced works (because, if the piece were of higher quality then the market would have recognized this fact).

For the investor, price becomes *the* indicator of quality (but not so for the art lover/collector). The collector can go about collecting with both passion and obsession -- without ever considering potential market profit (or loss). In general, the collector does not resell pieces. In contrast, the investor is keen on turning over pieces for profit.

Wagner and Wagner (2013, pp. 87 & 90) tell of court documents (revealed as the result of lawsuits) in which a gallery had received loans from various prominent art investors. The gallery had promised to each of these investors first choice (priority access) to the work of various painters that the gallery represented -- thus a clear conflict of interest.

Wagner and Wagner list the downsides of collecting art as an investment: (a) art works in general are illiquid, (b) the transaction costs are high, (c) the art must be properly stored and cared for, and insured, (d) art does not produce an income (as do stocks and bonds), (e) it can be faked or damaged (e.g., due to moisture, temperature, age), and (f) the art market is not well regulated and so prices can fluctuate wildly and/or be manipulated (since most bidders remain anonymous).

Thompson (2014) describes various cases in which dealers secretly purchased works (produced by the artists they manage) in order to boost the value of other works by those same artists.

The Wagners speak of how the price of art can distort its aesthetic appreciation and how "rising prices tend to be self-affirming" (i.e., cause "bubbles").

Jerry Saltz (2007), an American art critic, stated, "Essentially, the art market is a self-replicating organism that, when it tracks one artist's work selling well, craves more work by the same artist. Although everyone says the market is 'about quality', the market merely assigns values, fetishizes desire, charts hits and creates ambience."

In 2007 (before the Great Recession), Melanie Gilligan (an artist and writer) pointed out that many new billionaires earned their fortunes by becoming hedge fund managers, with some earning over a $1billion each year, by managing trillion-$ funds which were highly leveraged (i.e., on borrowed money). She points out that, at that time, such funds were secretive and unregulated, and that many hedge fund managers became collectors of Art. She argues that the high risks involved in purchasing Art (as an investment) are similar to the high risks involved in hedging and that this behavior can explain some of the astronomical prices spent on certain works of Art.

Thompson (2014) describes how billions of dollars are currently being spent to construct immense new museums in the mid-east (in Dubai, Qatar and Abu Dhabi). The Qatar royal family in 2011 purchased a Cezanne painting for more than 250 million dollars. [srch: Qatar royal family "The

Card Players"]

Fraser (2011) comments that, in 1986, the entrepreneurial economist William J. Baumol analyzed a few hundred years of art prices and concluded that there was no real return on art investments. {11.6}

However, in 2002, the economists J. Mei and M. Moses claimed that (based on auction prices) art investments could outperform other forms of investment. They formed both the *Mei Moses Art Index* and a consulting business, called "Beautiful Assets Advisors". Other economists have since concluded that the value of Art rises, not as a result of an increase in wealth, but as a result of an increase in *inequality* of wealth -- that is, when the top percentage of the wealthy accrues a much larger share of overall new wealth.

Fraser points out that, when the annual income approaches around $2 million per year, that is where one finds most of the art patrons. Fraser hopes that European museums will turn away from the art market of wealthy collectors. She argues that high-priced art has as "little to do with art as yachts, jets and watches".

Semuels (2013), a journalist for the *LA Times*, states that, as the wealthiest become even richer, and as new super-wealthy individuals look for alternative investments to the "shaky stock market", they consider investing in Art. She states that the Fine Art Fund Group (which advises wealthy clients on art investments) has recently acquired 120 new clients who have not before invested in art. Many of them are from Asia, Europe and Latin America and one of their clients recently spent $67 million on two paintings.

The global art market is now estimated to be worth around $60 billion. In the last 5 years the number of millionaires in China has increased by 90% while its number of billionaires has increased by 400%. Semuels states that Art is often not as successful as stocks: "From 1987 to 2012, the Mei Moses World All Art index showed an average annual return of 5%, while the Standard & Poor's 500 index added 9.6%."

In a way, it doesn't matter whether or not astronomical prices occurring within certain sub-genres of the Art market may actually turn out to be "mini-bubbles" (that may or may not burst in the future). Consider complaining to a stockbroker before the Great Recession that started in 2007. The broker might just as well say, "Yes. It could be a bubble, but

I'm riding it right now and making a lot of money. Hopefully I will know when to get out before it bursts."

If you are an investor in Art you will not want to buy your pieces at the height of a bubble because it then may take a long time (if ever) to recoup your losses (which you will not experience, except on paper, until you actually try to sell your now over-priced treasures). So it makes much more sense to purchase Art that you consider to be currently undervalued (that you believe will grow in future value).

Representation by Top Dealers/Agents

Josh Greenfeld (1966) is a screenwriter and novelist who, at one point wrote about the art dealer Leo Castelli (who is believed by some to be responsible for the explosive growth of Pop art). Greenfeld stated that, although Castelli claimed to have never himself done the following practice, Castelli said that other dealers would, and it involved manipulating prices. Since many times the bidders are anonymous, a dealer can bid up the work for one of his own artists at an auction. If someone else buys it then all the better, but if no one purchases it, then the dealer buys back his own work, which raises the perceived price for all other works by that artist.

Greenfeld recounted that Castelli claimed that only "myth making" will motivate the super wealthy to become willing to pay $800,000 for a little Cézanne painting and that Castelli was in the business of creating myths in the area of Art.

Castelli recounted how the publisher of an influential art journal wanted to write an article about one of his artists. Castelli selected an art professor to write the article. The professor said that it would take 6 months to write the article and charged 5 times what the journal could pay for the article, so Castelli paid for 80% of the professor's fee.

I wonder if readers of that review article ever suspected that the reviewer had been selected by the artist's agent and that the dealer had paid for the cost of most of the article.

Display in Influential Galleries

Braathen (2007) claims that, historically, the masses became aware of art when department stores started decorating display areas with it. He points out that both department stores and museums display precious items. In the case of the department store, it is both for consumption and for the entertainment of consumers; in the case of the museum, it is for appreciation by connoisseurs. He argues that the Art gallery fills a gap existing between these two venues -- it is both a display area for connoisseurs and a store with its own items for sale. While both institutions display art in largely the same manner, their financing is very different. Museums are financed largely by public and private donations and by membership fees while galleries are financed by sales of Art.

In general, the space in both museums and galleries are expected by the visitor to consist of "white cubes". Most gallery owners believe that a dilapidated or dark space will reduce the value of the works found within it. Gallery owners are successful to the extent that they can network and establish strong bonds with wealthy patrons of the arts. Patrons will not want to associate with a gallery that is considered to be failing or "unhip". In fact, stores that sell non-Art items (such a purses, shoes and clothing) like to associate themselves with the gallery mystique; for example, some clothing stores refer to themselves (or their offerings) as a "collection".

Wagner and Wagner (2013) state that certain galleries have great connections with high-powered collectors/investors, auction houses, and other galleries internationally. If a collector can find out that a previously less-known artist is going to be represented by such a gallery, then that artist's work should increase in value.

The top galleries are able to purchase display space at international art fairs and other annual, biannual (twice a year), or biennial (once every 2 years) events. They are able to promote selected artists' work to wealthy collectors, museum curators, and other connoisseurs of Art.

Display at International Art Fairs and Biennials

Peter Scheldahl (2006), an art critic for *The New Yorker*, discusses the importance of major art fairs for gallery owners (e.g., Art Basel in Switzerland and Miami, the Frieze Art Fair in London, the Armory show in New York, the ARCO in Madrid, and the FIAC in Paris).

Scheldahl tells of how art dealer Gavin Brown wanted to protest the commoditization of Art and, as a result, placed only one work in the large (therefore expensive) space he had paid for (perhaps as a protest against art fairs). The piece was a crumpled Camel cigarette pack, attached to a fishing line with a mechanism that moved it over the floor. Scheldahl states that it sold for $160,000.

In contrast to many USA and European artists, who feel that the growth of art markets and the "commoditization" of art is detrimental to Art, Peng (1992) argues the opposite. He was happy to see Chinese art becoming commoditized and sold through markets. {11.7}

Peng argues that the artist, in order to improve and produce, must be compensated for his/her labor. Peng argues that a fundamental goal of any artist should be to sell his/her work and that a market is an essential and safe mechanism for achieving this goal. He states: "An artistic environment without a market is a primitive wilderness that is actually harmful to the development of art."

Peng dismisses the argument that an Art market will result in lots of mediocre or shoddy pieces. His counterargument is that all societies are striving to improve and that a necessary first step (before establishing a submarket for refined, high taste in Art) is to establish markets for a variety of Art tastes and needs. He argues that, since there is no final arbiter over quality, money can just as well help to serve that purpose. He states that "artists use their art to disclose the secret of their souls while society uses money to affirm the value of these secrets".

Personality - Business Acumen - Creativity of Artist

Many connoisseurs of Art have stated that they invest as much in the artist as in the art itself. By this, they mean that they want to buy pieces from artists whose careers in Art will be successful. Therefore, an Art investor will want to purchase pieces from an artist who is good at networking (establishing connections with wealthy collectors and prominent dealers), who is disciplined and productive; who is articulate (and thus can put a good conceptual "spin" or "backstory" on whatever he/she creates). The more famous an artist later becomes, the more valuable will be those earlier pieces that the collector bought at a bargain.

Wagner and Wagner (2013) talk about the enjoyment of being in the company of artists who appear highly intelligent and who expound theories of Art which are over the heads of the listeners. If a collector feels that an artists ideas are complex, sophisticated and ahead of their time, the collector is more likely to want to obtain works from that artist.

Geography of Art

The location of the artist (or works of his/her art) can have a strong effect on its value. The Wagners give the example of Brazilian artists receiving very little attention (as compared to artists located in New York or London).

Top international Art centers also include: Paris, Vienna, Berlin, Saint Petersburg, Rome, Tokyo, Beijing, Florence, Barcelona, Basel (Switzerland), Madrid, Mexico City and Singapore. If an artist wants his/her work to gain international attention, then the artist has to relocate to a major Art center or be represented by a dealer with an international presence.

Image Quality

I have made image quality *the last and least* important dimension for evaluating artifacts of Art.

The investment (collectability) value of a work of art must depend, at least somewhat, on image quality -- but how much? If investment value were dependent *only* on image value, then any wonderful image found in a yard sale would be worth a lot, and images (that look like they were produced by toddlers) would never be worth very much. Unfortunately (or fortunately, depending on your perspective!), the connection between image quality and investment value is quite tentative; mainly because, the components used -- in evaluating in these two domains -- are largely non-overlapping. Just compare the dimensions used in Chapter 8 with those discussed in this chapter.

The last dimension mentioned in this chapter is that of image quality (and thus includes all dimensions discussed in Chapter 8). I include this dimension within the *Artifact Investment Domain* because, if I did not, then I would be claiming that the quality of the image has *nothing* whatsoever to do with the value of the artifact (on which that image resides) and that cannot be the case. Almost all *collectors*, when they acquire an artifact, will tell you that they acquired it for the image. Even art *investors* will not want to admit that they acquired a mediocre image (even if the real reason is that they believe that this piece will sell for much more in the future).

The art literati (experts, high priests, connoisseurs) who advise wealthy collectors of artifacts of Art would like their collectors to believe that they can accurately predict the value of an artifact based on the quality of the images produced by a given artist.

It turns out that it is much more difficult to judge (rank) an art work's *aesthetic value* than it is to judge its economic value. Consider an early image in some genre (e.g. cubism, surrealism, minimalism -- take your pick). From an *artifact* perspective, an early exemplar will have great economic value to collectors of works by that artist.

From an *aesthetic* perspective, however, some other artist, once that artist has learned of that genre, might have the skill to produce images that are much more esthetically interesting and appealing within that genre.

Which dimension (aesthetics or economics) will dominate, in terms of the Art market? Clearly, economic market value will dominate.

What we will end up with is a state of confusion (in the minds of the man-in-the-street *and* connoisseurs) concerning how valuable the *image* happens to be. Consider the Mona Lisa. It's market value is hundreds of millions of dollars, but is the bemused smile in the image really *that* much more esthetically superior to other images of seated, smiling young women? If you say "Yes", then you are continuing to confuse *market/artifact*-value with *aesthetic/image* value. Within the image space, an image by a minor, derivative artist *can* (easily) be superior to the image produced by the break-through, original artist. The result is that viewers will see images (that are universally admired and sought after by the collectors of artifacts) that are clearly inferior to images produced by unknown artists.

The main claim in this book is that every viewer/admirer of the visual arts should learn to separate *artifact from image* and understand that artifacts are judged by completely different criteria than those used to judge the aesthetic value of the images that appear on those artifacts.

Given that the art market is a market of artifacts (not images) then, if you want to become financially successful in Art, you would do well to focus on those artifact-oriented dimensions that matter the most to collectors. If, however, you just want to enjoy the aesthetics of images, then you will find that you are suddenly freed from the constraints imposed by the Art market. You may begin to see how images might actually compare to each other within their genres and you might arrive at the conclusion that many unknown artists have produced (and are producing) images that are more esthetically interesting and appealing than images whose corresponding artifacts are worth millions of dollars.

I have to warn you, again, that it is much more difficult to judge image quality than to judge artifact value. That is why most investors in Art concentrate on artifacts and, as a consequence, largely ignore images. Alternatively, collectors may wax eloquent about how some (clearly inferior) image (to the novice) is actually an incredible image. But if you listen closely, they will usually not be talking about the image *per se*, but rather about artifact-related aspects of the image (e.g., that this is the first example of that new genre invented by that now deceased artist whose limited supply of works all collectors now want to possess).

This confusion does not occur in music. When a musical artist invents a song, that artist does get credit for being the song composer. However, if another artist comes along and produces a more popular version of that song (even though it is obviously derivative, since it is a cover), then listeners will enjoy both and discuss, in frank terms, the relative *aesthetic* merits of both versions.

For example, John Lennon and Paul McCartney (of The Beatles) wrote *With A Little Help From My Friends* in 1963. However, English singer Joe Cocker did a radical reinterpretation of this song in 1968 and many listeners consider Cocker's cover to be esthetically superior to The Beatles' original version. Since no artifact (of either) exists, both versions compete equally and sales/downloads/views of each version represent the relative popularity of each. In each case, each listener will pay approximately $1 to obtain a single copy of either version. Currently, a single youtube.com version of this song, as performed by the Beatles, has over 10 million youtube views while a single live performance by Cocker has over 11 million youtube views.

Imagine if an artifact existed for each song version and imagine if (as in the visual arts) no music collector wanted to own a "mere copy". In that case, the Beatles' artifact would be worth many millions while the Cocker derivative artifact would be largely worthless, in spite of the fact that the Cocker artifact might consist (esthetically) of a more interesting rendition. But thankfully, this is not the case and each music rendition is purchased for essentially the same, nominal price.

The musical artist is rewarded in terms of the *number* of recording purchases (as opposed to the price of a single artifact, that can be bid up in price to astronomical heights, by demand from multiple, super-wealthy collectors or investors). To listeners, it doesn't matter that Cocker's version is derivative. They have no trouble stating whether or not they find Cocker's version esthetically superior; while at the same time giving credit to Lennon and McCartney for having created the original version.

In contrast, Art connoisseurs often find themselves trying to explain why some *inferior* image must be superior, largely because the inferior image is associated with an artifact whose value has been established to be very high by the Art (artifact) market. One result of this unrecognized confusion (between image and artifact) is a "push-back" by people who enjoy tricking connoisseurs into giving high judgments to art that turns out to be produced as a hoax.

Tricking the Art Experts

Consider the case of a work of art inside the Charles E. Young Research Library at the University of California at Los Angeles (UCLA). In the UCLA Special Collections there exists a framed oil-on-canvas painting. It was once regarded as an exemplar of a novel genre. It is a crude oil painting of a black woman washing clothes by hand in a large barrel. The piece is titled "Aspiration". In the 1920s in both New York and Chicago, art connoisseurs were interested in a new art movement called "modernism", which placed originality above skill. The painting was supposedly produced by an unknown painter, a Russian named Pavel Jerdanowitch.

Jerdanowitch called his unique, 2D style "disumbrationism", which in Latin means "anti-shadow". Art experts declared this to be a completely novel genre of modern art. A prominent French publisher selected "Aspiration" to appear in its prestigious art review titled *L'Art Contemporain*. Supposedly, Jerdanowitch was born in Moscow in 1890 and studied at a prestigious Art institute 1905-1910.

In August 1927 a writer, Paul Jordan-Smith, revealed to the *LA Times* that there was no such artist and that the paintings were a hoax.

Jordan-Smith painted the works himself as a joke. He had no art training and he wanted to make fun of international contemporary art critics. Jordan-Smith was angry that his wife (an amateur painter) had had her paintings negatively critiqued because they were not modern enough, so he submitted paintings to a modern art show in New York City under the name of Jerdanowitch.

It only took him an hour to make what he thought was the most crude work of art that he could produce. [srch: disumbrated art Pavel Jerdanowitch] Critics termed it "cutting edge", "intoxicating", "inspirational", "one of the finest artists of the avant-garde". He didn't know how to paint shadows, but he turned this detriment into a feature by coining the lofty-sounding term "disumbrationism". Some critics, clearly embarrassed by their gaff, attempted to claim that Jordan-Smith really did have talent and just didn't realize it.

From 2006 until the present, mockers of contemporary art have held an international Pavel Jerdanowitch contest, with the challenge to produce the worst paintings ever. To see their results, [srch: Pavel Jerdanowitch painting contest].

'Artifacting' a Work of Art

If it is the case that "artifact trumps image", then it becomes important to *artifact* any image.

Here I am using "artifact" as a verb. The process of "artifacting" something then becomes the process of turning it into an artifact, or making it (in some way) *more* of an artifact than it originally was. One method we have already discussed (in Chapter 2) is that of adding some brushstrokes to a *Giclée*.

Another method is to incorporate actual artifacts into a painting. For example, artist Jason Mecier produces what he calls "celebrity trash art". He collects objects from the trash of celebrities (or requests that they send some of their trash to him). Examples of celebrity trash might include used Q-tips, scissors, dental floss containers, toothbrushes, lipstick, buttons, tubes of glue, hair rollers, old batteries, and so on. [srch: celebrity trash art Mecier]

In a very real sense, his works are much *more* artifactual than a standard painting, because they contain actual artifacts from that celebrity and those artifacts are physically involved in creating the image of that celebrity.

While a photographic image of a standard painting may capture much of that image, a photograph of Mecier's works will not only fail to capture the extreme 3-D nature of his canvases, but also fail to contain those actual artifactual elements that make up the image.

What is *most* "artifact-ually" related to a celebrity? Probably that celebrity's DNA. I foresee, in the future, images being created out of a celebrity's DNA. An artist could take a celebrity's DNA; amplify it via various techniques, such as PCR (polymerase chain reaction) and then dye the resulting DNA and use it as a kind of "paint". (Note: this is not the same as having an image created of one's DNA profile, which has already been done. [srch: DNA art; custom DNA art])

Is Art a Good Investment? The Price Ratchet Policy

Some people become interested in Art because they believe that works of art never lose their value and that they provide a good hedge against other investments (that the value of Art will rise whenever stocks and bonds fall). We have all heard of cases where works of art that once sold for thousands of dollars are now selling for millions.

It is true that one rarely hears that a work of Art sold at a loss. This is the case because galleries and auction houses follow what the economist Thompson (2014) calls the "price ratchet" policy (p.141). If an artist sells works (at a high-end gallery or auction house) for a higher price, then the artist is welcomed back, with the requirement that all the works (by that artist) sell in that higher price range. However, if few (or none) of these higher-priced works subsequently sell, then the high-end galleries and auction houses will *not* allow the artist to lower his/her prices (as in normal markets of supply and demand). Instead, the galleries and auction houses will no longer represent that artist.

This price ratchet policy is very important to galleries and auction houses because it sustains the illusion that the price of a work of art will never drop (which is a great selling point for those who are trying to convince the wealthy to collect art as an investment).

The auction houses and high-end galleries spend a lot of money on publicizing the sales of works of art that broke price records. But when a work sells for a loss, no publicity is made of this fact. In cases when a work has to be sold at a loss (which can be millions less than the owner spent to acquire it), those sales are almost always arranged in a private manner and so information (about such losses) is hard to come by.

Consider the psychology of Las Vegas hotels (where gambling on slot machines is a major source of their income). The slot machines are placed, all together, in very large rooms with no walls or sound dividers. Every time a player loses money, there is no sound made. You lose your money quietly. However, whenever a slot machine delivers a winning jackpot (no matter how small) to its current player, the machine makes a loud racket, for all to hear. The overall psychological effect, when one is standing in one of these large open areas, is that of a great many people constantly winning.

In contrast, however, the truth is that the vast majority of the players are continuously losing (quietly) while, here and there, just a few individuals are winning. The same is true for works of Art. The impression that one gets (from the publicity on high-priced sales at auctions and galleries) is that works of Art are a fantastic investment, while the truth is that, when compared to stocks and bonds, Art is not a very good investment.

Thompson (p. 74) states that 2/3rds of the art investment funds (which are unregulated) that he has tried to track are now defunct. He argues that art market indices indicate that "the best that can be done" over the long-term is a 4% annual growth rate.

That work of art (that you have had in the attic for many years) just might sell for thousands more than when you acquired it, but your chance (that *your* acquisition will appreciate in this way) is similar to the chance that it will be *your* slot machine (among the legion of other machines in that Los Vegas hotel) that will deliver a big jackpot.

Success in the Market: Art vs. Music

Are the factors (that we have examined in this chapter) ever involved in someone's purchase of music? For example, will a music lover purchase (or refuse to purchase) a song because of who the singer's manager happens to be? Or what country the singer comes from? Or what other people have said about a song? Will people purchase a piece of music only because some famous person has also purchased it?

These phenomena are rather rare in Music because musical pieces have no chance of increasing in value by large multiples. Since they are not unique artifacts it will never come about that wealthy people will fight over a piece of music at an international auction. As a result, the aesthetics and appreciation of music are never distorted by such market forces. {11.8}

However, if we were to try to predict the future success of the career of a musical artist, then the same factors as we discussed above (personality, drive, productivity, connections in the musical industry, reviews by critics, where the artist is located, who's managing him/her, etc.) *would* be what we would use when making our predictions concerning their careers. However, the musical artist's career successes will *not* increase the monetary value of a song purchase or download.   That artist might sell many *more* songs, but each song will continue to sell for around one dollar.

Expensive *non-Art* Artifacts

People are always surprised at the astronomical prices for which some works of art sell, but how does this compare to other types of artifacts, outside of Art? Below is listed some *other* artifact types, along with their highest prices. (Do [srch: most expensive X] where X is replaced by the category of your choice).

1. Old Coins -- The most expensive US coin is the first dollar coin issued by the U.S. Federal Mint, in 1794. One such coin was sold for $10 million in 2013.   An example of an expensive European coin is the 1343 Edward III florin, which is valued at over $6 million.

2. Old Stamps -- Postage stamps began their existence around 300 years ago. Examples of expensive stamps are: the Swedish Treskilling *yellow* stamp. A printing mistake resulted in 3 such stamps back in 1855 (they were supposed to be green). Its estimated value is over $3 million. The U.S. Franklin Z-Grill stamp was printed in 1861 and has an estimated value of $8.8 million.

3. Classic Cars -- A 1904 Rolls-Royce 10 HP (only 17 were produced) sold at auction in 2004 for $7.3 million. A 1931 Bugatti Type 41 Royale Kellner (only 6 produced) was sold at auction in 1987 for nearly $10 million. In 2009 a 1957 Ferrari 250 Testa Rossa was sold at auction for $12.1 million.

4. Antique Furniture -- A Chippendale antique secretary cabinet (made around 1760) sold at auction for over $12 million. The Lichtenstein Museum acquired the Badminton Cabinet at auction for over $29 million. The cabinet was made in Florence during the time of the Medicis and took 30 craftsmen 6 years to build.

5. Ancient Manuscripts -- A first-print edition of Chaucer's "The

Canterbury Tales" (1478) sold in 1998 for $7.5 million. An illustrated book "The Birds of America" (1827 - 1838) by John Audubon sold in 2010 for over $10 million. The Magna Carta (1297) sold in 2007 for over $21 million. Leonardo daVinci's Codex Leicester, a document containing some of his scientific theories and drawings in many areas, including geography and astronomy, was acquired by Bill Gates in 1994 for over $30 million. He had the pages scanned and made available as digital files.

6. *Diamond Jewelry* -- A 6-carat blue diamond ring, mounted in platinum, sold in 2011 at auction for $10 million. An un-mounted heart-shaped diamond over 56 carats sold in 2011 at auction for $11 million. A rectangular pink diamond ring over 14 carats sold in 2010 at auction for over $23 million. A pink diamond, over 24 carts with rounded edges and mounted in a platinum ring, sold for over $46 million in 2010.

Again, a good backstory helps. Thompson (2014) recounts the sale of a charm bracelet (whose replacement cost was around $25,000), selling at auction for $326,500. It had been owned by the famous actress Elizabeth Taylor (who had also been married 8 times, including to Richard Burton, another famous actor).

7. *Sterling Silver Objects (single item)* -- An estimate of the cost of the most expensive, single-item sterling silver pieces can be obtained by looking at high asking prices on eBay. An Austro-Hungarian silver sculpture (consisting of a bowl held up by a base containing mermaids, cherubs and tree branches) made circa 1900 can be obtained for $80,000. A King Farouk Egyptian Palace sterling silver cigarette case can be purchased for $245,000. A King Edward VII Scottish silver centerpiece can be purchased for $195,000.

8. *Glass Paperweights* -- The first glass paperweights were made in Venice in the mid 1400s. The most expensive paperweight sold at auction in 1990 for $258,000. It was the "Basket of Flowers" produced in the 1850s by French manufacturer Clichy. A Clichy paperweight containing a glass rose sold at auction for $40,000 in 2009. Top modern, large paperweights (such as those made by Paul Stankard) sell in the range of $5000 to $15,000.

9. *Musical Instruments* -- The most expensive instruments tend to be violas and violins. A 250-year old violin (made by Antonio Stradivarius) sold for $3.9 million in 2007; another for $3.5 million in 2006. More recently, a Stradivarius violin sold for over $15 million at auction in 2011. Top classic guitars sell for much less. A Robert Bouchet guitar sold for

$122,500 in 2009. A guitar made by C. F. Martin (model OM-45) sold for over $500,000. A Fender Stratocaster electric guitar (owned by Eric Clapton) sold for nearly $1 million. (This is a good example of the value of a collectible item being influenced again by its "backstory" -- in this case, that the guitar was owned and played by Eric Clapton.)

Quality of Sound vs. Instrument Artifact Value

While musical performances do not result in artifacts, the musical instruments that are played during performances *are* artifacts. Thus a distortion can come about -- between the quality of the sound produced by a musical instrument, as opposed to the monetary value of that instrument (as a collectible artifact). This psychological distortion is analogous to that distortion between the quality of an image, as opposed to the monetary value of the artifact on which the image is displayed.

Does such a distortion occur in the domain of musical instruments? I happen to play both steel string and classical guitars and I have noticed that very expensive U.S. guitars will often sound no better than much cheaper guitars (such as those made in Japan or China). But does a psychological distortion occur at the very highest monetary range of musical instruments?

When violinists play a Stradivarius, they tend to agree that it sounds much better than competing, modern violins. However, acoustic researchers Claudia Fritz and violin maker Joseph Curtin in 2012 asked 10 top violin maestros to play a dozen violins while wearing some form of blindfold. Six of the violins were modern while six were either Stradivarius or Guarneri violins (made in the 18th century).

The maestros tested these violins for 2.5 hours and judged them according to playability, tonal quality, clarity and projection. *New violins were preferred* at a ratio of roughly 3 experts to 2. Maestros rated the *overall* qualities of the new violins as superior also. The researchers found no correlation between the quality of a violin and its monetary value. [srch: Fritz Curtin test classic vs. modern violins]

Music as Artifact? Wu-Tang Clan Case

To my knowledge, the closest attempt at turning music into an artifact is that being done by the Wu-Tang Clan, which consists of 8 (and often more) rappers and hip-hop artists. They plan on releasing *just one copy* of a 2-CD set, consisting of 31 tracks. The CD-set will be housed in an engraved Moroccan-style silver and nickel box. They plan to have the CD-set tour various galleries and museums (just like a visual work of art) and then hope to sell it at auction for more than $5 million. They intend to have the CD-set extremely well guarded, so that no one can make copies of the tracks (which were recorded in secret sessions).

Once some wealthy collector (or investment group or record company) acquires this CD-set artifact, there are 3 possible outcomes: (1) the owner may decide to keep the music private, with only his/her closest friends/colleagues able to listen to the tracks, (2) the owner may release the tracks for free on the internet, so that all can enjoy, or (3) the owner could be a record company that purchased the so-called 'artifact' in order to monetize it.

It is assumed that the owner of the artifact will also own the legal right to make and sell multiple copies (and downloads) of the song/music tracks. If the purchase price, say, ends up being $5 million, then if the owner believes that more than $5 million worth of sales/downloads will occur, then the owner will have made a profit on the purchase. Of course, once copies are made, the so-called 'artifact' will lose most of its appear *as an artifact*, since most listeners are interested *in the music* (not the plastic jewel-cases, text, silver-engraved box and printed images that makes up the physical CDs and their container).

There are three different views one could have toward this attempt (to turn music into a visual, art-style artifact):

1. *The Wu-Tang Clan view* -- Their view is that the high values one sees being placed on visual art artifacts are something for the Music world to envy and, if the Moroccan-style box and 2-CD set does end up selling for millions of dollars, then that is a very positive endorsement of the artistic value of music (as opposed to a musical work's standard endorsement, which consists of millions of individuals, each purchasing a track for $1). The Wu-Tang Clan's attitude is that music *should* be viewed and treated more "as Art".

2. *The Distortion view* -- Throughout this book I have argued that Music *benefits* from its lack of artifacts because it avoids the distorting confusion -- between image and artifact -- that plagues Art. From this point of view, it seems crazy that anyone would want to actually introduce this sort of distortion into Music. A work of music proves its artistic value when millions consume it (as opposed to a single, very wealthy individual paying

millions for a single item).

3. *The pragmatic view* -- Under this view, a work of music can be released in one of two ways: (a) as a work whose multiple copies are immediately available for sale and/or download or (b) as a purchase of the *legal rights* to all future sales and downloads. If a record company (or wealthy individual) acquires these legal rights, and if the music is viewed as having a potential market of millions of consumers, then the purchaser of these exclusive legal rights may very well pay millions of dollars up-front for those rights.

From this pragmatic point of view, the existence of an artifact (i.e., the CD "master set") is not of any major relevance. What is of value is the exclusive, *legal right* that is being obtained as part of the purchase.

The CD-set itself *will* also have some artifact value -- just as any album cover, with its art work, has as a collectible value, based on the rarity of the physical album. In the case of the Wu-Tang Clan's CD-set, the physical CD-set *will* be rare, since only *one* physical copy was ever made.

What might be its value (assuming that the music on the CD-set has, in some way, already been monetized)? Well, old albums *are* collectibles. How much are old album covers and old vinyl records worth? Currently, there are album collectors out there willing to pay several thousand dollars for selective items.

Perhaps the Wu-Tang CD-set will be worth much more since it will be well known that only *one* physical CD-set exists. But again, its real market value consists in the number of potential (paying) consumers of the *music* that is encoded on the CD-set, *not* the CD-set itself.

Expensive Paintings

In 2013 there were many paintings that sold at auction for tens of millions of dollars. These include: a 1977 William de Kooning abstract painting (that looks like a child could have painted it) titled "Untitled VIII", which sold for over $32 million. A Gerhard Richter painting, titled "Cathedral Square, Milan" sold for $37 million. A painting by Amedeo Modigliani, titled "Jeanne Hebuterne (au chapeau)" sold for over $42 million. A Pablo Picasso painting, titled "Femme Assise Pres d'une Fenetre" (Woman Sitting Near a Window) sold for over $44 million. A Mark Rothko painting, titled "Untitled (No. 11)" sold for over $46 million. A painting by Jean-Michel Basquiat, titled "dustheads" (looks like some teenager painted it very quickly and sloppily) sold for over $48 million.

A painting by Roy Lichtenstein, titled "Woman with Flowered Hat", sold for over $56 million (looks like a Picasso-styled cartoon of a Queen of Hearts image). An Andy Warhol work, titled "Coca Cola [3]" (looks like a retro-style, simple, black & white advertisement) sold for over $57 million. Jackson Pollack's "Number 19" sold for over $58 million. (As with most Pollack paintings, this consists of a dense mess of thin, overlapping strands of paint.) Andy Warhol's "Silver Car Crash (Double Disaster)" went for $105 million. It consists of 3x5=15 images concerning a crash.

A 1969 painting by artist Francis Bacon (actually, a set of 3 different paintings, each of the same surrealist, seated man) sold for $142 million. The most expensive sale-at-auction in 2013 was a Picasso, titled "Le Rêve" (The Dream), painted in 1932 and consisting of a flattened, distorted woman sleeping in a chair, with a penis coming out of her mouth and chin, which sold for $155 million. The all-time highest-priced artwork is a Cézanne painting bought by the Qatar royal family for over $250 million.

There are, of course, many other types of collectibles, including: beanie babies, pez dispensers, buttons, match boxes, dolls, shoes, movie props, vintage clothes worn by celebrities, and on and on.

Why Paintings Out-Price Other Collectibles

Clearly, the most expensive paintings, as a category, sell for much more than the most expensive items in other categories of collectibles. Why is that the case? I think there are a number of reasons:

1. Some items are too bulky and so take up to much space for many collectors. Items in this category would include automobiles and very large sculptures. Such items are also too heavy to be able to place multiple items in one's home (or rather, in one's mansion). A billionaire may have several large sculptures on their grounds, but they will not collect hundreds of such works (as they will collect paintings).

2. Some items are too small. A collection of hundreds of coins can fit into a single drawer. To impress one's peers within one's own home, the collector needs things that appear large, but that are also easy to transport; doesn't weigh too much, and are easy to see at a distance (as one enters a room) but is not in the way as one moves about. Most paintings fulfill

these constraints quite admirably.

3. Objects that are collected by a great many people will have the largest market and therefore generate the highest prices. Many more people (including the very wealthy) collect paintings, as opposed to collecting automobiles, stamps, glass or coins.

4. Paintings can serve two purposes simultaneously: to impress and to decorate the walls.

5. Museums of Art are, in general, much more popular with the viewing public than other types of museums. There are many more art museums than other types of museums. (When did you last visit a coin or stamp museum?) As a result, Art museums (sometimes with tremendous endowments) are actively involved in acquiring paintings. This demand will increase the value of paintings, as compared to other collectibles. In Chapter 12 we will see how a painting's ability to draw in a crowd to an Art museum could justify a purchase price of over a million dollars.

Chapter 12
ROLE of ART MUSEUMS

What is (or should be) the role of Art museums? Well, we know very well that the role of museums in general (that is, museums of categories *other than* Art, such as Natural History museums, Aerospace museums, Science Museums, Holocaust Museums, Automotive Museums, War museums, etc.) has much to do with the acquisition, storage, maintenance and display of *artifacts*, but in this chapter we are concerned specifically with Art museums.

I suspect that museum directors and curators (and those on the boards of museums) are regularly asking themselves what roles should their museum undertake, and just what should their museum's goal(s) be?

No Museums of Music

First, let us agree that there are **no** museums of Music because, as we have argued, performances do not leave behind artifacts (at least not anything corresponding to a canvas, as in Art). Whenever we speak of a museum "of music" it ends up containing only ancillary artifacts, such as the instruments played by certain famous musicians, or other physical items involved in the production of the music, such as: album covers, sheet music, clothing worn by the performers and recordings of performances.

The closest thing to a 'museum' of music is probably any sort of institution that stores and aggregates musical recordings, such as iTunes or Spotify, or any institution having a musical library (for example Clear Channel, which owns over a thousand radio stations). However, unlike an Art museum, no one ever physically visits the iTunes store (and when someone visits a radio station, they are usually there to converse with a DJ).

Art Museum as Storer/Preserver of Artifacts

Since the main role, for any Art museum, is to store and display *artifacts*, then the main issue becomes: What *sort* of artifacts should an Art museum collect and display? There are two main approaches a museum can take with respect to artifact collection and storage:

1. Collect only the *best* works of Art.

2. Collect a *representative sample* of artifacts from a given area and/or period.

Probably most museums, due to financial and logistical constraints, end up carrying out a mixture of these two strategies.

As a museumgoer I have often asked myself "Which strategy do I prefer for an Art museum to take?" This is actually a difficult question for me.

For many people, when a work appears in an Art museum, they immediately assume that it must be of very high quality. They view an Art museum as a gatekeeper; as a high priest in the realm of Art quality. We could even argue that, if a museum lets in mediocre pieces, then how will people know what is great vs. only good (vs. mediocre or downright awful)? I've seen museum goers (including myself) get very annoyed at an Art museum for displaying works of Art that appear to be of laughably inferior quality.

Most people believe that museums purchase *only* works that are of the highest quality. Galleries reinforce this idea whenever they refer to their most cherished and valuable pieces as "museum quality". What are galleries conveying to the potential collector when they use such a phrase? Obviously, they are conveying the idea: "This piece, that you see in my gallery, is of such high quality that it could appear in a museum, which represents, of course, the highest form of vetting."

Art Museum as Gatekeeper of High Quality Art

For a museum whose curators only want to display the very best works of Art, they now have a difficult decision to make, which is to figure out *which* works constitute high quality (and then how, financially, to obtain these works). It is a much easier strategy to acquire a broad sampling of works of art from unknown or up-and-coming artists. Such works tend to be much cheaper and therefore easier to acquire. Curators (who want only the best) can now justify this broad-based strategy by reasoning that, over time, those works of the highest quality will become evident. Furthermore, if they can maintain a large storage area (that is invisible to the public), then they can hold many mediocre works while attempting to display only the best ones (or those that they think are, or will become, later judged to be the best).

As the years go by (and their storage cellar becomes full) they can perform occasional "spring cleanings" and eliminate undesirable pieces.

From this point of view, an Art museum is somewhat like a curio shop or antique store. Those items that "move" (are purchased) maintain the financial solvency of a store and, every once in a while, the store owner must eliminate items that, it appears, will never sell and are now cluttering up the store so much that shoppers can no longer move about enough within the store to find those pieces that "move". {12.1}

Since museums are usually considered the top venue for an artist's work, the museum curator has tremendous influence, in terms of what themes, events and works of Art he/she decides to organize and display.

Just like galleries, there is a pecking order (in terms of prestige) of first-tier, second-tier, and third-tier museums. First-tier museums tend to be public institutions at major metropolitan centers and also certain, well-endowed private museums (e.g., the Getty Museum in Los Angeles, established by the oil wealth of Paul Getty, who was named by Fortune magazine in 1957 as the richest living American).

Some enterprising "guerrilla" artists have attempted to by-pass the museum gatekeepers by surreptitiously hanging their pieces on museum walls when the guards are not looking! [srch: Polish artist Sobiepan hang art national museum; Benote hang art Guggenheim museum].

Other "guerrilla" artists have done the same in galleries. [srch: French artist Guérineau hang art galleries]

In general, I prefer to see examples of only the *best* Art (within varying genres) at museums but, sometimes, I *do* enjoy seeing what a variety of artists are doing (or have done during some recent past era, or from some given location) -- even if those works turn out to contain mediocre or substandard pieces.

I think this ambivalence of mine occurs because storage and display of high quality works is not the only role of an Art museum. Museums also have the role of educating and entertaining the Art-going and Art-loving public.

Art Museum as Educator and Explainer of Art

Those who run Art museums are, fundamentally, lovers of Art. They want to not only display great Art, but also to pass on to others their knowledge of, and passion for, Art.

Part of the role of educating the viewing public should be, not only to display (perhaps along with an historical time-line) the greatest art, but also to explain *why* it is great. Explanations are especially needed for much of contemporary art and museums are obvious candidates for being those capable of explaining art.

In general, most museums do only a mediocre job of explaining the greatness of its Art collections to its viewers. Many museum stores contain books about the pieces contained in the museum and the viewers are expected to read those books (which is fine) but it would be nice if the works themselves (in addition to the title, author, year and materials used) had more extensive explanations associated with them.

Art Museum as Entertainment Venue

From both a cynical and practical point of view, a major role of any institution is to continue to survive, and Art museums are no exception. Public museums survive based on taxpayer's dollars. Private museums survive on membership dues and entrance fees (including parking fees) paid by its visitors. {12.2}

Ford and Davies (1998) state that the leaders of major cities invest in public museums for two reasons: (a) to improve the cultural "coolness" of their city (under the view that decision-makers want to live in a place with an excellent cultural reputation, because that makes them look feel more civilized and "hip") and (b) to attract tourists from other cities and countries.

Whether public or private, a museum's collection (or other collections on loan from other museums) can be viewed as a form of *entertainment* that is capable of drawing in ticket sales. Using this point of view, a museum can easily calculate the value of a piece of art that it might consider purchasing (or bidding on during an auction). One need only estimate the number of *additional* (non-member) visitors -- those who would not have visited if that piece had not been acquired by the museum -- and then multiply that number by the entry fee.

For example, assume that a work of art has enough notoriety (celebrity or curiosity) to attract an additional 10,000 visitors every year (approximately 200 extra visitors every weekend), for ten years. Assume that the admission fee to the museum is $15. In that case, it is worth it for the museum to pay up to $1.5 million for that piece! This figure can be easily calculated as: 10,000 new visitors per year x 10 years x $15/ticket = $1,500,000.

Sometimes very *bad, mediocre* or downright *awful* art can be a money-maker, and in such cases, connoisseurs of high quality Art may be shocked to see what is on display.

A good example of *very bad* art attracting large crowds is that of the botched attempt at restoration of a fresco painting of Jesus, titled "Ecce Homo", in a church in Zaragoza Spain. [srch: Ecce Homo Martinez restoration Gimenez]

Since this botched restoration occurred, the church has experienced around 40,000 visits per year and has been charging a fee to see the fresco. So very *bad* art can sometimes be as entertaining (and as much of a crowd-draw) as high-quality art.

What *is* Art? What is Authentic?

Whenever an Art museum acquires an artifact, it is assumed by the public to be: (1) a work of Art and (2) an authentic artifact. As a result, museum directors are always having to make a judgment as to what *is* Art (in addition to whether or not the piece is *high quality* art).

We have seen that the process of *framing* (Chapter 8) can turn a readymade object into art and also that, in conceptual art, the image may disappear altogether.

Thus, it can be very difficult for a museum director to determine Art from non-Art. But if it's Art, then the museum should, in the very least, carry art that is *authentic*.

Although a forgery of Art *is also* Art, it will usually not draw much of a crowd. In general, people are not attracted to fake artifacts and, occasionally, museums are embarrassed to discover that one of their prized possessions is not authentic.

Forgeries in Art vs. Music

In Chapter 2 we discussed the different monetary value of three hypothetical chairs (sat on by a nobody vs. Shirley Temple vs. George Washington). An example of a famous chair forgery is that of the Brewster Chair, which was used by William Brewster (one of the Pilgrims who helped to found Plymouth, MA in 1620).

In 1970 the Henry Ford Museum purchased what it thought was a Brewster chair. However, this artifact turned out to be a forgery. The carpenter who had made it described how he used seawater to age the wood. [srch: Brewster chair Henry Ford museum forgery]

The Henry Ford Museum directors were very savvy because they continue to display it -- as an example of how even museum experts can be fooled by a forgery.

Forgeries are common in Art. There are 3 types of forgeries: (1) the *copy*, (2) the *composite*, and (3) the *original*. In the case of the *copy*, the forger makes a copy that is as close as possible to an original work. In the *composite* (mash-up, pastiche) case, the forger combines elements from several works by the same original artist in order to create an ostensibly new piece -- one suddenly discovered in someone's attic. The most interesting, third type of forgery is the *original*. In this case, the forger produces a fake that does not combine pieces from other works by the original artist, but is still made to look like it follows the style of the original artist and displays content that the original artist was likely to have worked on.

Given the interest that collectors and investors of Art have in acquiring artifacts of Art (and the astronomical prices that they will sometimes pay for such artifacts), it is no wonder that forgery is common in Art.

In Music, forgery is rare but *plagiarism* does occur. In a sense, plagiarism is the opposite of forgery -- in plagiarism of music, the plagiarist takes the music of another artist and claims it as his or her own. In *forgery* of Art, the forger *creates* the fake work of art and then claims that this work was actually created by another, more famous artist. In both plagiarism and forgery, the faker is hoping to obtain a financial benefit from the consumption of work by a more famous artist, but in the case of *forgery*, the faker creates the fake and passes it off as famous, while in *plagiarism*, the plagiarist passes off work already created by another artist.

An example of plagiarism in music is that of Joyce Hatto, a British concert pianist who died in 2006. While she was ill, her husband, William Barrington-Coupe (a record producer) told Hatto's fans that he had recordings of her performing compositions by famous composers, such as Chopin, Tchaikovsky, Rachmaninoff, etc. The recordings received much praise from reviewers. Shortly after her death it came to light that her husband had used the recordings of famous pianists and had attributed them to his wife. The discovery was made because these recordings still had metadata on them that indicated their actual sources.

Why did plagiarism occur in this case? Here, the plagiarist was pitching a product whose value was not necessarily the quality of the sound, but that the sound had been produced *by a certain individual*. Fans of Hatto were thrilled to be able to obtain these supposed recordings of hers. Her husband Barrington-Coupe claimed to have himself sold around 8000 Hatto CDs during 2005 to 2008. Barrington-Coupe claimed that he did it out of love for his wife and that Hatto never knew of the deception.

I imagine that, if one could find a new recording of a guitar performance by, say, the deceased Beatle, George Harrison, then many people would be willing to pay to hear it. In that case it could be a motivation for creating a forgery of such a recording (but I am not aware of such a case).

Since forgeries are common in visual Art, experts have developed many techniques for detecting forgeries. These include: (a) examining the chemical composition of materials used in a painting (e.g., with spectrophotometry techniques), (b) examining the frame, along with any nails or mounting marks, (c) using carbon dating and other isotope analysis, (d) employing x-rays to look under the surface of the painting, and (e) performing a detailed analysis of the painting's provenance (i.e., any document history of ownership, purchase, and/or transfer).

Protection from plagiarism of digital Music and digital Art is an active area of research and involves incorporating *watermarks* into digital files when they are created. A watermark is a small pattern that is embedded in the digital file (or the image or audio recording). It is small enough to be unnoticed by the viewer (or listener) but encodes data about the work. If a file is illegally copied then the watermark will also be copied and can be used to provide evidence of original ownership.

Since forgery, in general, is rare in Music, few techniques have been developed for music forensics, but those that do exist involve: (a) examining some of the digital encoding features that are used in the making of audio files, e.g. Yang et al. (2008) and (b) looking for statistical correlations between audio wave forms, e.g. Kraetzer et al. (2007).

Authenticating Art

In most cases, authentication is the end result of a process in which several Art forensic experts supply their opinion about a given work's origin.

A fascinating case is that of an attempt by various Art forgery experts to determine whether a painting (with practically no provenance) of a young woman, dubbed "La Bella Principessa", had been painted by Leonardo daVinci. See Grann (2010). [srch: Portrait of a Young Fiancée La Bella Principessa Leonardo]

Kemp (2010) is an art expert who wrote a book about his analysis of this painting and he believes it to be painted by Leonardo. Other experts disagree. Another forensic expert, Peter Paul Biro, claimed to have found a fingerprint *on* the painting itself, which he claimed is very "comparable" to a fingerprint found on another, unfinished painting by daVinci. Unfortunately, he has claimed to discover fingerprints on other paintings (for other clients, who later claimed that he conned them) and thus the possibility has arisen that the fingerprints themselves on La Bella Principessa were forged.

If it's an authentic daVinci, then it's estimated value may be around $150 million; if not, then it's probably worth around $30,000.

In some cases, an artifact is not deemed authentic until certain specific experts have given it a "thumbs up". For example, any potential Claude Monet painting must first be judged authentic by a handful of experts associated with Wildenstein & Co. which is one of the most influential dealers in art, with galleries all over the world. It is currently managed by billionaire Guy Wildenstein.

David Joel believes that he has an authentic 1875 Monet painting, titled *Bords de la Seine à Argenteuil* (Banks of the Seine at Argenteuil). The painting is of a scene near Monet's home and has Monet's painted signature. Joel purchased it for £40,000. If authenticated, it could be worth several million dollars. Extensive analysis of the painting by non-

Wilderstein experts, including records of provenance, infrared and X-ray photography, chemical analysis of the paint, etc., all indicate that the painting is authentic, but without the Wilderstein stamp of approval, it remains unauthenticated.

In different countries there exist different methods for determining authenticity and there are different Art authorities, depending on the type of painting. For example, in France, the custom has been that a descendent of the painter determines authenticity. In the Netherlands, a committee of 6 experts determines whether or not a Rembrandt painting is authentic. [srch: art fake-or-fortune]

Chapter 13
LIFE, BRAIN, MIND,
COMPUTERS and ART

Universal Constraints on Art Aesthetics

John Barrow is a cosmologist. In his book *The Artful Universe: Expanded* (2005), he discusses differences and similarities between Science and Art and what Science might reveal about Art. He states that both arose from individuals making careful observations of reality.

Scientists ended up focusing on universal hidden, objective truths while artists ended up celebrating the idiosyncratic, the subjective, the metaphoric and the diversity and complexity of human experience.

Barrow claims that only recently has Science begun to understand how diversity and complexity can arise from the simple laws that appear to govern the universe. One way -- in which diversity and complexity arise -- is as a result of what scientists refer to as "symmetry breaking".

To a scientist, the term "symmetry" is quite abstract and (in addition to referring to visual symmetries) refers to any law that remains invariant under various perturbations. For example, the law of gravity is "symmetric" with respect to location. That is, the law of gravity works the same no matter where one is located.

Symmetry breaking comes about when a given law is actually applied. Barrow gives the example of a needle, balanced on its tip. In a gravitational field it will soon fall. When it does, it will do so in some particular direction. The result is a non-symmetrical outcome from a symmetrical law. Thus, symmetry has (in this case) been "broken". In his book he gives many examples of the complexity of the world arising as asymmetrical outcomes from the application of universal, symmetrical laws.

Complexity and diversity also arise from *chaos*. In physics the term "chaos" refers to systems that are extremely sensitive to initial conditions. Many systems, described by means of simple, differential equations (used to model weather, the stock market, and neurons), exhibit extreme sensitivity to initial values. For example, if a weather equation is given an initial input that differs by, say, just 0.00000000000001, then the resulting weather could end up being profoundly different. (This effect is sometimes described as the "butterfly effect" because the way a butterfly flaps its wings might determine, from a mathematical point of view, whether or not a hurricane later arises.)

Barrow claims that the physical laws of the universe influence human artistic sensory and behavioral experiences, due to the fact that humans have evolved under these laws. Both Art and Science are constrained by the same, underlying reality (along with its chaotic and symmetry-breaking diverse outcomes).

Constraints on Life and Art

In his book Barrow spends much time describing how Life is constrained to a very narrow domain within the universe and how intelligence life is further constrained. For example, animals that live in water could never develop fire (and thus never develop new materials). If temperatures on Earth were too cold or too hot, then the biochemistry of Life would become unsustainable.

If the universe were not expanding then the light from the stars would have long ago baked the Earth -- because the light from other stars only weakens by the square of the distance; while the number of stars that we observe would be increasing by the cube of their distance from us -- thus the amount of light hitting the Earth would have been much greater than the weakening of that light (due to its greater distance from the Earth). The fact that the Universe is expanding enables humans to enjoy a dark sky at night. (For Art to arise, first intelligent Life must arise.)

If the Universe weren't extremely old then Life would again not exist -- because Life is constructed out of complex atoms, and scientists now know that it takes billions of years for such atoms to form (and escape) from stars and thus become available as building blocks for Life.

Life is also constrained to a limited size range. The strength of a muscle is due to the cross-section of the muscle tissue and thus increases by area (a relationship of squaring). In contrast, as size increases, the mass (and thus weight) of an object increases by volume (a relationship of cubing). Thus, if animals became too large, their muscles would not be able to support their weight. (It is this squaring vs cubing difference that makes it impossible to scale up a small bridge, made out of clay, to become a much larger bridge of the same material).

In the other direction, as creatures become smaller, it becomes more difficult for them to store and manipulate the information required for high levels of intelligence. The invention of fire was extremely important for human evolution. Barrow points out that very small creatures make use of the fact that, at such small scales, adhesive forces overcome gravity (enabling lizards to climb up sheer, vertical walls). To start a fire requires overcoming these adhesive forces (e.g., enough friction and force to create sparks) which becomes impossible for very small creatures to achieve. At very small scales, the adhesive forces (e.g., that make the book pages stick together) would make turning those pages (of even a tiny book) impossible for very small creatures.

Order, Complexity and Aesthetics

Is there a mathematics underlying aesthetics in Art? Barrow describes the work of the American mathematician, George Birkhoff, who attempted to *quantify* the aesthetic appeal of various objects. Birkhoff (1933) arrived at a general equation that consists of a balance between order and complexity.

Aesthetic Measure = Order / Complexity

He then applied this formula to the domain of vases. To do so, he had to first quantify the Order and Complexity of any given vase. He defined the *complexity* of a vase in terms of its curves, inflexions, corners and end points. He defined the *order* of a vase in terms of four features: (1) **H** - the number of horizontal distance relations (of the Order elements), (2) **V** - the number of vertical relations, (3) **HV** - interrelations between H and V, and (4) **T** - the number of parallel relations between vertical tangents and inflexions (i.e., changes in curvature).

Birkhoff analyzed and demonstrated that classical Chinese vases have a highly constrained aesthetic measure. He was also able to produce his own aesthetically pleasing vases by applying his formula during vase design. Thus, aesthetic appeal may lie in a region in which there is a particular tradeoff between order and complexity.

As creatures become more complex, their brains must store and manipulate more information within a given volume. *Fractal* structures are those that can create greater areas within a given volume. Thus brains (lungs and veins) exhibit a fractal (i.e. self-similar branching) structure. Many other phenomena in Nature exhibit fractal forms of order and complexity, including: clouds, trees, waves and coastlines. Thus, one could argue that the human mind would have evolved to recognize and appreciate fractal forms of order. As an example, Barrow discusses how a mathematical analysis of Jackson Pollack's paintings has revealed that they contain a fractal dimension.

Relying on current theories of human evolution history, Barrow argues that the African savanna should be viewed by modern humans as more aesthetically appealing than, say, dense jungle (where a predator might hide) or extreme desert (where there would be less food and water).

The savanna consists of "scattered tree cover, which offers shade and escape from ferocious predators, interspersed with grasses; yet there are long vistas with frequent undulations that allow good views, orientation, and way-finding" (p. 133). Barrow then displays a number of paintings of man-made countrysides and shows how they are much more like savannas than like other natural landscapes. He argues that their aesthetic appeal for humans is due to their important role in human evolutionary survival.

Barrow argues also for constraints on what is musically appealing, due also to our evolutionary past. Being able to track and analyze sounds would give any animal an increased ability to survive. He discusses how two physicists, Richard Voss and John Clarke (1977), analyzed a variety of musical forms (e.g. a Bach Brandenburg concerto, rock music, Scott Joplin piano rags) and noticed that they all share a similar type of *power spectrum*, which has to do with the average behavior of time-varying elements, along with their frequency.

In contrast, different forms of *white noise* (those static-y sounds on the radio late at night) and *dark noise* (e.g. the sounds of floods and train crashes) lack the aesthetic appeal of human-generated speech and music.

According to Barrow, our minds evolved to survive in Nature and thus have structures that internally track and model the laws and outcomes of Nature (along with their complexity -- due to symmetry breaking, chaos effects and fractal dimensions). These evolved brain structures will influence how we respond aesthetically to various images and objects of Art.

Neural Constraints on Art Aesthetics

V. S. Ramachandran is a neuroscientist at the University of San Diego in California. Ramachandran and Hirstein (1999) propose a set of eight principles of artistic experience. They believe that artists make use of these principles (either consciously or unconsciously) to heighten the viewer's aesthetic experience of an image. They claim that these principles arise due to how the brain is organized and that this organization came about as the result of evolution (thus conferring increased survival). These eight principles are:

1. *Peak Shift* -- For example, after a rat learns to press a food lever when shown a rectangle (versus a triangle), the rat will respond even more strongly to an *elongated* rectangle. That is, the rat responds more strongly to an image that is a heightened version of the original image. Another example is that of baby seagulls pecking at their mother's beak to get the mother to release her catch of fish. At the end of her beak is a red dot, which the chicks peck at. Baby seagulls will peck more vigorously when displayed a heightened version of the mother's beak -- such as a longer beak with a larger red dot, or even a thin stick with 3 red dots on it.

Ramachandran and Hirstein claim that their Peak Shift principle can explain the aesthetic pleasure derived when viewing some forms of abstract art and/or cartoon caricatures.

For any feature that the brain extracts, the Peak Shift principle can be used to explain how caricatures/exaggerations of that feature will elicit a stronger aesthetic reaction. If seagulls were ever to become intelligent enough to create and display art, then they would find an image of a long oval, with 3 very large red dots at one end, to be an extremely aesthetically pleasing form of abstract art.

2. *Perceptual Binding* -- Viewers experience pleasure when a set of apparently disparate splotches suddenly "come together" to be recognized as an object. Ramachandran and Hirstein claim that it is of survival value to be able to recognize camouflaged objects in the environment and that the brain evolved to discover correlations between visual features. For example, by noticing correlated textures and colors, the visual system can recognize, say, an animal that is creeping along the ground (vs walking, running, or panting while resting).

3. *Feature Isolation* -- The human brain is very expensive to maintain (in

terms of energy consumption) and has limited processing capability. As a result, the brain will attempt to isolate a given feature, so that the attentional system can become more carefully focused. Ramachandran and Hirstein claim that this isolation principle can be used to explain why sparse line drawings are often more aesthetically pleasing than full-color images.

4. *Contrast* -- While the principle of perceptual binding can unite features that are spatially somewhat distant from each other (e.g. recognizing that the front and back legs of a cheetah are part of the same animal), the principle of *contrast* usually occurs when very *different* features (or feature values) are spatially close to one another. These feature values may exist within the same feature dimension.

For example, color contrast occurs when two very different colors are placed right next to each other. The attentional system would have evolved to notice such contrasts (e.g. to be able to recognize an object from its background). Contrast can therefore be predicted to heighten aesthetic pleasure.

5. *Symmetry* -- Many researchers have pointed out that, in general, animals prefer to mate with others of their species who display symmetry (asymmetry being an indicator of disease). Thus, symmetry recognition would also have evolved to be aesthetically pleasing.

6. *Generic Viewpoint* -- This is the principle of interpreting an image from the most statistically probable viewpoint or (stated in a complementary fashion) avoiding interpretations that are statistically unlikely. Ramachandran and Hirstein give the example of one foreground square ob2 occluding the corner of another square ob1 (that is partially behind ob2). Consider Figure 13.1a.

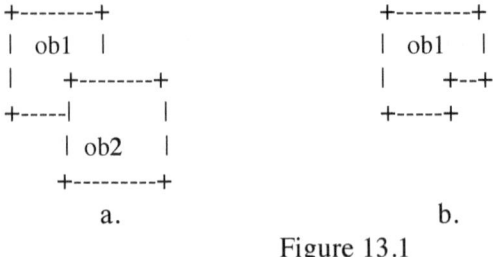

Figure 13.1

There do exist alternative interpretations -- one alternative is that ob2 is actually not in front of ob1 but that ob1 happens to *not* be a complete square but is missing its corner (exactly that part of the corner that appeared occluded in the initial interpretation, as in Figure 13.1b). However, people rarely arrive at this type of interpretation. Instead, the visual system selects that interpretation that is statistically more probable (in this case, that ob1 is square in shape but is being partially occluded).

7. *Perceptual Problem Solving* -- An image that is difficult to interpret may often yield more pleasure than one that is immediately recognizable. Ramachandran and Hirstein argue that the extra labor expended (say, to spot a hidden predator) would bestow an evolutionary advantage on those who are willing to work harder in examining ambiguous images. Thus, images that require more perceptual and conceptual "work" on the part of the viewer can serve to heighten aesthetic pleasure. {13.1}

8. *Visual Metaphors* -- This principle involves mapping two disparate images to non-image-based concepts that are similar in some non-image space. The example they give (from literature) is Shakespeare's Romeo stating, "Juliet is the sun". Although, at the image level, Juliet has nothing to do with the image of the sun (e.g. the sun is circular while Juliet is not); at a conceptual, non-image level, both the sun and Juliet exhibit warmth and radiance.

Ramachandran and Hirstein claim that recognizing such visual metaphors requires categorizing and comparing images at different levels of abstraction (capabilities that would, again, be advantageous from an evolutionary point of view).

They admit that their 8 principles are just a start (in attempting to find universal principles of art aesthetics) and they mention areas for further research, such as examination of principles that might underlie recognition and use of *style*. They also admit that much of Art is "idiosyncratic, ineffable and defies analysis" (p. 34).

Algorithmic Art

Both digital images and image-producing software interfaces are becoming more and more common. It is very likely that, over time, more and more artists will create images on virtual canvases by digital means. Instead of having to deal with messy blobs of oil, water color, or acrylic paint, they will 'paint' on a digital canvas and, once a work is completed, the artist can use a large, high-quality printer to generate a physical canvas, which could then be touched up with a few (or many) real brush strokes, in order to make it more like an artifact.

But rather than using the computer simply as an interface, the computer can be used more directly to generate Art.

The computer is a universal device. That is, a computer (if given enough memory) can mimic any other computing device. The computer accomplishes this task by understanding some language of commands. When given an algorithm (i.e., some sequence of commands designed to accomplish some task) in that command language, the computer then executes the algorithm, by carrying out each command, as specified.

All programming languages contain, minimally, 6 types of commands:

(1) *Arithmetic, logical and/or string commands* -- These commands cause the computer to add, subtract, multiply or do other types of operations on the information content at particular locations in the computer's memory. For user convenience, certain memory locations are commonly given mnemonic names. (It is easier to remember the name NUM_CANS than some numbered location in memory, such as 32456800190077.) For example, the command:

CATS + DOGS

will cause the computer to find a number at some location named CATS; then find the number at some other location named DOGS and then add them.

Since each named location can have its value altered, such named locations are called "variables" (because their values can vary over time).

An example of a *string* operation is concatenation. Suppose that "|" stands for the concatenation operation and that the information stored at the variable PEG is the string: "how" and the information stored at the variable GY is the string: " are you?" Then the command:

PEG | GY

will return "how are you?" while the command:

GY | PEG

will return " are you?how"

Examples of *logic* operations are: &, ~, =, >, v. For example, if the variable ON has a value of 32 then the statement:

ON > 19

will return TRUE.

If JOE_LIKES_MA has the value TRUE and MA_LIKES_JOE has the value FALSE then the statement:

JOE_LIKES_MA **&** MA_LIKES_JOE

will return: FALSE

(2) *Memory related commands* -- these commands include fetch and store commands. *Fetch* commands retrieve the content of memory at a given location and *store* commands move it to another memory location. A common example of a fetch-and-store command is the *assignment* statement, which usually has the following form:

variable-name := operations on variable-names.

An example is: PETS := DOGS + CATS

This assignment statement (commands are also called statements) causes the contents at the locations named DOGS and CATS to be fetched, then added together and the resulting sum is then stored at a memory location named PETS.

Here is an assignment statement that bumps up the value of a variable (here, named COUNT) by one:

COUNT := COUNT + 1

If COUNT has the value of, say, 33 then 1 will be added to it and the new value will be assigned back to COUNT.

Clusters of memory locations can also be accessed by name. For example, a cluster of 1000x1000 memory cells can be specified and given the name CANVAS1. Next, the value of 8 (which could represent some color) could be placed at (row 30, column 255) in this cluster by executing the command:

CANVAS1(30, 255) := 8

(3) *Loop control commands* -- These commands tell the computer how many times to execute a set of commands, or to execute some set of

commands until some condition arises. Here are two examples of loop commands:

do IM := 1 **upto** 100 **begin** <commands-1> **end**

until JOB = STOP **do begin** <commands-2> **end**

The first statement will repeatedly execute whatever appears in the <commands-1> area exactly 100 times and each time these commands get executed, the variable IM will be bumped up by 1. For example, when <commands-1> is executed the 87th time, the variable IM will be equal to 87 during that execution phase.

The second command above keeps executing <commands-2> until a condition occurs. In this case, the loop-halting condition is that the value of the variable JOB must equal the value of the variable STOP. If JOB fails to ever equal STOP then the computer will keep executing this loop forever.

(4) *Read and Write commands* -- *Read* commands cause the computer to access some external source of data and bring one or more data items (from that source) into some location in the computer's memory. *Write* commands cause information in the memory to be placed on some external medium. A common result is that this information will be displayed on a computer screen (or printed out on some printer). Write commands can include commands that *draw* elements (such as lines). Here is an example of an assignment command, followed by a loop command that contains within it a write command:

```
HYPHEN := "-"
Do X := 1 upto 9
    Begin
        Write X
        Write HYPHEN
    End
```

Executing this set of commands will cause the following output to appear:

1-2-3-4-5-6-7-8-9-

(5) *Conditional commands* -- These commands are usually of the form:

> **if** <condition-is-true>
>   **then** <commands-3>
>   **else** <commands-4>

The if-then-else command enables a computer to check for some condition and take a different path of execution, based on the state of that condition. An example is:

> **if** MARY < 20 & MARY > 12
>   **then write** "Mary is a teenager"
>   **else write** "Mary is not a teenager"

Very complex, distinct execution paths can be created by embedding other if-then-else commands inside the **then** or **else** portion of a given if-then-else command.

(6) *Specification commands* -- These commands specify what kinds of names to give to locations (or clusters of locations) in memory and also what kind of information will go into those named locations. Here is an example:

> **define** ON **logical**

The **define** command specifies that the variable ON contains only a value of either TRUE or FALSE.

An important type of specification command is one that lets the user create new commands out of combinations of existing commands. One example is the subroutine command. It usually has the form:

> **subroutine** *Name* (param-1, param-2, ...)
>   **begin**
>   <commands-that-manipulate-those-parameters>
>   **end**

When someone uses a subroutine (by using its *Name*), the variables specified in the parentheses next to the new command name are passed to the parameters. Whatever computations are specified, that manipulate those parameters, will then be carried out.

Here is an example. For ease of reading, some of the commands are not completely fleshed out, but are stated in a kind of pseudo-English:

subroutine SQ-SPIRAL (**loc, ang, len, extend, limit, color**)
   begin
       start at **loc**
       do X = 1 **upto limit**
          begin
             Draw a line with **color** and length **len**
             Turn by angle amount **ang**
             len := len + extend
          end
   end

The user can then issue a command, such as:

SQ-SPIRAL((25,35), 90, 4, 3, 8, 13)

In this case, **loc** = (25, 35); **ang** = 90; **len** = 4; **extend** = 3, **limit** = 8 and **color** = 13. (We will assume here that 13 codes for some grey color.)

As a result of this command, the computer will draw a square-shaped spiral (similar to Figure 13.2 below) on a cluster of memory cells that represent a virtual canvas, with the spiral's center starting at location: (row 25, column 35). The spiral will consist of a line that starts by being 4 units in length, but whose length each time increases by 3 units (since **extend** = 3). Thus, the first line drawn will be of length 4, but the next line will be of length **len+extend**, which will be 4+3=7. The variable **len** will now become 7 (due to the command **len := len + extend**) so the next time, when the value of **extend** is added to **len**, it will then become 7+3=10, and so on.

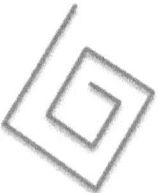

Figure 13.2
A square spiral produced by SQ-SPIRAL

This process will continue until the variable X reaches the value of **limit** (which, in this case, is 8). Therefore, this particular spiral will contain 8 lines, each attached to the line before it and angled by 90 degrees (since **ang** = 90).

By changing the values sent to SQ-SPIRAL's six parameters, different types of spirals can be drawn. With some additional modifications to SQ-SPIRAL, it could be made to draw spirals consisting of sequences of any kind of object (as opposed to just lines). With more modifications it could be made to generate spirals in which each line (of a given square spiral) has a different color, thickness, etc.

I define the term "*algorithmic art*" to refer to any art that occurs as the result of an artist combining and manipulating these 6 general types of commands. For example, the artist could embed the SQ-SPIRAL command within another loop command that repeatedly calls on SQ-SPIRAL, but with the starting location of each spiral being made to vary. The digital canvas could then be filled with a dense "jungle" of overlapping square spirals, each with different turning angles, different starting locations, different numbers of components and different types of elements making up the general spiral pattern.

Let us call this resulting artwork: "Spiral Jungle". While it might take a non-algorithmic artist weeks to produce "Spiral Jungle" by hand, it would only take minutes for the computer to generate it -- that is, once the algorithm for "Spiral Jungle" has been specified.

Algorithmic vs. Non-algorithmic Art

The approach in algorithmic art is quite different from that of standard, non-algorithmic art. In the standard approach, the artist has some image in mind and sets about to create it, using whatever tools are at his/her disposal. In algorithmic art (at least in the early stages of this art form), the artist will more likely take existing algorithms and modify them, in order to see what kinds of capabilities they have (or how they can be extended).

The beginning algorithmic artist will most likely produce hybrid works of Art -- that is, mixing standard virtual brush strokes with more complex patterns being produced algorithmically.

Over time, however, artists (and art-oriented engineers) will want to improve the commands (i.e. description language; see Chapter 6) available to artists. The most important improvement will be to enable the artist to create new commands, not by directly specifying combinations of commands (as we have done above) but by showing the computer what the artist wants, by means of a mixture of commands and *examples*.

For instance, suppose the artist wants to create a spiral consisting of undulating, wavy lines, in which the line not only grows in length with the growth of the spiral, but each subsequent line also *thickens* as it undulates. In this case, rather than having to figure out how to specify directly the commands needed to do this, the artist should be able, instead, to select the spiral command, select the line portion of the command, click on an *example* button, and then draw (with a virtual brush) a wavy line that increases in thickness as the artist draws it.

Upon seeing this wavy-thickening line example from the artist, the computer should then be able to automatically create a new spiral command -- one that now produces wavy, thickening lines as a spiral is grown outward. The computer will then ask the artist what he/she wants to call this new command, and then create a visual palette for this new command so that, next time, the artist will now have this new command available for his/her convenience.

Low-Complexity Art

Jürgen Schmidhuber (1997) is a computer scientist who has done research into an area of algorithmic art that he terms "low-complexity art". He uses this term because he is interested in the kinds of images that can be created by relatively small algorithms.

Schmidhuber claims that low-complexity art is computationally hard to achieve, but this statement may be misleading to other algorithmic artists. Schmidhuber is actually referring to a theorem in computer science that states that, in general, there is no way to find the smallest algorithm for representing a given piece of data (such as an image). However, the goal of algorithmic art is not to find the very smallest algorithmic description for a pre-existing image, but rather, to produce interesting images by means of an ever-expanding set of algorithmic tools (along with an interest in what kinds of images can be produced by relatively concise algorithms).

At the end of his paper Schmidhuber predicts that creating low-complexity art will become easier over time, because a "virtual atelier" will be developed that will enable artists to specify algorithmic art via hand movements. He imagines a scenario in which an artist wears a virtual-reality glove (so that a computer can track the artist's hand motions) and then the virtual atelier constructs the object that the artist specified via hand motions.

Computational Art

Casey Reas is a Professor of media arts at UCLA, concentrating in a branch of algorithmic art that he calls "computational art". He states that producing an image, involving lots of lines and circles (or moving images), can require over a page of computer commands (when stated in a standard programming language, such as Java) and this requirement causes many young artists to avoid computational art.

Along with his thesis advisor and another student, Reas developed a new programming language for artists, called "Processing".

For examples of his computational art, see [srch: Casey Reas art-by-numbers]. Processing is an open-source programming language; that is, many people can extend the language and make those extensions available to others. {13.2}

An Artist's Apprentice for Algorithmic Art

What distinguishes algorithmic art from a standard, art software interface (such as Adobe Illustrator) is that the commands used in algorithmic art involve combinations of more complex looping and conditional controls. In general, artists will want an interface that makes it easier to specify these types of commands. Here we are going to imagine portions of such an improved interface.

During the middle ages and the Renaissance, young artists would become apprentices to master artists and would help the master artist in producing works of art. Let us imagine that a human artist (call her Artecia) is engaged in algorithmic art and has access to a virtual art apprentice, named APPREN.

Our hypothetical APPREN can carry out sophisticated looping and conditional commands, which enable it to act somewhat like a helpful apprentice, capable of being involved in the construction of any digital image that Artecia is planning to create. Let us assume that APPREN and Artecia both have access to a virtual canvas and to various image work areas on a computer screen.

Here is an example of a more sophisticated control command -- one that could be issued to APPREN:

wherever find <spec1> **do** <commands-5> **with** prob = 1/3

This command states that, wherever the software system APPREN finds a sub-image (specified by <spec1>) on the virtual canvas, APPREN will carry out <commands-5>, but only on 1/3rd of those specifications that were found.

For example, suppose Artecia has already used looping commands (with embedded spiral commands) to create many spirals (along with other objects) on her virtual canvas. At some point, Artecia decides that she wants to replace a random 1/3rd of these spirals with some other kind of object. To do so, she issues the "**wherever find** ..." command above, in which spec1 will refer to those sub-images generated by past spiral commands.

In the area <commands-5> Artecia places whatever commands will cause whatever replacements she wants to achieve. For example, if in the <commands-5> area she places some loop command, then perhaps Artecia is specifying that each spiral is to be replaced with multiple other objects (created by that loop command).

The "**with** ..." portion specifies constraints and/or variations. In this case, "prob = 1/3" indicates that <commands-5> (whatever they happen to be) are to be executed on a randomly selected 1/3rd of the spec1 sub-images that APPREN finds.

As mentioned earlier, another command could be: **example**

When APPREN encounters this command, it asks the user (Artecia in this case) to draw an example of what APPREN is too look for in the image, or it waits for Artecia to circle an area (on the virtual canvas) which contains an example of what APPREN is to look for.

Thus, from Artecia's point of view, it is as though she has access to an apprentice -- one who can carry out multiple operations under potentially very complex conditions, in which portions of those operations can be specified by a mixture of algorithmic commands and examples.

Future of Digital Art

Due to its many conveniences, digital photography and digital cameras now dominate analog photography and analog cameras. The same process will occur with digital vs. analog art. Digital art enables the artist to make many changes at once. It enables the artist to undo those many changes at the touch of a button.

With the development of virtual artist apprentice interfaces, it will become easier and easier for artists to tell their software apprentices what they want.

One could add an audio, speech-recognition interface. The artist could then speak to the software apprentice while working on a digital canvas and state verbally: "Generate 80 spirals at random locations all over the canvas; then replace a random 10% of them with small images of cats, each in one of 4 different example positions." APPREN would then request, "Please indicate the 4 example positions."

The artist could then indicate those cat positions (perhaps cats sitting, standing, jumping, or hissing) by pointing, or drawing, or by defining those positions in terms of other algorithmic commands.

Chapter 14
ELEMENTS of MUSIC and ART:
A COMPARISON

Throughout this book I have contrasted Art with Music, but they possess many elements in common. What are the basic elements of Art and how well do they correspond to those of Music? It is somewhat surprising that the elements of Art and Music correspond as well as they do.

Here is my list of elements of Art: color/hue, lightness/darkness, texture, line, micro-spatial arrangement, repetition/variation, 2D vs. 3D (binocular & perspective), background vs. foreground, enclosures, macro-spatial arrangement, symmetry, contrast/dominance, density, simplicity vs. complexity, unity, and content.

It's interesting that these 16 visual elements have a close correspondence to the basic elements of Music. Let us examine each in turn. I will use "X ~ Y" to indicate that element X (in Art) corresponds to element Y (in Music).

1. *Color/hue ~ tonal quality.* Color in Art corresponds to tonal quality in Music. Each pixel of an image can be one of a wide variety of color hues. Each note of music can be played by a different type of instrument, in which each instrument has a different tonal quality (e.g. middle C played on a trumpet vs. on a guitar vs. on a piano).

2. *Light/dark ~ soft/loud.* Light/dark colors in Art correspond to soft/loud sounds in Music. Just as parts of an image are darker (or lighter), sections of music are louder (or softer).

3. *Surface texture ~ wave form.* Visually, textures range from smooth to bumpy to jagged. Acoustically, a waveform can also be smooth or jagged (saw-tooth shaped). A more jagged texture, in Music, will sound more "scratchy". For example, the acoustic "texture" of a violin is slightly scratchy, as compared to a flute, which is smoother.

4. *Lines ~ scales.* A line drawn across a canvas (that can go up or down, be straight or curved) corresponds to a sequence of notes in music. A smooth line that rises (falls) corresponds to a chromatically rising (falling)

glissando sequence (e.g. sliding a finger up/down the string of a violin while bowing). A sequence of rising horizontal dashed lines can be viewed as corresponding to musical notes rising chromatically. Bigger vertical spaces between dashes can be mapped to scales of notes in which intervening notes are skipped. A straight, horizontal line across a canvas corresponds to a single musical note being held for some duration.

5. *Micro-spatial arrangement ~ chord progressions.* If we look at a canvas, say, from left to right and view a piece of Music as producing a mental image (also left to right) in time, then any notes played at the same moment in time (thus creating chords) corresponds to visual elements placed above/below one another on a canvas.

In this sense, Music could be said to trace out a sequence of vertical spatial arrangements (each a vertical column) that, over time, creates a 2-D acoustic "image". Since the notes in the chords can be from different instruments (i.e., different colored hues), a colored 'image' can be traced out as a temporal progression of chords. Temporally, vertical spatial arrangements are created simultaneously in Music while horizontal spatial arrangements are created across time.

6. *Repetition/variation ~ repetition/variation.* Repeated visual elements correspond to repeated musical elements. Visual variations within a repetition will correspond to musical variations.

7. *2D vs. 3D (binocular & perspective) ~ 2D vs. 3D (bi-aural).* Normally, an image is not 3-dimensional. The effect of 3D occurs when each eye sees a slightly different image. On a physical canvas, 3D occurs when the image is built up enough to protrude into the 3rd dimension (that of approaching-to/receding-from the viewer).

The same 3D effect occurs acoustically when the listener's two ears receive slightly different timings in signals. In such a case, the listener will perceive the source of a flute-sound as coming from, say, to-the-right-of and behind the source of a guitar sound.

3D can also be created in Art by vanishing lines (perspective). Visually, perspective fools the eye into perceiving depth through use of lines and shading. Musically, the ear can be fooled into perceiving depth -- e.g. a sound approaching from the right -- if that sound is made louder over time while being shifted leftward.

8. *Background vs. foreground ~ sustained vs. intermittent.* Visually, a background is created by repetition (of similar textures, lines or colors) and foreground is created by individual elements placed over, and occluding this background. In Music, a background is created by sustained low volume sounds (by continuously or periodically generating a sound or a beat). Intermittent sounds then will stand out (acoustically) against this background.

9. *Enclosures ~ phrasing.* In an image, enclosures consist of simple geometric forms (e.g., circles, triangles) and complex forms (e.g. outline of a hand with fingers).

Phrasing in music corresponds to enclosures in Art. Just as enclosures are structural elements at macroscopic scales (larger than a pixel), so too in Music, phrasing consists of structural elements larger than the duration of a single note (or chord). For example, a song may have lines of verse that are sung across repeated chord progressions. A progression of, say, 4 chords may be referred to as progression A. A different progression will be referred to as progression B. An overall phrase may then be described as ABBA. Thus, A encloses B in the sense that the pattern begins and then ends with A.

Just as enclosures (visually) can be small or large, so too can musical phrases. Some phrases involve just a few notes, while others organize musical segments that may extend across many minutes of time.

10. *Macro-spatial arrangement ~ composition.* The spatial arrangement of different image elements in Art corresponds directly to the temporal arrangement of different musical elements in Music. In fact, the term "composition" is used in the same way, in both Art and Music, to describe both the process (and end result) of placing elements (visual vs. acoustic) in relationships (spatial vs. temporal) with one another.

11. *Symmetry ~ harmony & rhythm.* Visually, symmetric patterns are those that are balanced in some way (or related to one another by certain, mathematical relationships). {14.1}

Many philosophers and scientists have explored different types of spatial relationships that are visually pleasing. In Music, the corresponding elements are both harmony and rhythm. Musical notes that are in certain relations with each other, (such as the octave, the third, or the fifth notes of the major scale) are pleasing to the ear. {14.2}.

In addition, musical rhythmic structures are almost always symmetric in some way, due to their repetitive nature.

12. *Contrast/dominance ~ contrast/dominance.* Once symmetry (harmony) is established, the artist (musician) can create contrasts by inserting visually non-symmetric (or acoustically dissonant) elements. Visually, some elements will dominate others (in size or intensity of color). Musically, one element can dominate another also, in terms of relative loudness (or uniqueness of tonal quality, or in terms of its bi-aural spatial position).

13. *Density ~ tempo.* In Art, a dense image will contain many more elements than a sparse image. In Music, the density of a piece is increased by raising its tempo. All other things being equal, a piece with a faster tempo will contain a greater number of notes within the same time duration (thus, a greater density).

14. *Simplicity/complexity ~ simplicity/complexity.* In Art, some visual elements dominate others (e.g., are larger or with more intense colors). Some images contain many small elements (see density above) while others may contain just a few, large elements. Musically, the same types of structural variations can occur. Some musical pieces will have a few, long-held notes, while other (virtuoso) pieces will contain many rapidly performed varying micro-notes.

We spent an entire chapter on the issue of image complexity in Art. I am sure that the same could be done for Music (e.g. less complex music can be more compressed).

15. *Unity ~ theme.* In Art, the notion of unity is that many of the elements in the image, in some way, fit together -- they all occur under a single, organizing principle. This unity could be due to Nature (e.g., that it is "natural" to encounter the image of a stream running through a meadow with grass and trees growing along it.) or due to some abstract concept, such as the concept of "purchase" (e.g., a scene in a store in which a customer buys an object from the store owner). In Music, unity is established by a theme, which is a melodic line that is repeated at various times throughout the piece.

16. *Semantic content ~ lyrical content.* An advantage that the visual medium has (over the musical medium) is that the eye will quickly

recognize an enormous variety of natural (and man-made) objects -- often from just a few sketchy lines (as in cartoons). The closest musical element, that corresponds to these content-based visual elements, is the lyrical element -- in which the human voice generates a language stream while at the same time producing musical sounds.

For example, an image may illustrate a boy petting a dog. A corresponding musical element would consist of a singer singing the lyrics "a boy is petting a dog". In the case of music, these particular lyrics (for those who understand English) will cause the listener to recall (or construct) images in their mind of boys petting dogs.

The correspondence is far from perfect because, in the case of the image, the viewer sees exactly what type of boy is petting exactly what type of dog (its size, length of fur and exactly how that dog is positioned is space, etc.).

In the case of Music, the listener will be employing both memory processes and imaginative processes. In both cases, semantic content has been conveyed to the music listener (or art viewer).

By using language that is sung, music can communicate abstract ideas, such as love, destruction, foolishness, etc. but images in Art allow also for use of language. For example, the title of an artwork (which is in language) is usually considered part of the work. The title could, for example, be "leniency" and this will cause the viewer to analyze the image in terms of this abstract concept.

In addition, images can include text within them. In this case the viewer will read the text and that text will evoke knowledge that may not occur directly in the image. For example, an image of lions at rest could include a sign (in the image) that states "elephant nearby" which will cause the viewer to imagine some (non-illustrated) elephant.

Music Genres vs. Art Genres

How far can we push this correspondence between Music and Art? Can very high-level structures, such as styles or genres of Art be related to styles/genres of Music?

Consider the art genre of amorphous, abstract, cloud-like paintings, such as those produced by Mark Rothko. Such styles could be placed in correspondence with the musical styles characterized as New Age "mood" or "atmospheric" music. In a Rothko-style painting, much of the canvas will be covered by repeated vague splotches of similar colors. Likewise, in "atmospheric" music, much of the music will consist of similar patterns being repeated, over and over, with just slight variations.

Consider the genre of surrealism in Art, such as works produced by Salvador Dali. Within this genre, realistic images are distorted (e.g. Dali's images of melting clocks). [srch: Dali "Persistence of Memory"]

I would argue that surrealism has a correspondence with atonal, neoclassical music. There is even a genre of music that is called "surrealist music", in which surrealist techniques are used to generate music. These techniques include: collage techniques (in which non-harmonic musical structures are juxtaposed), romantic techniques (e.g., dream-like passages are embedded – recall Debussy's musical piece "Claire de Lune"), echo techniques, lyric techniques (in which nonsensical or semantically odd phrases are sung), and so on.

The style of country music could be related to the genre of Western-cowboy styles of Art.

Psychedelic music (e.g. by The Doors, Jimi Hendrix and Jefferson Airplane) can be placed in correspondence with psychedelic art. What actually relates them to each other is the shared experience (both visual and musical) of when the listener/viewer is under the influence of a psychedelic drug (e.g., LSD, mescaline, psilocybin).

Just as the multiple contours around a psychedelic poster under black light will cast an undulating effect, so also the echoing, glissando and guitar sounds of the music of that style create an undulating effect.

I think we have to be careful not to push these types of analogies too far. For example, can we place Pablo Picasso's Cubism style in correspondence with certain styles of jazz? In any case, it's interesting to notice just how many reasonable correspondences can be found, even across complex structures, such as styles/genres.

Why do Art and Music Elements Correspond So Well?

At first I was surprised to see just *how well* the fundamental elements of Art correspond to those of Music. However, from an evolutionary perspective this is perhaps not as surprising.

The brain has evolved to extract information from both image and sound sequences. The main difference between an image and a sound in Nature is that, commonly, sounds decay away rapidly, while the objects that generate images tend to remain. Thus, the brain had to evolve to extract spatial (and other) relationships from the rapidly decaying temporal sequences of acoustic information. For example, a listener would want to quickly recognize a lion from its growl and build a mental map of where that lion might be located (and how it is moving) in relation to the listener. As human language evolved, the brain would have evolved to discover more complex acoustic patterns (while at the same time also evolving to interpret more complex visual patterns).

The kinds of information (via both visual and acoustic senses), that the brain would want to extract, would tend to involve the same fundamental elements. For example, consider a line. A line can correspond to a trajectory in Nature. It would be very important to be able to follow an imagined path back to one's home, or to follow the trajectory of a thrown object (or of a moving source of food, such as a pheasant). The sound of an animal coming toward/away from oneself would consist of an acoustic trajectory. Over time, as Art and Music evolved, lines (as trajectories in both media) would remain as fundamental elements.

Consider other elements -- distinguishing a loud sound (e.g. an angry opponent) from a quiet sound (e.g. a whimpering child in distress) would also be important; as would distinguishing bright vs. dark objects within the visual medium.

In addition, the brain is always employing both senses simultaneously and so an evolving brain would be seeking correspondences between what the acoustic world is revealing, alongside what the visual world is revealing.

Recently, researchers at the Institute for Neuroscience and Psychology at the University of Glasgow performed functional Magnetic Resonance Imaging (fMRI) studies of volunteers who were blindfolded and asked to listen to different types of sounds (e.g., a crowd of people talking, birdsongs, traffic noise). They discovered unique patterns of activity (associated with different sounds) in the early *visual* cortex (Vetter et al. 2014). Before this research it was not known that sounds are also processed by certain *visual* parts of the brain.

How Experiencing Art and Music Differ

So what is *different* about Art and Music? Answer: Time and qualia.

While both music and art are appreciated over some temporal duration, in the case of music, the sounds arrive in a temporal sequence. The listener cannot "peek ahead" but must wait for these musical structures to unfold. In contrast, the image arrives to the eye all at once. After this initial arrival, the viewer may then focus attention on different areas of the image.

The qualia of the experience is also fundamentally different.   Hearing the following words sung: "a small, dead terrier, with matted hair, by the side of a dirt road" has a different type of emotional impact, as opposed to seeing an image of that dog. In general, the image carries much more detail. Music (without lyrics) corresponds better to abstract art than to realistic art.

So the main differences are in terms of the spatial organization within images (vs. sounds) and the sheer amount of extra information conveyed visually (in terms of number of bits needed to re-generate an image versus a musical sequence)

But even if one were to only compare music with images that are equal (in terms of number of bits), the *qualia* of the experiences would remain fundamentally and profoundly different. A totally deaf person (from birth) can never really know what the subjective experience of music is really like. Similarly, a totally blind person (from birth) can never really know the experience of seeing, no matter how much acoustic information they process.

Chapter 15
TECHNOLOGY and FUTURE of ART

Art has always been profoundly affected by technological developments (e.g. the camera). The technologies I will discuss here are oriented around the computer and consist of: (1) Evolutionary Programming, (2) Artificial Intelligence (AI) and (3) Neurocomputing

When I say here "Future of Art", what I really mean is "some future activities of artists that I believe will either come about or, if they already exist at some level, will increase in their activity".

Evolutionary Programming

Evolutionary programming is a technology that can produce products (even intelligent software) by means of selectional pressure being applied to randomly varying populations that are capable of self-reproduction. To do so the programmer does the following:

1. *Create an initial population of reproducing entities* -- Each entity is represented by both a genotype and a phenotype. A development function is then defined that, when given a particular genotype, produces a specific phenotype. The development function achieves this by interpreting the genotype as a series of instructions that, when executed, result in the phenotype.

The genotype usually consists of some type of artificial DNA. In the case of evolutionary programming, an artificial form of DNA is used, which can be a binary code (consisting of 0s and 1s) or some set of computable functions.

2. *Apply selectional pressure to the population of phenotypes*-- Selectional pressure is applied to the phenotypes (not the genotypes). In the case of living entities, such as mice, the selectional pressure would include (a) changes in weather and food supply and (b) changes in the number and behavior of other creatures that prey on the mice.

These selectional pressures will *differentially* reduce the mouse population. Those mice that happen to be superior (with respect to a particular type of

175

selectional pressure) will tend to survive and reproduce. For example, mice who are better at finding food, attracting mates, avoiding predators and finding shelter in harsh weather would tend to out-survive those who are less capable.

3. Replicate the population differentially and with random variations -- The new offspring that are produced will be random variants of their parents. Variation in parental offspring is achieved by two processes: (a) random *recombinations* of the genotypes of the two parents and (b) random *mutations* made to the genotypes of the resulting offspring.

In the case of genotype sexual recombination, a number of *crossover* points are chosen at random and artificial DNA segments are taken from each parent to produce an offspring genotype.

For example, assume that the artificial DNA of Parent1 is CDDDCCCD and of Parent2 is ABBBBAAB (see figure 15.1). Assume that two crossover points are selected at random, between the 3rd and 4th position and between the 7th and 8th position. In this particular case the crossover points are at the locations indicated by the vertical lines: CDD | DCCC | D and ABB | BBAA | B.

These crossover points are lined up and offspring are produced by taking artificial DNA from Parent1 (or Parent2) until a cross-over point is reached, and then by taking DNA from the other parent (and switching back again when the next crossover point is reached, and so on, as indicated in Figure 15.1.) For Parent1 and Parent2, the results from this form of sexual recombination will be: Child1 = CDDBBAAD and Child2 = ABBDCCCB.

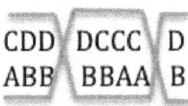

CDD DCCC D
ABB BBAA B

Figure 15.1
Recombination of parental genes by means of crossover operations.
Here, there are 2 crossover points.

Let us assume that **G** and **H** represent mutations. If a random mutation occurs, say, on the 4nd position of the first child and on the 2th position of the second child, then the final two offspring genotypes will be: CDDHBAAD and AGBDCCCB.

4. Apply the development function to the new genotypes to produce new phenotypes. These new phenotypes are then added to the population and this 4-step cycle repeats.

Over multiple generations, those variants who perform in a superior manner (with respect to the selectional pressure) will dominate the population.

In Nature, a population is obtained from a given animal species. The genotypes will be the DNA of each member in that population. The development function will consist of all internal cellular processes that cause animal bodies to grow and the phenotype will consist of both the body (with its sensory and motor capabilities) and the brain (with it ability to make decisions and perform different types of behaviors).

If the environment selects for greater intelligence then the more intelligent creatures will out-reproduce the less intelligence ones. In each case, what evolves depends upon the nature of the selectional pressure.

In Nature, the selection pressure comes, not only from external factors (such as weather) but from competition within a species, and between species. For example, millions of years of co-evolution (between evolving sonar in bats and evolving evasion flying patterns in the moths that the bats prey upon) has resulted in the strange type of fluttering patterns of flight that many moths exhibit (e.g., by bringing their wings together and dropping, they can throw off bat sonar).

Creating Art via Evolutionary Programming

In the case of Art, the *genotype* can be a sequence of visual (i.e. spatial, color, shape, position, etc.) manipulation functions. The development function will be realized by an interpreter that executes the sequence specified in the genotype and *the resulting phenotype will be the image*.

The selection pressure will arise from the aesthetic taste of one (or more) viewers.

Now we are ready *to evolve Art*. The steps above produce a population of genotypes (via random processes, due to the throwing of many dice). Each member in this population consists of an initial *random* sequence of image-making and image-altering functions. The development function is then applied to each member to produce the corresponding image (phenotype).

For simplicity, let us assume that the population is always kept small and fixed in size (say, 25 images). The viewer then applies his (or her) aesthetic taste and selects which image (or images) will survive (and which will not). The genotypes of pairs of surviving images are then sexually mated with each other (undergoing both random *recombinations* and *mutations*) and the developed phenotypes (i.e., offspring images) are then displayed.

The viewer repeatedly applies his/her aesthetic selectional taste to each new population of images. Over time, the population of images will tend to conform to whatever aesthetic sensibilities are being applied (as selectional pressure) by the Art lover or Art connoisseur.

An early example of this process was implemented by Karl Sims (1991). To see images (and videos) that he evolved, go to www.karlsims.com.

Art Without Artists

Normally, the Art environment consists of *art consumers* and *art creators*. The technology of *evolutionary Art* eliminates the need for art creators. Every art consumer can now become a creator of art, simply by acquiring evolutionary art software and then acting as an aesthetic *selector* of art -- selecting those images that satisfy that consumer's own taste (i.e., the consumer supplies the selectional pressure).

One can easily imagine future homes/apartments containing large, flat-screen TVs in which images are being constantly generated via evolutionary technology.

There would be two modes of display. In the *selectional* mode, the flat-screen would display multiple images and request the viewer to select one or more for further evolution. In the *favorites* mode, the flat-screen would save (and display, in sequence) those images that the viewer had indicated are worth saving.

Any time the viewer is viewing his/her favorites, the viewer could switch to selectional mode and the favorites would then become the initial seed population for subsequent artificial evolution. The viewer would then be shown multiple (new offspring) images for approval (to become the parents for producing yet newer generations of images) or for rejection (and thus elimination from the population of images that will be allowed to undergo future replications).

Over time, the viewer could issue simple commands (via a remote control) that would group different images into different genres or sub-genres (species or subspecies) and evolve, from those, yet other species/genres. The flat-screen software could maintain an evolving tree of branching species (subpopulations of images) and the viewer could traverse this branching Tree of Art (analogous to a Tree of Life) to decide which populations (genres) would undergo random mutations and sexual recombinations to produce new offspring images. The Art lover would then select those deemed worthy of producing offspring (according to whatever aesthetic sensibilities the Art lover happens to want to apply at that moment).

This scenario is no longer futuristic. One can already obtain free software for evolving images (but the software is, at this time, rather restrictive). [srch: evolvotron]

Creating Art by artificial evolution is mainly that of creating Art by means of selectional pressure. The only human labor required in producing new images is that of examining one or more images and deciding which one gets to survive and replicate (either solely, via mutation, or sexually in pairs, via recombination and mutation). This human labor is much less than the labor required to create an image from first principles (as is normally done by an artist).

A Comment on Genotype vs. Phenotype

Why does an evolutionary Art system apply mutation and recombination *to the genotype* (i.e., the code that creates the image). Why not apply mutation and recombination directly to the *phenotype* (to the image itself)?

Answer: Recall how mind-bogglingly immense the image space is (Chapter 4). If we were to apply a mutation to the image itself then a mutation might result in altering just one pixel's value. This change would hardly be noticeable. Instead of 50 generations (of selection) to bring about major changes in image "offspring" (when given a parent image) we would require tens of thousands of applications of selectional pressure.

Consider the case in biology. If we alter the DNA of some creature then, when it undergoes development, this change in DNA will create a somewhat different creature.

In contrast, if we were to just make changes to the resulting creature directly (to its phenotype), we would end up altering, say, just one cell in the creature's body. A living entity, such as a frog, contains thousands of millions of cells. It would be very inefficient to search in the space of configurations of cells making up such creatures. Instead, Nature creates new creatures by modifying their DNA (genotype) in a single cell and then by developing that cell into a new creature (phenotype).

Recall when, in Chapter 4, we compared each image to a star and clusters of related images to galaxies (with empty space containing all noisy, amorphous images). This type of image "universe" is so very, very much more enormous than the actual universe that we need some way of "jumping" large distances. That is, we need to go from galaxy to galaxy (not from one location to some other location that is just a few feet, meters, or even miles away). Thus, in evolutionary programming, we must restrict our search (for new images) to those images that are produced by altering some "genetic code" -- this code is then passed to some development function. This approach (of recombination/mutation plus development) will create images that are different enough that they are worthy of having selectional pressure applied to them.

Could One Evolve Movies, Books, Music?

The main bottleneck, when using evolutionary technologies to evolve cultural works, is the time that it takes a participant to make a selectional judgment. In the case of 2D images, a human selector can probably view a 5 x 5 grid of 25 distinct images and select the most appealing one (or two) within a minute. Thus, evolution can progress rather rapidly. By the time an hour has gone by, the selector will have gone through 60 new generations (each of 25 images) and, thus have selected a few favorites from a potential space of 25^{60}, which is roughly equal to around 10^{83} (or more atoms than exist in the known universe!).

Notice that, while the selector has only made 60 decisions, each decision was a selection from 25 different image possibilities and there were 60 different cases of selection -- each over a different population of 25. As a result, an *enormous* space of possibilities is being explored by means of a relatively small number of selectional decisions.

Any decision made early on is going to greatly narrow the remaining space of decisions. If only one image is selected from the first population (of 25) then none of the resulting offspring (that could have come about from mutating or mating those other, rejected potential image "parents") will ever be considered.

The difficulty with using selectional pressure (coupled with mutations and sexual recombinations) to evolve music, books or movies is that, for these works, it can take a long time to listen to, view, or read them. Thus, applying selectional pressure is extremely time consuming.

Consider a song that lasts 4 minutes. If two "parent" songs are "mated" to produce 25 different song "children" then it will take the human selector 25 x 4 minutes = 1 hour and 40 minutes to listen to these songs, in order to select the one (or several) for subsequent evolution. To make 60 such judgments, in the case of images, took 1 hour. In contrast, to make 60 selection judgments (over a population of 25 songs) will require 100 hours! (Listening to 25 variant songs each time requires 25 x 4 minutes = 100 minutes. Performed 60 times requires 60 x 100 = 6000 minutes = 100 hours.)

Since the changes to each song will be a *random* mixture of two songs (in the case of recombination), it could take a very long time to produce a song that is appealing throughout its performance. It will probably take many more than 60 selectional decisions. Remember, when the judge picks two songs to mate, the offspring are *random* recombinations of those two songs.

It is very likely, from a small population of 25 songs (as offspring), that none of them will be free of errors (in timing, in melodic line, in harmonic structure, etc.)

Now consider trying to evolve a short story. Let us assume that the story is *very* short, consisting of just 10 pages, each with 1000 words per page. Let us assume that it takes 3 minutes to read each page, which is 30 minutes per short story. To read a population of 25 variants will take 25 x 30 minutes, which is 12.5 hours. To make 60 selectional decisions will take 60 x 12.5 hours = 750 hours. (At 10 hours per day, this task will require 75 days or over 2 months!)

Again, given two offspring (that will consist, initially, of ungrammatical and incoherent short story "parents") there will exist offspring that are less coherent. Over time, the human selector will slowly (very slowly!) evolve a more coherent story, but the labor required might be better spent just writing a story from first principles (using plot and character development techniques employed by story writers).

The problem (of the time taken to perform selectional pressure) will be much worse for a book or movie, in which it can take several hours to read a partially evolved book (or watch a partially evolved movie).

Could crowd-sourcing be employed? One could imagine that many people, all working together on the web, could each read (watch, listen to) a small population of variant cultural works and then decided which ones to select for further evolution. But the problem here is that each judge will have his/her own distinct criteria for what to select for. Unless there is some way to force a large pool of judges to apply the *same* selectional pressures, the results will be incoherent.

So, unless this "incompatible judge pool" problem is solved, evolutionary techniques will remain constrained to the domain of 2D, static images. Within this domain I foresee evolutionary techniques becoming more and more popular because it enables anyone with an aesthetic sense to produce works of Art without the need for an artist to create them.

Artificial Intelligence and Meta-Art

Artificial Intelligence (AI) is a subfield within computer science that is concerned with designing software (and computing hardware devices) that exhibit human-level intelligence (Russell and Norvig, 2010).

Cognitive processes that underlie human intelligence include: representing and comprehending the thoughts conveyed by human language; achieving goals through planning and plan execution; reasoning and arguing about beliefs; and processes of learning and invention.

One major approach in AI is the use of symbolic structures (which include logical formulas as a subset). Knowledge about the world can be represented in terms of symbolic structures and logical rules can be applied to those structures to reason about how to achieve different tasks -- even creative tasks. For example, consider this symbolic rule-of-invention:

IF some symbolic structure of the type $G(b, c)$ exists,
THEN invent a new structure by modifying it to become $G(b, b)$.

In the area of mathematics, this rule-of-invention can be used to create a new mathematical operation. For example, if this rule is applied to $+(b, c)$ (which represents adding 2 different numbers) it will create $+(b, b)$ which can be renamed as the new operation of *doubling* a single number. If this rule is applied to $x(b, c)$ it will create the new operation of $x(b, b)$ which is the new operation of *squaring* a single number.

In the area of story telling, the same rule-of-invention can be used to create new types of actions (at least new to the program that is applying the rule). For example, if a story-telling system already knows about the concept of **kill(b, c)** then this rule will create **kill(b, b)** which is the new event of a character **b** committing *suicide*.

Over the years, a number of AI invention systems have been built, which have invented simple short stories (Turner, 1994), invented new chemical structures (Lindsay et al. 1980) and which have discovered or re-invented various laws of physics.

For example, the BACON system (Langley, 1981) re-discovered many physical laws, including: Ohm's Law (concerning current, voltage and resistance), Snell's Law (of refraction of light), Newton's Law (of gravity), Kepler's 3rd Law (of planetary motion), Galileo's laws (for pendulum motion and acceleration), and many other laws.

The EURISKO system (Lenat 1983) had rules (called heuristics) of invention that were designed to not only be creative, but also to invent yet other rules of invention. Thus, EURISKO could improve its own invention capabilities. EURISKO has been applied successfully to different task domains, including computer chip design and competitive, multi-player games.

If this rules-of-invention approach can be applied to the above domains, then it should also be applicable to Art, which would result in artificially intelligent systems that invent art on their own.

Harold Cohen: AI and Meta-Art

Harold Cohen is an artist and professor emeritus of visual arts at the University of California, San Diego.

During the 70s he learned AI techniques at Stanford University. In the 80s and 90s he developed more and more advanced versions of an art-creating program that he titled AARON, which is a rule-based symbolic-manipulation system in which symbolic structures and rules are used to generate images.

Cohen describes the art produced by AARON as "meta-art" because he produced AARON (which he considered to be a work of art) and AARON itself produces its own art (thus becoming meta-art).

In AARON, different rules interact to produce line drawings of various sorts, which Cohen himself then colors in. Early versions of AARON produced doodle-like drawings (non-representational) but this early version had conceptual (symbolic) structures concerning repetition, balance, foreground vs. background, inside vs. outside, and symmetry. Intermediate versions of AARON produced contour images (reminiscent of cave paintings) by manipulating stick-figure-like internal representations. Instead of drawing the stick figures directly, AARON used these stick-figures to guide the drawing of contour images.

Later, more advanced versions of AARON drew human figures in jungle-like environments. For examples of works of art by AARON, see (McCorduck 1990). The front cover of McCorduck's book displays a painting produced by AARON. [srch: Pamela McCorduck Aaron's Code]

AARON has a very distinctive, human-like style, with both impressionistic and realistic elements. To modify that style would require Cohen to alter the rules of the program (or the way in which those rules are applied and varied). These variations result from random processes that Cohen has also coded into AARON.

AARON is not capable of learning. AARON cannot learn from experience because it does not maintain any memory of the past works of art that it has produced. As a result, AARON cannot compare and contrast different prior works. Another reason why AARON cannot learn -- either from its own creations or the creations of others -- is that AARON cannot see what it has produced. AARON is blind! A blind artist will be able to generate images on canvas but will not be able to appreciate the visual subtleties (or lack thereof) of what has been produced.

Over the last few decades there have been tremendous advances in Artificial Intelligence. Sophisticated planning, reasoning, comprehension and learning systems now exist. Consider the WATSON program (Ferrucci et al. 2010), which beat the top human champions at the game of

Jeopardy, winning the top prize of $1million. This program combines many AI capabilities (of memory, reasoning and language comprehension) into a single system.

A key capability, in order to produce an artificially intelligent artist, must be an ability to process, represent and recognize images -- that is, to see. This is a capability that the WATSON system also lacks.

However, recent advances in artificial neural networks (ANNs) have resulted in robust vision systems.

Challenges in Computer Vision

Recognizing specific objects (or categories of objects) in images poses many challenges. Consider how a specific object, such as a particular chair, might be recognized within some scene containing that chair. Let us assume that this chair has been photographed against a white background and that a 2D image of this chair is stored in the computer's memory -- as those pixels making up the chair image (along with their color values and locations). Let us call this set of pixels ChairImage-1. A number of problems arise in using ChairImage-1 to recognize images of the same chair within some scene.

1. *Variation in object position and size* -- Given a scene with other objects and containing this particular chair within it, the chair can appear anywhere within the scene. If some learning system is trained to spot a chair by matching the pixels in ChairImage-1 against the same pixels in the scene, then if the chair is shifted (even just slightly) in the scene, the values of those pixels (in ChairImage-1) will fail to match those in the scene. The same problem will arise if the chair's image in the scene happens to be larger (or smaller) in size than the original chair image. The ChairImage-1 pixels will no longer match the enlarged (or shrunken) image of the same chair.

2. *Variation in orientation* -- As a chair is rotated (or viewed from different angles), completely different 2D images will arise. The same chair, as viewed from the side (or from the back) will look very different than when viewed from the front. At each angle of orientation, the image of most objects (unless they are completely symmetrical, such as a sphere) will look very different.

3. *Partial occlusion by other objects* -- Most 2D images are of items in 3D

space. In such cases it will be very common that some other object (or objects) in the foreground will be partially occluding the object to be recognized.

4. *Variation in color, lighting and shading* -- Photographic scenes of multiple objects will vary in their color, depending on lighting conditions. Also, larger objects nearby will cast shadows on other objects. If the computer is looking for specific pixel values, they will not be encountered under these very common, alternative lighting conditions.

Recognition of more complex objects, such a people, involves even more variation. Consider recognizing your maternal grandmother. Let us call her Grannie. You can recognize photographs of Grannie in spite of the fact that she may be standing, sitting, sleeping, walking, smiling, laughing, frowning, or wearing different clothing. You will recognize images of her in which she is older or younger (with more or fewer wrinkles and with changing hair color).

Recognition of *categories* of objects also involves dealing with many forms of variation. For example, to recognize the category DOG requires recognizing many different types of breeds (German Shepherd, Doberman, English setter, poodle, etc.) in which the dogs may be in different positions (sitting, standing) or engaging in different actions (running, barking) with different colorings, lightings, shadows and partial occlusions.

Over the last decade, artificial neural networks (ANNs) have advanced to such an extent that they have now, in just the last few years, reached human-level (and even human-superior) capability in recognizing thousands of different objects (or categories of objects) within millions of different scenes. How has this been accomplished?

Artificial vs. Biological Neurons

An artificial neuron is a greatly simplified version of a biological neuron. The biological neuron consists of the following components (see Figure 15.2):

A. *Dendrites* -- a branching structure that receives inputs from other neurons. This branching structure can receive inputs directly from over 100,000 other neurons. Each little dendritic bulb will make contact with a corresponding bulb at the tip of the axon of another neuron.

B and C. *Soma (i.e., nucleus and cell body)* -- It is in a region of the soma that an electrical pulse is generated, which travels along the axon.

D and E. *Axon (with myelin sheath)* -- The axon is single long fiber, along which the neuron's electrical pulse travels (as output). This fiber branches as it extends outward. As a result, a single neuron can send a signal to over 100,000 other neurons. The myelin sheath acts as an insulator that coats the axon.

F. *Axon Terminals* -- Each little bulb on the end of an axon makes contact with a little dendritic bulb on the dendritic branch of another neuron.

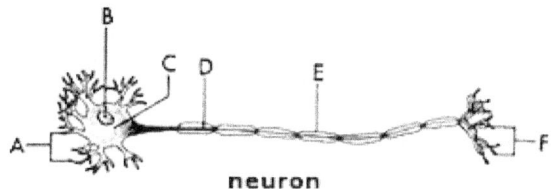

Figure 15.2 Schematic of a Biological Neuron

When neurons make contact with each other, they don't actually physically touch one another. At the point of connection (between an axonal bulb and a dendritic bulb that are in contact) there is a tiny gap, called the synapse.

When the electrical pulse (traveling along the axon of some neuron n1) reaches the synapse, the signal is changed into a set of small molecules (called neurotransmitters) that diffuse across this synaptic gap -- from the axonal presynaptic bulb of neuron n1 to the dendritic post-synaptic bulb of neuron n2.

The neurotransmitters are molecules that act like keys (on axonal side of the synaptic gap of n1) that fit molecular locks (on the dendritic side of n2). When these molecular keys fit their corresponding locks, that event causes the receiving neuron n2 to become more (or less) likely to fire (i.e., send a signal along its axon to other neurons).

Thus, signaling between neurons is electro-chemical, because the electrical pulse from neuron n1 is converted into molecular structures that then affect the subsequent firing of neuron n2.

As neurons communicate (by the electro-chemical means just described) their synapses *change in structure* (in terms of the number and types of synaptic keys and locks).

It is believed that memories are storied, not in the soma of each neuron, but in their changing synaptic structures. The human brain contains on the order of $10^{10} = 100$ billion neurons, with an average connectivity of $10^4 = 10,000$. That is, each neuron connects (via synapses) to approximately 10,000 other neurons. As a result there are approximately 10^{14} synapses in a human brain.

Neurons are slow when compared with a computer chip in a laptop (which can execute about 1 billion instructions a second). Neurons fire at a rate of approximately 100 times per second. Thus, the brain updates about 10^{14} x $10^2 = 10^{16}$ synapses per second. When compared to your laptop, this is $(10^{16})/(10^9) = 10^{(16-9)} = 10^7$, so the human brain is still $10^7 = 10$ million times more powerful than a standard computer chip (in terms of synaptic updating capability).

However, if the current rate of technological progress keeps up, within 30 years a computer laptop will be able to simulate all the neurons of a human brain in real time for under $1000.

Biological neurons are much more complicated than artificial neurons because the biological neurons consist of living cells and, as such, they must stay alive (while also achieving their signaling and computational functions). Thus, a living neuron must receive nutrients (via arteries), expel waste products, turn on different segments of its DNA, and engage in other functions. These life-related processes are usually ignored in most *artificial* neural models.

In Figure 15.3, we are only going to consider the simplest type of *artificial neural network* (ANN). Each artificial neuron in an ANN contains the following components:

1. *Weights* -- Assume that artificial neurons AN1, AN2 and AN3 are each connected to another neuron AN4 (see Figure 15.3). The synaptic connection between them (e.g., an axonal bulb of AN1 being near a dendritic bulb of AN4) is represented by a *weight* w(1, 4), which in the figure has a value of w(1, 4) = 0.5. In Figure 15.3 w(2,4) = -0.5 and w(3, 4) = 1.0.

Commonly, each weight is a fractional number between -1 and 1. Thus, the state of the molecular locks and keys of the biological synapse are abstracted down to a single, fractional number.

2. *Inputs* -- Each artificial neuron, that receives signals from n other artificial neurons, will have n input lines. In Figure 15.2 neuron AN4 has 3 inputs. Each input is modeled by another number, called an *activity* or *activation*, which represents the average firing rate of that neuron. In the figure, we have assigned an activity of 50 to AN1, 18 to AN2 and 13 to AN3. For example, AN1 = 50 represents the fact that neuron AN1 is firing, on average, 50 times a second.

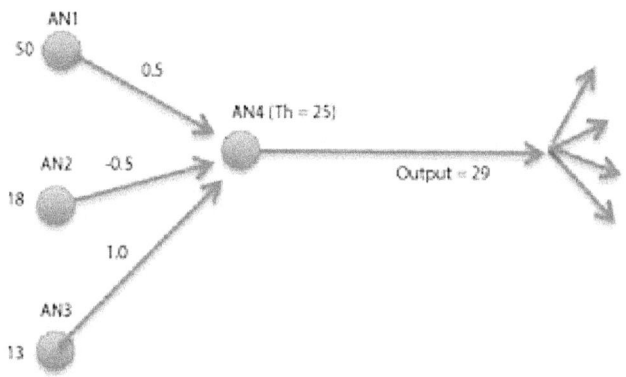

Figure 15.3
An ANN consisting of 4 artificial neurons.

3. *Gating function* -- This function decides when a neuron "fires" and sends it computed activation on to other neurons. The gating function sums up all the weight-modulated activations (coming in along all input lines) and then decides whether or not to fire. In this case, the weight-modulated summation will be:

$(0.5 \times 50) + (18 \times -0.5) + (13 \times 1.0) = 25 + -9 + 13 = 29$

The simplest gating function is a *threshold function*. In the figure the threshold for AN4 is Th = 25. Thus, neuron AN4 will not fire unless its total weight-modulated, incoming activation exceeds 25. In Figure 15.3 AN4 receives a weight-modulated activation of 29 and that happens to exceed the threshold (of 25) and so an output activation of 29 will be passed on to other neurons via it axon. The branching output line, emanating from neuron AN4, represents that neuron's axon.

Artificial neurons learn by adjusting their weights. They learn mainly in two modes:

1. *Supervised Mode* -- In this mode, the neurons are given an input signal and told what the output signal should be. The output currently produced is compared against the desired output and when there is a discrepancy, the weights of the neuron are adjusted so as to increase the likelihood that it will produce the desired output in the future.

2. U*nsupervised Mode* -- In this mode, a multi-layer network of neurons learns to produce an output pattern (which appears on its output layer of neurons) that is identical to the input pattern. Such networks do not require a supervisor (to tell them what output to produce for each input) because they are being asked simply to reproduce, as output, whatever the input pattern happens to be (for an example, see Figure 15.8).

Pattern Recognition with a Single Artificial Neuron

Here is a simple example of how a single neuron might learn (in the supervised mode) to prefer one visual pattern over another. Let us consider just two, very simple, black and white visual patterns -- one for the letter H (in Figure 15.4) and one for the letter A (in Figure 15.5).

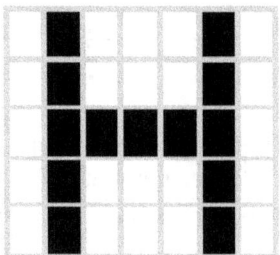

Figure 15.4
Simple visual pattern for letter H

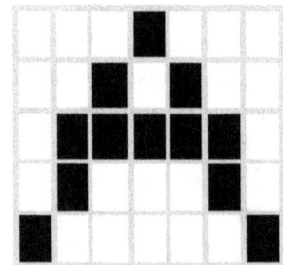

Figure 15.5
Simple visual pattern for letter A

To process such images, we will have a single neuron, which will receive 35 inputs from a "retinal grid" -- one that has the same shape and number of cells as those in Figures 15.4 and 15.5 -- namely, 5 rows x 7 columns = 35 binary cells (where 0 represents a white cell and 1 represents a black cell). This neuron appears in Figure 15.6.

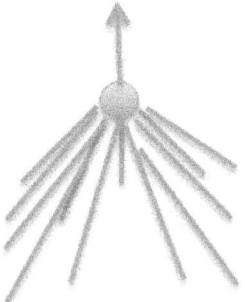

Figure 15.6
A single neuron, ANha, receives 5 row x 7 columns = 35 input lines (not all shown), in which each line is weighted with a value between -1 and 1.

We want a single artificial neuron to learn to prefer the H-pattern over the A-pattern. Let us call this neuron ANha (Figure 15.6). ANha will receive, on its input lines, an image from an artificial 'retina' composed of 35 different binary values (7 per row times 5 per column).

Let us assume that the 35 weights (on these retinal input lines) are set randomly between -1 and 1. Whenever ANha sees the H-image, we will want it to learn to output a high activation value. Whenever ANha sees the A-image, we will want it to output a low activation.

How can this be accomplished? First, let us refer to each cell in terms of its row-column location. For example, in the H-image, at retinal location [1,2] (i.e., row-1, column-2) there will exists a black cell (input of 1) while in image-A there exists a white cell (providing input of 0 to ANHa).

To prefer the H-image over the A-image, our neuron needs to *increase* the weights that have black cells on its "retina" when an H pattern is presented to it, since black cells at these locations are increased evidence <u>for</u> an H visual pattern.

Since we want this neuron to output a low value for an A-pattern, the neuron needs to *decrease* the weight on any input line where there is a black cell for the A-pattern.

Some black cells are shared across both patterns. Shared locations include: [3,2], [3,3], [3,4], [3,5] and [3,6]. A black cell at these locations provides evidence for <u>both</u> an H and an A visual pattern. These weights will be raised (when the neuron is learning about the H pattern) and lowered (when the neuron is learning about the A pattern), so these weighted lines will end up being in a mid-range.

Over time, as the neuron is trained on a variety of similar H (and A) patterns, the neuron will learn to weight its input lines so that lines that tend to be black (when it is an H pattern) are weighted high while lines that tend to be black (when it is an A pattern) are weighted low.

Thus, an artificial neuron can be viewed as a device capable of learning to produce different outputs, based on whatever 2D patterns are fed to them as inputs. The weights can be viewed a form of evidence for (or against) some particular type of pattern.

Suppose activity at a location [4,5] on some retina provides strong evidence *for* some pattern P while activity at a location [5,5] provides strong evidence *against* P. In this case, the weight on the [4,5] input line should be close to or equal to 1 while the weight on the [5,5] input line should be close to or equal to -1.

The activity on the retinal cells need not be binary (0 or 1). Suppose activity at [3,4] = 100 and its input line has a weight of -0.5 while activity at [5,5] = 20 and it's weight is 1. In this case, the receiving neuron (ignoring all other inputs) will receive an activation of $(-0.5 \times 100) + (1 \times 20) = -50 + 20 = -30$. This negative activity will provide evidence *against* pattern P occurring on the retina.

Combining Neurons into Layered, Feedforward Networks

Instead of a single neuron receiving its input lines from a 2D retinal region, we can have a layer of k neurons, where each of those neurons receives the same inputs, but each neuron can have a different set of weight values on its own input lines. As a result, each neuron can be looking for *different* patterns in the *same* input.

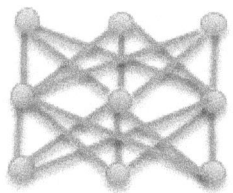

FIGURE **15.7**
Multiple layers of k neurons.
Here, there are three layers of neurons where k = 3.
placed above some retina (not shown).

Those k neurons can then each send their outputs to a layer of neurons above them (Figure 15.7). This new layer can then combine the patterns that were extracted by the layer below, to recognize patterns that consist of *combinations* of patterns that were extracted in the layer below.

Neural Learning without Supervision

In the H vs. A case, some teacher is needed -- to inform the network concerning which images are to be preferred. In the unsupervised case, however, no such supervision is needed. Instead, a network (consisting of 3 layers of neurons labeled input, hidden and output) is trained to produce, on the output layer, the *same* image as that which was placed on the input (retinal) layer (see Figure 15.8). Such an ANN is called an *autoencoder*. The network gets trained on multiple images. Call these images Im-1 up to Im-n. After training, the network will have learned when it is given, say, Im-6 as input to reconstruct that same Im-6 image on the output layer. Thus, no teacher is needed since the autoencoder is learning how to reconstruct (on the output layer) the same image that it is presented on the input layer.

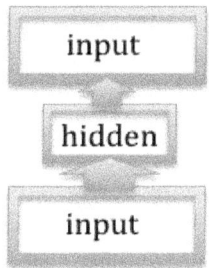

FIGURE 15.8
Autoencoder neural network with 3 layers (multiple neurons within each rectangle) and two layers of weights (thick arrows).

When the autoencoder network is starting off, the weights will have randomly set values (between -1 and 1). Whenever the network does a poor job of reconstructing an image (say, Im6) on the output layer, then the weights of the network will be adjusted to improve its performance. Different images are fed, repeatedly, to the network until all input images are properly reconstructed on the output layer (the top layer in Figure 15.8).

In an autoencoder network "auto" stands for the output being a reconstruction of the input and "encoder" refers to the fact that the first layer of weights (the larger arrow in Figure 15.8) encodes the input image into a pattern of activity across the neurons in the hidden layer. The second layer of weights (the smaller arrow in Figure 15.8) decodes this hidden-layer activity back into the original image.

Thus, an autoencoder neural network learns to both encode each image (into an activity pattern across hidden layer neurons) and then, when given that hidden activity pattern, to decode it back into the original image.

The number of neurons in the hidden layer must be *fewer* than the number of images being learned by the network. Why is this the case? Suppose the hidden layer has 50 neurons in it and that there are 50 images for the network to learn to reconstruct (on its output layer). In this case, each different neuron (in the hidden layer) could learn the pattern for each different image of those 50 images. The network would be able to successfully perform the reconstruction of each image, but the network would, in essence, have *memorized* those 50 images.

However, if the autoencoder has only, say, 10 hidden-layer neurons, then, to reconstruct the images (on the output layer) it will have to learn to extract any patterns that are *shared* across many images and to learn how to *combine* these patterns in order to reproduce the images.

By forcing the autoencoder to encode each image (into a smaller hidden layer), the autoencoder is forced to discover weights in the network that enable *combinations* of neurons in the *hidden* layer to represent the different images. That is, we want the hidden layer to form a compressed, efficient representation of all the features that are being used to reconstruct all the images. This efficiency (of representation) will greatly increase the network's ability to *generalize* to images that it has *not* yet seen.

Another way to look at what the autoencoder is doing is to consider a person who is being asked to learn the following input-to-output mappings: 2, 2 --> 5; 3,2 --> 6; 2,3 --> 6; 4,4--> 9; 5,4 --> 10; 4,5-->10.

If the learner just memorized the values above (given the inputs above) then the learner will not be able to generalize to new inputs. However, if the learner extracts the underlying rules being used (in this case, that the numbers are being added, with an additional one being then added to the result) then the learner will be able to generalize -- that is, predict what output will be generated for future, *unseen* inputs. In this case, the learner will be able to predict: 6,7-->14 even though he/she has not seen this example.

In summary, the first set of weights in an autoencoder neural network take an input image and encode (compress) it into a concise representation (as activity on the hidden layer). The second set of weights then decode (un-compress) the hidden layer activity back into the original image.

A nice generalization property of such a network of neurons is the following: if a partial image is presented to the network (e.g., part of some object is occluded in the input image), then the network will be able to reconstruct the entire image. As a result, such networks can recognize objects after being shown only a portion of that object.

Recent Improvements on Artificial Neural Networks (ANNs)

Here I will briefly mention improvements that have been made to the ANNs already discussed, in order to achieve (in just the last decade) impressive performance (in some cases, beating out humans) in recognizing objects and object categories.

One example of ANNs beating humans is the task of recognizing different traffic signs along street scenes (an ability that machines will need to have if robotic automobiles are to become successful alternatives to human-driven autos).

1. *Convolutional ANNs* (CANNs) -- In such artificial neural networks a smaller retinal area is shifted repeatedly across a larger retinal area (Krizhevsky et al. 2013).

Figure 15.9 shows the general approach of convolution. The large gray square in the figure represents the retinal area (in which different images are received during learning). The smaller squares represent a set of neural inputs that are fed to the next neural layer. During learning, this smaller square is shifted systematically across the larger image in an overlapping manner.

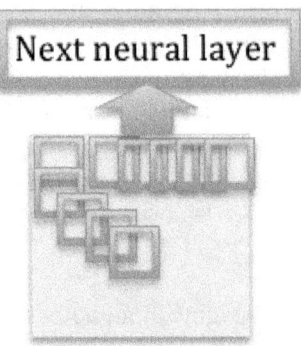

FIGURE 15.9
A convolutional neural network.
Only a subset of the shifted and overlapping
(i.e., convolved) areas are shown here.

As a result of convolution, the weights being formed for the next layer of neurons become able to handle patterns that might appear at *any* location on the artificial retina.

2. *Hierarchical ANNs* (HANNs) -- There are many different forms of hierarchical organization in artificial neural networks. Here we consider networks that sample a retinal area at different levels of granularity. For example, instead of passing a retinal cell value to one input line on a neuron, the values of 4 nearby cells are averaged and that averaged value is sent along a weighted input line to the neuron.

Figure 15.10 illustrates a simple hierarchical neural network. At the top of the figure (left to right) are shown 3 neurons: Hhi, Nmed and Hlow, with each sampling the retinal input at a different level of granularity.

For simplicity, each neuron has just 4 input lines. Nhi receives 4 (weighted) inputs, in which each input consists of an *average* of a 2-by-2 square. Thus, Nhi is sampling (in a slightly blurry manner) a total retinal area of 2x2 = 4 cells. Nmed also receives 4 (weighted) inputs, but in this case, each input is an average of a square of 3x3 = 9 cells, and so Nmed is sampling a larger total area. Nlow is also sampling 4 areas, but each area is the average value of 4x4 = 16 cells – an even larger area.

Thus, Nlow is receiving input from a total area of 4 times each 16-sized area (which covers the entire image).

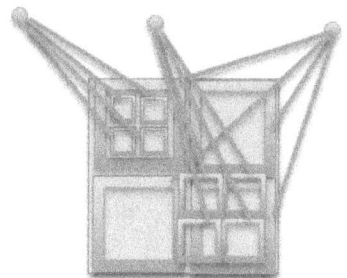

Figure 15.10
Hierarchical artificial neural network (HANN). Only 3 neurons are shown.
The leftmost neuron is Nhi. Its 4 input lines are sampling
the average value of areas each consisting of 2x2=4 cells.
The middle neuron is Nmed. Each of its input lines is sampling the average value of a
3x3=9 cell area. The rightmost neuron is Nlow, which is sampling the largest areas (and
therefore with the lowest resolution).

If we restrict the input lines to 4 while increasing the area being sampled, then Nlow will be looking for the most vague (blurriest) patterns, but these will be patterns that appear across the entire artificial retina. Nlow learns the largest-scale (but blurriest) patterns while Nhi learns more detailed patterns (but only occurring over much smaller areas).

HANNs are very good at learning to recognize objects no matter how large (or small) they happen to be within a given scene. HANNs can be combined with standard ANNs, along with the technique of convolution.

3. *Deep Artificial Neural Networks* (DANNs) -- This class of ANNs (Bengio 2009) consists of many hidden layers (between the input and output layer). Each layer learns to find and use combinations of patterns from the layers below. A hidden layer is formed using an autoencoder ANN and then the activation patterns (on the hidden layer) are used in yet another autoencoder. Thus, this second autoencoder is learning to encode/compress and decode/expand, not a set of images, but the representations that were learned by the first autoencoder.

Researchers have discovered that, by doing this, with multiple, "stacked" autoencoders, artificial neural networks can learn many different forms of (compressed) representations -- ones that are useful in recognizing objects hidden in complex scenes.

Requirements for An Artificially Intelligent Artist

The core features of the AARON system were designed and implemented several decades ago. Given all the recent advances in Artificial Intelligence (AI) -- which include advances in artificial neural networks (ANNs) -- at some point an AI-savvy artist will come up with an greatly improved AARON-like "meta-art" system.

Since Aaron was Moses' brother in the Bible, let us refer to this hypothetical future meta-art system as MOSES2.

What are the technological challenges in constructing a MOSES2 artificial artist and what technologies currently exist to address these challenges?

First, let us consider any arbitrary, human artist, in common art-creation scenarios, who we will refer to (again) as Artecia. One capability that any artist, such as Artecia, must exhibit is to be able to access multi-media sources.

A human artist such as Artecia can read the newspaper, watch TV and browse the internet. As she does, she learns new things about events and people in the world. She also learns about new forms of Art being produced by other artists. Both of these sources of multimedia information (images and text) modify Artecia's state of knowledge and trigger new goals in her, in particular, the desire to create some new image.

To model these capabilities, MOSES2 will need the following AI subsystems:

1. *Natural language processing (NLP) subsystem* -- There now exist NLP probabilistic systems that can translation between different languages. They actually learn to translate by examining corpora of pre-existing translations. They learn both probabilistic language models and probabilistic translation models. A probabilistic language model contains information about which types of words are likely to precede (or follow) other words. For example, suppose you were asked to place the following words into their most likely order: "man the the fat ate steak old juicy"

You will most likely produce: "the fat old man ate the juicy steak". Why? Well, statistically it is more likely that word "juicy" is a modifier of "steak" than of "man", "old" or "ate". It's much more likely, (when examining any corpus of English text) that people eat steaks (not the other way around). We also tend to say "fat old man" more often than "old fat man". Thus, a bag of words (if it comes from human-generated speech or text) can be reordered, using statistical methods, into a reasonable, grammatical sentence without even necessarily needing a grammar -- as long as a system has acquired probabilistic information about how words (or categories of words) are most likely to combine.

Similar statistical "data mining" techniques can be used to gather information about how words should be translated. For example, given a dual-language corpus, when the word "pen" appears in the context of "write with pen" in the English part of the corpus, then the Spanish translation for "pen" will more likely be *pluma* in the Spanish part of the corpus; while in the context of "pig pen" the Spanish translation will more likely be: *pocilga*.

In spite of these advances, NLP systems -- capable of mapping text into meaning structures -- are still at a relatively primitive level. However, even with shallow semantic and statistical structures, an NLP subsystem could extract some concepts from text and feed that to both learning and creative subsystems.

2. *Vision processing subsystem* -- We have already discussed how recent ANNs are now capable of learning to recognized objects (and categories of objects) after having been trained on thousands of images. Such systems produce compressed representations from multiple image-training scenes. These representations could then be fed to our hypothetical MOSES2 system.

As Artecia remembers (or examines) her past paintings (or views the paintings of others), she learns about new categories of Art and also about new art techniques, which she can then later use in producing her own art pieces. Thus, modeling Artecia via AI technology will require machine learning capabilities.

3. *Machine Learning (ML) subsystem* -- A major area of research within AI is that of machine learning. There are many types of ML systems now in existence. They are characterized by the amount of feedback they receive during learning. There are 3 broad types of feedback:

(1) *Supervised* -- in this case, the ML system is told what type of output it should produce, given some input that it has been shown, (2) *Unsupervised*

-- in this case, the ML system learns to group together different inputs, based solely on noticing features of similarity. As a result of these groupings a ML system can form new categories. (3) *Reinforcement* -- in this case, the ML system is given simple positive or negative feedback. It is not told what it should do, but simply that something it did do has either a positive (or negative) effect.

Let us consider our human artist, Artecia, within the above learning contexts. She goes to her art teacher with an idea and he tells her to try producing a certain type of image. This would fall within the supervised learning context. While she is painting, she notices that certain techniques result in similar effects and so she now reorganizes these techniques in her mind (thus, performing unsupervised learning). Later, she shows a partially finished work to a friend, who makes a face. As a result of this negative feedback, Artecia makes alterations to her work (thus learning via reinforcement).

4. *Inspirational and Creativity subsystem* -- We have already discussed how AI systems can employ rules to create new concepts and/or operations. We have also discussed how applying operations of mutation and recombination can also result in new structures. Another method for creativity involves the use of *analogical reasoning*. In this form of reasoning, new structures are created by mapping a structure in one domain to that within another domain. For example, the Minstrel (Turner 1994) story-invention system makes use of analogical reasoning to create novel stories.

Assume that Artecia has finished a painting and is now searching in her mind for new inspiration. What new image will she attempt to create? She recently had a fight with a friend, who yelled at her. On the news Artecia has also recently read about a dam breaking and the damage caused by the resulting flood. She suddenly imagines objects rushing out of a woman's mouth. Her new idea for a painting ends up consisting of an angry woman, with an enormous mouth, with fish and people and houses and other items flowing out, along with some form of liquid, and destroying other people in its path. Artecia came up with this idea by mapping one domain (dams, rivers and water flow) to another domain (anger and speech), mediated through an analogical similarity (the notion of a flow). She titles her work "Friendship's Angry Flood".

As Artecia paints, she examines what she had produced so far. If she dislikes some aspect of it, she will modify or paint over that area and start again. Thus, an AI image invention system would need a way of evaluating what it has produced so far.

5. *Aesthetic Evaluation Subsystem* -- Since AARON could not see what it had produced, it could not begin to evaluate its own output. Our hypothetical MOSES2 system will need to be able to see what it is producing as it creates it. It will also need methods for evaluating what it producing, so that it can make changes during the process of creation. Aesthetic forms of evaluation will need to be applied (along both image-related and concept-related dimensions).

a. *Image-related dimensions* -- These will include: balance, repetition, foreground vs. background, complexity, density, and so on (see both Chapters 8 and 14).

b. *Concept-related dimensions* -- As we saw in our hypothetical scenario above, Artecia was inspired to produce "Friendship's Angry Flood" by mapping abstract, conceptual relationships (such as friendship and conflict between friends) into the domain of images (such as that of a dam breaking). Thus, Artecia is not just judging the image that she is producing in terms of the image content itself, but also in terms of *non-visual*, conceptual themes that inspired the on-going creation of the image in the first place. (This capability is similar to Ramachandran and Hirstein's *Visual Metaphors* aesthetic.)

Thus, when our hypothetical MOSES2 system rejects some aspect of an image under production, its aesthetic subsystem must evaluate an ongoing image in terms of both imagistic and thematic criteria. These judgments could be encoded as rules. Clearly, both imagistic and conceptual rules are needed because conceptual rules of aesthetics can alter the way imagistic aesthetic judgments are applied.

For example, if the overall thematic intent is one of, say, happiness, then an imagistic aesthetic rule may be to select light colors over dark colors. However, if the intent is one of sadness, then, in this conceptual context, the imagistic aesthetic (for colors) may be altered to now prefer dark colors.

Once Artecia has some theme in mind, she must then plan out how to realize that theme. That is, she must replace this vague theme with a more concrete, imagistic realization. As she works out (in her mind) what specific scenes (or sub-scenes) she is going to produce, at some point she will feel that her ideas are fleshed out enough to merit starting to put them down on a canvas. If a MOSES2 system is going to behave like a human artist, it therefore must also have a planning subsystem.

6. *Goal and Planning subsystem* -- There are many goal/plan AI systems currently in existence. For each goal that such a system has, it will also have one or more plans, that when executed, have a high probability of achieving that particular goal. Each step in a given plan will have preconditions that must be met before that step can be carried out. These preconditions become new subgoals for the planning system. Those subgoals may need additional planning (and plan execution) in order to be achieved.

The most primitive AI planning systems generate a complete plan (along with sub-plans for each sub-goal) and stop there. More sophisticated planning systems are able to re-plan while they are in the mist of executing their current plan. Re-planning involves selecting a different plan (or different step in a plan) to achieve a goal when the current sub-plan is not working during plan execution. More sophisticated planners are even capable of changing their high-level goals.

In the case of Artecia, she may be half way through producing her piece "Friendship's Angry Flood" when she decides that some effect she is attempting to achieve is not working. After struggling with different approaches and techniques, she decides to change the types of objects coming out of the mouth of the woman in her painting. In this case, she had abandoned a specific sub-goal and replaced it with another.

7. *Emotional/Affective subsystem* -- Over the last few decades there has been an increased appreciation of the importance of emotion (and recognition and expression of emotion) in AI and robotic systems (Picard, 1997; Scherer et al. 2010). In humans, emotions influence the kinds of memories that are retrieved and how reasoning and planning systems progress. Emotions provide motivation for pursuing goals and also provide reward and punishment to learning subsystems.

As Artecia paints, she finds that she is no longer enjoying herself. She feels frustrated. Once this feeling becomes strong enough, it will cause her to change her current approach to whatever subtask she happens to be engaged in. A MOSES2 system would therefore also need an affective subsystem.

I predict that it just a matter of time before some AI savvy artist decides to combine these various AI and ANN subsystems to produce a MOSES2. If done well (perhaps by a team consisting of multiple artists, cognitive scientists and AI engineers), it could become as sophisticated in the art domain as the WATSON system currently is within the Jeopardy game domain.

Robot-Generated Art

As robots become more common, the MOSES2 system could be transported to an actual, physical robot. Let us call this robotic artist MOSES3. Unlike MOSES2, MOSES3 will be embodied.

The main advantage that MOSES3 will have over MOSES2 is that MOSES3 will be able to directly produce artifacts. That is, it will be able to move about in 3D space, physically grasping physical brushes and painting a physical canvas with physical gobs of paint (oil, acrylic, water color or other), just like a human artist.

I believe that autonomous, robotic artists will come into existence within the next three decades.

Algorithmic Exploration for Novel Genres in Image Space

The image space is so mind-bogglingly enormous that I foresee future generations of artists using evolutionary, algorithmic (with apprentice), artificial neural and Artificial Intelligence (AI) techniques to explore the image space. Recall that the image space already contains all possible images (for a given canvas size) that might ever be produced.

In a very real sense, then, when an artist creates an image, the artist is not only inventing a novel image, but also discovering a pre-existing image (in the sense that this image already exists within the image space of all possible images).

Historically, it has been human artists that have discovered new genres of images (e.g., Picasso). In the future, however, AI software systems could be exploring the image space while humans are sleeping. Once a software system has found an interesting, novel genre of Art, that system could inform human artists, who could then spend their time applying their (human) skills and imagination in producing variations on this newly discovered genre.

Alternatively, once a human artist has invented a new genre, then robotic artists could help that inventor create new artifacts within that genre.

As robots become more and more intelligence, Art will be produced by collaborations among humans and robots

Chapter 16
SUMMARY and CONCLUSIONS

The *art lover* appreciates (and gains aesthetic pleasure from) high quality images produced by artists. The level of appreciation is increased when the art lover learns more about how the artist created the image, what labor was required, and also what goals the artist was trying to achieve in creating the work. This knowledge alters the judgments that the art lover makes when deciding how the work compares with other works within that genre.

The art lover also assesses the aesthetic quality of the work within its historic context and weighs its value in terms of how innovative the image is/was, with respect to other images within that same historical context.

The art lover assesses how engaging a work is, along with how much current (and past) mental effort he/she has had to expend in order to become fluent in cognitively processing that work. The processing of any image includes deciphering any conceptual content that the image is claimed to generate in the minds of other viewers.

The *art collector/investor*, if he/she is also an art lover, will go through the same processes as above. However, the art collector/investor specifically goes through a different, *additional* process of assessment -- *not* concerning the quality of the image, but of the market value of the unique *artifact* that the artist has created (on which the image exists).

This assessment uses a very *different* set of dimensions, which include the artist's prestige/attention profile, the artist's personality (e.g., ability to articulate a good theory and/or backstory, along with promotional and business skills), present and perceived future demand by wealthy collectors, the authenticity of the artifact and so on.

In this book we have briefly explored a number of *contrasts* in Contemporary Art, including:

- Image vs. Artifact vs. Recordings
- Art vs. Music (in terms of both market and psychology)
- Objective vs. Subjective Descriptions of Art

- Uninteresting vs. Interesting Images in The Image Space
- Simple vs. Complex Images
- Dimensions of Monetary *Value* vs. Image *Quality*

Hopefully, our examination of these contrasts has shed some light on the nature of Contemporary Art and has helped to explain some of the strange phenomena that occur in Contemporary Art -- phenomena that tend to have the viewing public shaking their heads in (often mocking) disbelief.

What conclusions might we now draw? The conclusions listed below are framed in terms of advice to Art lovers, collectors and investors:

1. Form *your own* Art opinions and judgments. Don't let so-called Art experts decide for you. When they make a claim about some work or aspect of Art, make them justify their claim with clear, well-organized reasoning. This reasoning should include: (a) those features that make the image to be of high aesthetic quality, (b) why the image is innovative (if it is) (c) what conceptual content the image elicits and (d) what level and type of processing fluency is required to extract this content.

2. Don't be seduced into admiring something that seems ridiculous to you on the surface, and requires a lot of theoretical statements (or -isms or backstories) to overcome its obvious (imagistic) weaknesses.

3. Keep the realm of the *artifact* separate (as much as possible) from the realm of the *image*. You *can* enjoy, admire and love images of Art without letting them become distorted by the monetary realm of artifacts.

4. Don't let Art "artifact snobs" belittle your love of images of Art. It's OK to own a poster of a famous artifact whose image you love. Try to treat Art more like Music. Share your joy of images of Art with others. You do *not* have to become the sole possessor of some unique artifact in order to consider yourself a connoisseur of Art.

5. Don't become overly impressed by the monetary value of an artifact.

6. If you are collecting Art *as an investment*, then concentrate on those dimensions that *will* increase the value of your collection (and so it's OK to own a Rothko painting, even if the image is just an amorphous blob).

7. If you are operating within the investment domain, make sure that your artifact is *authentic* and has a strong *provenance* (documentation to support

its authenticity). Know the market demand for your artifacts (or get a professional who knows them to advise you).

8. When you talk with an Art investment professional, focus on those dimensions that will most determine its future value. That means discounting the aesthetic quality of the image with respect to the other, more market-oriented dimensions.

9. As a collector/investor, since your investment may *not* always increase in value, make sure to *restrict* your acquisitions to those artifacts whose images you truly love (i.e., do *not* be fooled by the Price Ratchet policy, as described in Chapter 11). In that way, even if they lose in monetary value, you can still enjoy them *as images*.

10. Understand and appreciate why artists sometimes create wacky Art and unsellable, crazy installations. Keep track of these wacky events. They will give you a good backstory to tell to others about those artists whose artifacts you happen to own.

11. Always continue to educate yourself about art techniques, skills, theory, and historical context -- because your judgments will change along with your changing knowledge of Art.

12. Do *not* assume that any work, appearing in a museum, must be of high aesthetic quality. Museums acquire artifacts for multiple reasons (e.g., viewer entertainment, risk-assessed investment strategies, education) and those reasons do not always lead to acquiring only works of the highest aesthetic quality.

13. Every time you look at the same image (or similar images within some genre), your brain will be modifying itself -- changing its organization -- in order to make your recognition of that image (and your conscious and subconscious relations to that image) more cognitively efficient. Your brain will also be generalizing and so, with more viewings of images, more insights (across images and image genres) will come to mind. As with any other behavior, the more you engage in it, the more efficient and natural it will become. Therefore, when you find images that others seem passionate about, really examine them on your own before forming your own judgment.

14. If you are not an artist, then allocate some of your leisure time; select a genre of Art and try to *create* works of art yourself. Attempting to create

Art will greatly enhance your *critical* appreciation of Art. If you end up becoming skilled as a 2D (canvas) artist, then I advise you insert/attach 3D objects in/on your canvases. The more 3-dimensional your artworks are, the more difficult it becomes to produce an image of your artifact that can capture its 3D aspect. As a result, your artifact will better retain its monetary value (due to its uniqueness and superiority to any image taken of it). {16.1}

In Music, those who most appreciate the musical (vocal and performance) skills of musical artists are those who know something about the structure of music and have tried, themselves, to write songs, or to perform at venues. Those who play an instrument (or sing) are in a better position to really appreciate the top music performers and composers. The same is true for Art. Those who have tried to reproduce great works of Art (whether in canvas, sculpture, cinematography, etc.) will have the greatest appreciation for what a high quality work really consists of (as opposed to something that can be quickly dashed off).

Before I decided to write this book, I found the world of contemporary art to be largely incomprehensible. In contrast, I now feel that much of the behavior of well-known artists (along with gallery owners, museum curators, critics, connoisseurs, etc.) actually makes sense -- even the behavior of those ultra-wealthy individuals who, to impress their peers (or attract viewers to their venues) are willing to pay millions of dollars for a given artifact. Finally, the behavior of many art viewers (who swarm around any highly iconic artifact, such as the Mona Lisa, but not around any of its reproductions) also now makes more sense.

We have seen why price replaces aesthetic judgment in the high-end Art market -- because it is so much easier to rank works in terms of monetary value than in terms of image quality.

We have examined how any image (in the digital realm) can be equated with a *minimal description* of three *objective* elements which, when combined, are able to reconstruct that image. These elements are: (a) the computational complexity of the image (i.e., number of steps required to produce the image), (b) the algorithm being executed (that will consist of a set of functional operations -- whose organization reveals the inherent structure of the image) and (c) the description language and language interpreter that is required for executing that algorithm.

These three computational elements correspond, respectively, in the realm of standard (non-digital) Art, to: (a) the labor an artist puts into creating a work, (b) the overall goals and plans of the artist, which direct that labor, and (c) the skill-set that the artist made use of to construct and carry out that plan (skills acquired through possibly many years of experience).

We have seen that the focus on a *minimal* description of these three elements is actually a way of requiring parsimony and efficiency when developing an algorithm (a plan) for generating an image, and also when carrying out a set of instructions (i.e., image-manipulation functions).

In general, the more labor expended (whether conceptual, in generating the plan, or physical, in carrying out a plan), the more complex an image will become, but only if that labor is efficient.

At least in this way, Art is like Science: High quality science seeks parsimonious theories of Nature. Likewise, high quality images should result from parsimonious plans and efficient methods for carrying them out.

Finally, the image space is so very mind-bogglingly *immense* that novel genres and amazing images will *never* be exhausted (even if mankind where to live on for another 10 billion years and continually produce art at an ever-increasing rate, even with the help of artificial neural networks and autonomous, AI robots). For the image (and Art) lover, the inexhaustibility of the image space is wonderful news. {16.2}

Let the exploration of Art continue!

ENDNOTES

In Chapter 1: Image vs. Artifact

{1.1} Music does have psychological distortions of its own but this book focuses on Art and so I only discuss Music in those cases were the contrasts between Art and Music help to shed light on the nature of contemporary art.

{1.2} The current price for downloading a song from an internet website (like iTunes) is about $1. To download the contents of a CD costs around $10.

{1.3} The derivative artist must not excessively alter the lyrics or melodic structure of a song. If a derivative music artist (ma-2) does so, then ma-2 must first obtain explicit permission from the copyright owner.

{1.4} One exception is that of Marilyn Monroe, since her image, while very iconic, is in the public domain and thus not under copyright protection. [srch: Marilyn Monroe art]

In Chapter 2: Value Multipliers

{2.1} Many market bubbles have occurred throughout the last few centuries. A recent bubble was in the USA housing market, which helped cause the great recession of 2008. In this case the US Government created extremely favorable borrowing terms for acquiring housing, which created an artificial demand for homes, thus raising their prices and leading to speculation. At the same time the US Government relaxed regulations, which allowed for more speculation in this area, leading to a bubble. Japan experienced a real estate bubble around 1985 to 1990.

{2.2} There exist other cases, outside of Music and Art, to support this claim (namely, that people, even experts, take their cues for how to judge something from the surrounding environment). For example, if one places cheap wine inside a wine bottle with an expensive label, then wine experts will most likely rave about that wine's wonderful bouquet. However, if an expensive wine is placed inside a bottle with a cheap label, then wine experts will most likely criticize the wine's taste and aroma.

In 2001, Frédéric Brochet (a researcher at the University of Brussels) asked 54 wine experts to describe a white vs. red wine, but he had tinted the white wine with red food coloring to appear red, so both wines were actually from the same bottle. None of the wine experts noticed. In another experiment, he served an average Bordeaux red wine, but poured it out of two different bottles. The experts did not notice that it was the same wine and praised the taste of the wine (poured from the more expensive label) as being superior to the same wine (poured from the cheap label).

In 2011 Richard Wiseman (a psychologist from Hertfordshire University) purchased many different types of wine and conducted an informal study in which over 500 subjects were asked to decide whether the wine they received was cheap or expensive. Their performance was at chance-level.

Clearly, people tend to associate increased quality with the prestige of the wine's label and with the monetary value of a bottle. These associations can bias (distort) the subject's actual perception of the wine's taste.

{2.3.} Recently, there was a case in which a work of art by a Chinese artist (which had sold at auction for $3.7M) was mistakenly dumped as trash by cleaners at a Honk Kong hotel. [srch: Snowy-Mountain mistaken trash] For other situations in which Art was mistaken as garbage, [srch: art mistaken garbage].

{2.4} Although infamy is a negative form of celebrity, it could enhance the value of Art. For example, a spoof article was posted of George Zimmerman (who gained USA national attention for being tried and acquitted for the second-degree murder of the black teenager Trayvon Martin in Florida). The spoof showed a fabricated image of Zimmerman holding a painting and claiming he has sold it at auction on eBay for $100,000. This story went viral and the fact that it was believed by many supports the general notion that infamy could help in the sale of artworks. [srch: George Zimmerman paintings]

{2.5} An example of a great music promoter is David Geffen.

In Chapter 3: Recordings of Artifacts

{3.1} A major alteration -- often made to famous songs from the 1920s and 1930s -- is to remove entire segments! During that time period, it was common for songs to have introductory lyrics. Modern versions often jettison these introductions. Here are just a few examples of famous songs, in which listeners today have probably never heard the introductory lyrics when the songs are performed:
"Embraceable You" -- George and Ira Gershwin, 1930
"As Time Goes By" -- Herman Hupfeld, 1931
"The Lady Is A Tramp" -- Richard Rodgers and Lorenz Hart, 1937

If you listen to Ella Fitzgerald sing "The Lady Is A Tramp", sometimes she will include the introductory lyrics and sometimes leave them off. I have never hear Frank Sinatra include them in his versions of this song.

Imagine if visual artists were to do the equivalent to paintings; that is, remove an entire portion of some famous painting before displaying it. I have not come upon this type of alteration every being applied to an iconic image in Art.

Because songs require a fixed amount of time, it is common for different arrangements to eliminate verses, in order to satisfy various time-related performance constraints. The following has probably happened -- a painting being sliced in half because of some space requirement -- but I suspect that such an event is quite rare.

{3.2} An exception is the case in which the artifact has been damaged. The damage could be sudden (e.g. caused by some vandal), or could be the result of many years of environmental effects (e.g., pollution, mold, bacteria). In such cases, art experts will try to repair and restore the image, but the goal is always to achieve an image as close as possible to the original.

In Chapter 4: The Image Space

{4.1} The notation used here, for example, 10^9, can also be represented using a superscript; namely, 10^9. It can also be represented as $10**9$. All are an abbreviation for 1,000,000,000. The superscript number (or number right after the $\wedge$ or **) is called the exponent. It might look small, but it can represent an enormously large quantity. For example, $10^{1000} = 10^{\wedge}1000$ and represents a number that consists of a 1 with one thousand zeroes following after it!

{4.2} For simplicity, I have ignored the Theory of Inflation, in which the universe, just after the Big Bang, is thought by many physicists to have undergone an extremely rapid expansion. (This speed of expansion is many times the speed of light but note that, while light has a maximum speed in the vacuum of space, space itself has no limit on how rapidly it can expand!) [srch: cosmology inflation big-bang speed-of-light]

{4.3} Note that the same phenomenon tends to occur in *other* realms of human endeavor. For example, mathematicians naturally concentrate on *interesting* functions, such as addition. However, if one actually considers the space of *all* possible functions, then there are many variants of addition. Consider just one variant of addition (let us call it ADD3). Instead of *infix* notation (e.g. "2+2=4") I will use *prefix* notation (e.g. "+(2, 2) = 4"). I will define ADD3 to be just like ADD -- except for the case in which the number 3 is used in the addition. In this case, ADD3 will produce 1 more than ADD would have produced. For example, ADD3(2, 5) = 2+5 = 7, just like ADD. However, ADD3(201, 3) does not produce 204; instead, it produces: ADD3(201, 3) = 201+3+1 = 205.

Even though ADD3 is identical to ADD for nearly all pairs of numbers, ADD3 is technically *a completely different function* than ADD because ADD3 behaves differently than ADD on certain pairs of numbers.

If some function F1 produces a different output than another function F2 (even for just a *single* set of inputs) then, technically, it is a completely different function.

There are an immense number of such strange (and one might say, pointless) functions and mathematicians tend to never consider such functions. So just as artists tend to restrict themselves to interesting images, mathematicians tend to restrict themselves to interesting functions.

{4.4} As technology improves, a flat screen could be replaced with a device that displays holograms. In this case, no special viewing glasses would be needed.

In Chapter 5: Describing Art Objectively

{5.1} Even analog entities, such as the varying bumps and pits in the groove of a record, or the varying amounts of dabs of paint on a canvas, can be replaced with binary encoding, at any desired level of precision (resolution).

{5.2} Eight bits can represent 256 different binary patterns, from 00000000 up to 11111111 and thus a different color can be assigned to each of these distinct binary patterns. Each bit has 2 possibilities and so, for n bits, there will be 2^n possibilities. In this case, it is $2^8 = 2x2x2x2x2x2x2x2 = 256$. If each pixel requires 8 bits, then 2 million pixels will require 16 million bits. Eight bits is so common that it has its own name: "byte"; e.g., 16 million bits consists of 2 million bytes (or 2 megabytes) and is abbreviated 2MB.

In Chapter 6: Image Complexity

{6.1} It is known in computer science that, in general, it is impossible to prove that a given description is the *minimum* description for generating a given output. Therefore, in this book we will use the term "minimal" (vs. the term "minimum"). By "minimal" we will mean that we are looking for a reasonably short description.

A preference for minimality (simplicity) is a common constraint, used in all fields of human endeavor. For example, when scientists invent theories to explain natural phenomena, they always prefer to first try minimal (simple) theories, before trying more complex theories. This approach is called "Ockham's Razor" (or "Occam's Razor") after William of Ockham, who was a Franciscan Friar, philosopher and scientist in the 14th century. He argued for always first seeking the most parsimonious/concise explanations for any phenomena.

{6.2} A standard type of (sequential) computer is selected because some computers contain parallel processors and can execute, say, 100 instructions at the same time. Such a computer could be up to one hundred times faster than a strictly sequential computer. By fixing the class of computers used, the computational complexity of different images can be compared without ambiguity concerning the number of computational steps required.

{6.3} When I was a child my father told me a story of a famous medieval clock repairman, who had studied clocks for years. It turns out that no one was able repair a large clock in a certain medieval town and so this master repairman was asked to attempt it. The master repairman examined the complex device and then took out a small hammer and hit a specific spot on the clock mechanism. The clock suddenly came to life and worked perfectly! The repairman then presented a large bill and the townspeople objected. They said, "It only took you one hit with your hammer to repair this clock." The master repairman replied, "But it took me *years* of study to know exactly *where* to apply that hit. You are paying, not only for my current labor, but for my skill level, which required years of effort to attain."

{6.4} The compression technique we have discussed (of replacing repeated patterns of an image with a description of the pattern, along with the number of repetitions) is a *non-lossy* compression technique, because, when uncompressed, the original image will be reproduced.

There are forms of compression that are *lossy*, because once such lossy techniques are used, the original image cannot be perfectly recovered. That is, the process of expansion will result in errors appearing in the resulting image (which usually show up as a blurring or lack of crispness in the resulting, re-expanded image).

{6.5} The same is becoming true for cinematography -- digital movies are now starting to dominate analog movies (those made using chemical emulsions). The conveniences of digital creation and manipulation (in production, editing, post-production, transmission, etc.) are greatly superior, when compared to analog processes.

In Chapter 7: Issues in Judging Images of Art

{7.1} If x > y were to represent the relation of "x is the boss of y" then the hierarchy above would represent the fact that worker w44 bosses workers w66 and w77 but that neither w44 nor w55 is the boss of the other. If we were to add (w44 <> w55) then we would conclude that w44 can also boss w88 and w99 while w55 can also boss w66 and ww77 (since they would be viewed as equivalent, in terms of their bossing relationships with others).

{7.2} Also, hopefully, there will exist overall similarities across different individual landscapes; for example, everyone will agree that there exists a separate mountain range for, say, impressionist sub-genres.

In Chapter 8: Dimensions for Judging Images of Art

{8.1} One can have images that appear simple but that took great skill to produce. Such images have a hidden level of complexity. As mentioned (in Chapter 6) calligraphic art may appear simple but require much skill to produce and thus exhibit complexity within apparent simplicity.

{8.2} If one were wealthy enough, perhaps one might buy, say, a cruise ship; cut it in half; build an Art building to house one of the halves, and then display that *as Art*.

{8.3} This phenomena -- of the conceptual cart before the horse -- occurs in other areas (outside of Art). For example, the famous jurist, legal scholar and theorist of justice and jurisprudence, Wesley Newcomb Hohfeld, argued that many judges probably arrive at their legal judgments largely by means of subconscious (and therefore possibly biased and prejudicial) operations. After they already had a judgment in hand, they would then come up with legal arguments to support it. Anyone reading the legal opinions of these judges might think that they had used their legal reasoning (appearing in their opinions) to arrive at their judgments, but according to Hohfeld, it had been the other way around. [srch: jurisprudence Hohfeld legal concepts judicial reasoning]

In Chapter 9: Conceptual Art vs. Image Conceptual Content

{9.1} This analysis (by the creator of this conceptual piece) ignored the fact that the actual lines-of-transmission must have occurred on (or above) the surface of Earth (not through the center of the Earth) due to the necessary use of transmission cables (laid on land or along the bottom of the oceans) and/or the use of satellites (above the Earth). So no fax message actually went *through* the interior of the Earth.

{9.2} Reena Spaulings is a fictional artist who was created by artists John Kelsey, Emily Sundblad and other collaborators

In Chapter 10: Theories of Artistic Appreciation

{10.1} Nicolas Bullot is a cognitive scientist in the ARC Centre of Excellence in Cognition and its Disorders at Macquarie University, Australia. Rolf Reber is a professor of psychology at the University of Bergen, Norway.

{10.2} Bullot and Reber (2013) refer to the third mode of art appreciation as the mode of *artistic understanding*. It appears that, in their paper, each later mode includes the prior modes; that is, their *design stance* mode appears to include the *exposure* mode and their *artistic understanding* mode (which adds the mode of analyzing an artist's contribution to Art within its historical context) appears to include both exposure and design stance modes. I think that the phrase "artistic understanding" is a rather vague phrase and, thus, I think it is clearer, in my discussion of these modes, to keep each mode separate from the others. Therefore, in my discussion of their modes I prefer to refer to this final mode as the *historical context* mode. In this way I can focus on what is unique about each mode of appreciation.

{10.3} A simple example of three different *styles*, say, when making doodle-based images, would be if one set of doodles always contained straight and jagged lines, while another style always contained curved and loopy lines; yet another doodle style could contain mainly hashed lines with scattered small circles. Obviously, styles can become very complex.

{10.4} For more discussion of Warhol's work within it historic/social context, see Danto (1998).

{10.5} If Jacques had been working on a *physical* canvas and had covered over one of his prior images with the final image, then Art forensic experts (using spectral analysis techniques) might later x-ray his canvas to discover the existence of this underlying image, e.g. [srch: Picasso Woman Ironing hidden revealed]. The ability to uncover a prior image in a *digital* file would depend on the file's meta-data (for example, if the artist had used digital layers to create the image and if the file saved this layered structure).

{10.6} For a survey of pigeon visual discrimination abilities, see Delius et al. (1999).

In Chapter 11: Dimensions for Judging Artifacts of Art

{11.1} W. Grampp is a Professor Emeritus of Economics at the University of Chicago in Illinois.

{11.2} M. Bull is a Lecturer of Fine Art at Oxford University.

{11.3} W. Ullrich is a Professor of Art History at the Kalrsruhe College of Arts and Design in Germany.

{11.4} J. Baudrillard was a French philosopher, sociologist and political commentator.

{11.5} T.Veblen was an American economist and sociologist who lived a century ago.

{11.6} A. Fraser is a performance artist based in New York.

{11.7} Lu Peng is a Bejing-based art historian and curator.

{11.8} Music *is* influenced by market forces but they fall into different categories. For example, to appeal to alienated and rebellious teenagers, the Kiss band members started dressing up in a combination of outlandish glam and Goth-like costumes, which some of their hard-core fans emulate when attending their concerts. But this type of "market force" is very different from the price "bubbles" that occur in the Art market.

In Chapter 12: Role of Museums

{12.1} There is a general law of storage that I call the "refrigerator law". Over time, my refrigerator gets so full of items (that I no longer care to consume) that it becomes hard to find those items that I actually *do* want to eat. Perhaps I bought something to try out and it turned out to not be tasty enough to finish, or perhaps someone else in my household tried a culinary experiment that did not turn out as well as had been hoped. So it becomes time to clean out the refrigerator to make room for the tried-and-true objects that are always enjoyed. This problem occurs for any type of physical storage space -- over time, the items that fail "to move" end up pushing out the better items. Finally, a decision must be made to remove these sedentary items. The "refrigerator law" applies to Art museums as much as it applies to refrigerators (closets or commercial warehouses).

{12.2} For example, entry to the Getty Center museum in Los Angeles is free, but to park there currently costs around $15.

In Chapter 13: Art, Brain, Mind, Computers and Art

{13.1} A good example of aesthetic pleasure being derived by discovering a hidden pattern in visual images is that of books of images produced by Magic Eye Inc. Each Magic Eye image consists of a blurry-looking, amorphous pattern that, when one relaxes one's eyes and focuses slightly past the image, a 3D scene (with now clearly recognizable objects) suddenly appears. The effect is always quite striking, exciting and pleasurable.

{13.2} For more information about the language called Processing, see: http://en.wikipedia.org/wiki/Processing_(programming_language).

In Chapter 14: Elements of Music and Art: A Comparison

{14.1} An example of an aesthetic, spatial, mathematical relation is the golden ratio. See http://en.wikipedia.org/wiki/Golden_ratio.

{14.2} See http://en.wikipedia.org/wiki/Harmony.

In Chapter 15: Technology and Future of Art

{15.1} In the biological case, DNA consists of 4 nucleotides that are combined to make 20 amino acids (which are then interpreted during biological development to produce the different types of proteins that make up an animal's body and brain). The genotype of, say, a mouse would consist of the DNA for that mouse. The phenotype would be the mouse body that developed from that particular sequence of mouse DNA.

In Chapter 16: Summary and Conclusions

{16.1} Adding 3D elements to a canvas will not protect the artist indefinitely. As holographic technology improves, consumers in the future will be viewing digitally generated holograms that reveal all 3D aspects of any 3-dimensional artifact, with the same visual verisimilitude as the original.

{16.2} Recall that our flat-screen image space (FSIS) consists of $10^{4,000,000}$ images. Suppose, hypothetically, that *only one* in every 100 billion trillion images in our flat-screen image space (FSIS) is of any potential interest. How many of these potentially exciting or interesting images are there?

Let us refer to this restricted sub-space of images as PEI-FSIS (i.e., Potentially Exciting Images within FSIS). One hundred billion trillion is 10^2 x 10^9 x $10^{12} = 10^{(2+9+12)} = 10^{23}$. To calculate the size of PEI-FSIS we divide 10^{23} into $10^{4,000,000}$. This calculation yields: $10^{(4,000,000-23)} = 10^{3,999,977}$. So PEI-FSIS contains $10^{3,999,977}$ images. This number remains mind-bogglingly enormous!

REFERENCES

Barr Jr., Alfred H. (1936). *Cubism and Abstract Art*, The Museum of Modern Art, NY.

Barrow, John S. (2005). *The Artful Universe: Expanded* (2nd ed.), Oxford University Press.

Baudrillard, Jean (1981). *For a Critique of the Political Economy of the Sign* (translated from the French by Charles Levin), Telos Press, St. Louis MO.

Bengio, Y. (2009), Learning deep architectures for AI, *Foundations and Trends in Machine Learning*, vol. 2, Issue 1, pp. 1-127, 2009.

Birkhoff, George D. (1933), *Aesthetic Measure*. Harvard University Press.

Braathen, Martin (2007). The Commercial Significance of the Exhibition Space, in *The Price of Everything -- Perspectives on the Art Market*, Whitney Museum of American Art.

Bull, Malcolm (2011), The Two Economies of World Art, in J. Harris (ed.) *Globalization and Contemporary Art*, Wiley-Blackwell, Malden MA. pp. 181-5.

Bullot, Nicolas J. and Reber, Rolf (2013), The artful mind meets art history: toward a psycho-historical framework for the science of art appreciation, *Behavioral and Brain Sciences*, 36 (2), 123-137.

Carruthers, P. (2006), Why pretend? In S. Nichols (ed.) *The Architecture of the Imagination: Essays on Pretence, Possibility, and Fiction*, 89-109, Oxford University Press.

Carruthers, P. (2009). Mindreading underlies metacognition. *Behavioral and Brain Sciences*, 32 (2), 164-182.

Cho, H. and Schwarz, N. (2006). If I don't understand it, it must be new: Processing fluency and perceived product innovativeness. *Advances in Consumer Research*, 33, 319-320.

Coremans, P. B. (1949), *Van Meegeren's Faked Vermeers and De Hooghs: A Scientific Examination*. J. M. Meulenhoff, Amsterdam.

Danto, A. C. (1998). *Beyond the Brillo Box: The Visual Arts in Post-Historical Perspective*. University of California Press, Berkeley, CA

Delius, J. D.; Emmerton, J.; Horster, W.; Jager, R. and Ostheim, J. (1999), Picture-object recognition in pigeons, *Current Psychology of Cognition*, 18 (5-6), 621-656.

Ferrucci, D, et al. (2010), Building Watson: An Overview of the DeepQA Project, *AI Magazine*, 31 (3).

Fritz, C.; Curtin, J. Poitevineau, J.; Morrel-Samel, P. and F-C Taod (2012), Player preferences among new and old violins, *Proc. of National Academy of Sciences of the U.S.*, Vol. 109 (3), p. 760, Jan 17.

Ford, S. and Davies, A. (1998). Art Capital, *Art Monthly*, No. 213, Feb. pp. 1-4.

Fraser, Andrea (2011). L'1%, C'est Moi, *Texte zur Kunst*, no. 83 (Sept.), 114-27.

Gilligan, Melanie (2007). Hedge Fund, *Texte zur Kunst*, No. 6 (June), 76-82.

Grampp, William (1989), *Pricing the Priceless: Art, Artists and Economics*, Basic Books, NY.

Grann, David (2010), The Mark of a Masterpiece. *The New Yorker* magazine, July 12.

Greenfeld, Josh (1966). Sort of the Svengali of Pop, *New York Times Magazine*, (May 8).

Herrera, Hayden (1983), *Frida: A Biography of Frida Kahlo*, HarperCollins Publ. NY.

Kelemen, Deborah (1999). Function, goals and intentions: Children's teleological reasoning about objects. *Trends in Cognitive Science*, 3(12), 461-468.

Kemp, Martin with P. Cotte, (2010), *La Bella Principessa. The Profile Portrait of a Milanese Woman - The Story of the New Masterpiece by*

Leonardo daVinci, Hodder & Stoughton, London.

Kraetzer, C.; Oermann, A.; Dittmann, J. and A. Lang (2007), Digital Audio Forensics: A first Evaluation on Microphone and Environment Classification. In *Proceedings of ACM Workshop on Multi-Media and Security (MM&SEC'07)*, Dallas, TX.

Krizhevsky, A.; Sutskever, I. and G. Hinton (2012), ImageNet Classification with Deep Convolutional Neural Networks, *Neural Information Processing Systems*, Vol. 25.

Kruger, J., Wirtz, D., Van Boven, L., & Altermatt, T. W. (2004). The effort heuristic. *Journal of Experimental Social Psychology*, 40(1), 91-98.

Langley, P. (1981). Data-driven discovery of physical laws. *Cognitive Science*, 5, 31-54.

Lenat, D. (1983). "EURISKO: A program that learns new heuristics and domain concepts". *Artificial Intelligence* (21): pp. 61–98.

Lindsay, R. K.; Buchanan, B. G.; Feigenbaum, E. A. and J. Lederberg (1980), *Applications of Artificial Intelligence for Organic Chemistry: The Dendral Project*, McGraw-Hill Book Co.

McCorduck, Pamela (1990) *AARON'S CODE: Meta-Art, Artificial Intelligence, and the Work of Harold Cohen*, W. H. Freeman & Co.

Peng, Lü (1992). Heading Toward the Market, *Jiangsu huakan* Vol 142, No. 10, (translated by Mia Liu (2010) in Wu Hung (ed.) *Contemporary Chinese Art: Primary Documents*, The Museum of Modern Art, NY pp 290-92).

Picard, Rosalind W. (1997), *Affective Computing*, MIT Press.

Ramachandran, V. S. and Hirstein, W. (1999), The Sciences of Art: A Neurological theory of Aesthetic Experience, *Journal of Consciousness Studies*, Vol. 6, No. 6-7, pp. 15-51.

Russell, S. and Norvig, P. (2010), *Artificial Intelligence: A Modern Approach* (3rd. edition), Prentice Hall.

Saatchi, Charles (2011). The Hideousness of the Art World, *The Guardian*

(Dec. 2).

Salganik, Matthew J. and Watts, Duncan J. (2008), Leading the Herd Astray: An Experimental Study of Self-fulfilling Prophecies in an Artificial Cultural Market, *Social Psychology Quarterly*, Vol. 71, No. 4, pp. 338-355.

Salganik, Matthew J. and Watts, Duncan J. (2009), Web-Based Experiments for the Study of Collective Social Dynamics in Cultural Markets, *Topics in Cognitive Science*, Vol. 1, pp. 439-468.

Salganik, M. J., Dodds, P. S. and Watts, D. J. (2006), Experimental Study of Inequality and Unpredictability in an Artificial Cultural Market, *Science*, Vol. 311, February 10, pp. 854-856.

Saltz, Jerry (2007), Seeing Dollar Signs, *Village Voice*, Jan. 16.

Schapiro, M. (1937), Nature of Abstract Art, *Marxist Quarterly*, Jan/Feb.

Scheldahl, Peter (2006). Temptations of the Fair, *The New Yorker* (Dec. 25), p. 148.

Scherer, K. R.; Banzinger, T. and Roesch, E. (2010), *A Blueprint for Affective Computing: A sourcebook and manual*. Oxford University Press.

Schmidhuber, J. (1997), Low-Complexity Art, *Leonardo:, Journal of the International Society for the Arts, Sciences, and Technology*, Vol. 30, No. 2, pp. 97-103, MIT Press.

Semuels, Alana (2013). New wealth taking art market to new heights. *www.latimes.com*, Dec. 8th.

Sims, K. (1991), Artificial Evolution for Computer Graphics, *Proceedings of the 18th annual conference on computer graphics and interactive techniques (SIGGRAPH91)*, pp. 319-328, Assoc. for Computing Machinery (ACM), NY.

Smith, Lisa F.; Smith, Jeffrey K. (2006), The Nature and Growth of Aesthetic Fluency. In P. Locher, C. Martindale and L. Dorman (eds.), *New directions in aesthetics, creativity and the arts*. pp. 47-58, Baywood Publishing, Amityville, NY.

Stecker, R. (2005), *Aesthetics and Philosophy of Art*, Roman & Littlefield.

Thompson, Don (2008). *The $12 Million Stuffed Shark*, Palgrave Macmillan.

Thompson, Don (2014). *The Supermodel and the Brillo Box*, Palgrave Macmillan.

Turner, S. R. (1994), *The Creative Process: A Computer Model of Story Telling*. Lawrence Erlbaum Assoc.

Ullrich W. (2009), "Icons of Capitalism: How Price Makes Art" in J. Bradburne, P. Dossi, B. Groys, F. Nori, P. J. Sacco, J. Stallabrass, W. Ullrich (2009), *Art, Price and Value: Contemporary Art and the Market*. Centro di Cultura Contemporanea Strozzina, Florence.

van den Berg, Karen and Pasero, Ursula (2012). Large-Scale Art Fabrication and the Currency of Attention, in M Lind and O. Velthuis (eds.), *Contemporary Art and Its Commercial Markets: A Report on Current Conditions and Future Scenarios*. Sternberg Press, NY, pp. 156-65.

Varnedoe, Kirk (2006), *Pictures of Nothing: Abstract Art Since Pollock*, Princeton University Press, Princeton NJ.

Veblen, Thorstein (1899). *The Theory of the Leisure Class: An Economic Study of Institutions*, Macmillan NY, 1902.

Vetter, P.; Smith, F. W. and Muckli, L. (2014), Decoding Sound and Imagery Content in Early Visual Cortex, *Current Biology*, 2014.

Voss, Richard F. and Clarke, John (1977), "1/f noise" in music: Music from 1/f noise, *Journal of Acoustic Society of America*, Vol. 63, No. 1, Jan. pp. 258-263.

Wagner, Ethan and Wagner, Thea W. (2013), *Collecting Art for Love, Money and More*, Phaidon Press, NY.

Watanabe, S.; Sakamoto, J. and Wakita, M. (1995). Pigeons' discrimination of paintings by Monet and Picasso. *Journal of the Experimental Analysis of Behavior*, 63 (2), 165-174.

Wilson, Fred (2001). Mining the Museum in Me, in L. Cohen (ed.) *Pictures, Patents, Monkeys and More ... On Collecting*, Independent Curator's Intern. NY.

Wolf, Thomas (1968). Bob and Spike, in T. Wolf (1989), *The Pump House Gang*, Black Swan, London.

Yang, R.; Qu, Z.; Huang, J. (2008), Detecting Digital Audio Forgeries by Checking Frame Offsets, In *Proc. of ACM Workshop on Multimedia & Security (MM&Sec'08)*, Oxford, UK.

About the Author

Michael Dyer is a professor of Computer Science at the University of California at Los Angeles (UCLA). He received his Ph.D. in computer science (CS) from Yale University in 1982. He also has an M.A. in anthropology from Temple University (Philadelphia, PA), an M.S. in CS from the University of Kansas and a B.A. in English from Dartmouth college (Hanover, NH).

He works within the field of Artificial Intelligence (AI) and his research interests are focused within the AI subarea of Natural Language Processing (NLP). Specifically, he is interested in producing computer programs capable of representing, learning, and understanding the meanings conveyed in human language text. The research issues he investigates include: the co-evolution of language and brain, the acquisition of language and comprehension of text via symbolic, neural and statistical techniques.

He has explored a wide variety of specific NLP tasks, including: story comprehension and question answering by machine, automated story invention, editorial understanding, argumentation (in legal and economic texts), humor/irony analysis, machine translation of one language into another, and language learning. Over the years he has published over 100 articles in computer science conferences and journals. He is author of the book: *In-Depth Understanding*, MIT Press, 1983.

In the areas of Art and Music, Dyer is both an amateur glass blower and singer/songwriter. Dyer's glass blowing techniques include Venetian-style glass blowing, glass casting and flame work. Over the years he has produced vases, paperweights, glass wall hangings, and sculptural forms. Some of these works can be seen by clicking on "My Glass Blowing" at the bottom, left-hand side of: michaeldyermusic.com

In the area of music, Dyer has self-produced a dozen CDs (in both soft-rock and light-blues genres). One of these CDs is a radio-play/musical titled "Dragon's Blood". Samples from his CDs can be heard at: www.cdbaby.com/Artist/MichaelDyer

INDEX